# Helping Students Overcome Depression and Anxiety

# Helping Students Overcome Depression and Anxiety

## A Practical Guide

KENNETH W. MERRELL

**THE GUILFORD PRESS**
New York   London

© 2001 The Guilford Press
A Division of Guilford Publications, Inc.
72 Spring Street, New York, NY 10012
www.guilford.com

Printed in Canada

This book is printed on acid-free paper.

Last digit is print number:  9  8  7  6  5  4  3  2

**Library of Congress Cataloging-in-Publication Data**

Merrell, Kenneth W.
   Helping students overcome depression and anxiety : a practical guide / Kenneth W. Merrell.
      p.   cm. — (The Guilford practical intervention in the schools series)
   Includes bibliographical references and index.
   ISBN 1-57230-617-3 (pbk.)
      1. Depression in children—Treatment. 2. Depression in adolescence—Treatment.
   3. Anxiety in children—Treatment. 4. Anxiety in adolescence—Treatment. 5. School
   children—Counseling of. 6. Students—Counseling of. I. Title. II. Series.
RJ506.D4 .M47 2001
618.92′8527—dc21                                     2001018804

# About the Author

**Kenneth W. Merrell, PhD,** is Professor and Director of the School Psychology Program at the University of Oregon. His research and clinical interests focus on assessment of and intervention for behavioral, social, and emotional problems of children and youth, and he has authored numerous journal articles, books, and published assessment instruments in these areas. He is also a frequent workshop presenter on these topics. Dr. Merrell has extensive clinical experience working with children and youth in school settings, and is a licensed psychologist and certified school psychologist. He is the editor of The Guilford Practical Intervention in the Schools Series.

# Contents

# Acknowledgments

This book would have never been written without the assistance, support, and inspiration of a number of individuals with whom I have had the privilege of interacting over the past few years. During the 1990s, my interest in internalizing disorders of children and adolescents was sparked by my interaction with several colleagues and graduate students who had a tremendous enthusiasm for the possibilities in this area and who helped inspire me to "jump with both feet" into a program of scholarly and clinical work that resulted in the publication of the Internalizing Symptoms Scale for Children (ISSC) and, eventually, this book. I also owe a debt of gratitude to a number of prominent scholars and clinicians whose work has resulted in many of the advances that we now have in helping young people with internalizing disorders. Most of the ideas in this book, particularly those ideas in the chapters on treatment, are directly influenced by or borrow heavily from the work of these scholars and clinicians. The efforts of the pioneers in this field, and those of others whose work has helped to put the topic of internalizing disorders of children "on the map," are also gratefully acknowledged. As I have conducted numerous training workshops on this topic for school professionals over the past few years, the feedback I have received from those in attendance has been critical in shaping the format and emphasis of this book, and more specifically, in making the intervention strategies that this book promotes realistic for day-to-day work in the schools. My thanks go to the entire staff at The Guilford Press for their efforts in making this book a reality. I am particularly grateful to Chris Jennison and Seymour Weingarten for their confidence in my ideas for this book, for helping me to shape and focus those ideas, and for allowing me to break some new ground with *The Guilford Practical Intervention in the Schools Series*. I also greatly appreciate the work of Barbara Watkins, Guilford's developmental editor, whose insightful and challenging comments regarding how to make this book as practitioner-friendly as possible were instrumental in improving this book. Finally, thanks to my family for keeping me grounded and for everything else.

# About This Series

Concerns that extend beyond basic academic instruction are impacting the work of educators. Student discipline problems, dysfunctional families, poverty, the conflict and stress of changing times, antisocial behavior, and legal mandates are just some of the nonacademic challenges facing educators today. The rapid and occasionally painful changes that characterize our times inevitably affect our educational systems and demand sophisticated responses and initiatives.

In the midst of these changing times, one of the most visible and dramatic challenges in our schools is the increasing population of students who are considered to be "at risk" for negative outcomes. Some of the more notable negative outcomes for these students include school dropout, a lack of functional academic skills, substance abuse problems, antisocial behavior and delinquency, mental health problems, chronic health problems, and participation in various dangerous and high-risk behaviors. Our educational systems have responded to the needs of this growing population through the work of mental health specialists who support teachers and administrators in meeting the complex needs of at-risk students. During the 20th century, the professional fields of school counseling, school psychology, school social work, school nursing, special education, and educational consultation have grown rapidly in response to these problems and needs.

The specific concerns and demands placed on these educational support service professionals change over time in response to the changing needs of at-risk students, new legal mandates, emerging research findings, and various professional and social trends. Some approaches for working with at-risk students that were considered state-of-the-art only two or three decades ago are now considered woefully outdated. Without question, educational support service professionals have a strong need for new techniques and tools to use in working with students, parents, and teachers. Not only do these tools and techniques need to be effective and based on sound empirical evidence, they also need to be practical and easy to use. Given their multiple demands and heavy caseloads, educators and mental health professionals have no time to invest in esoteric assessment and intervention techniques. What they need are practical and effective solutions that they can put to immediate use.

*The Guilford Practical Intervention in the Schools Series* responds to the need for practical and efficient tools for working with at-risk children and youth in school settings. The books in this series will be diverse in terms of the specific issues addressed. However, all books will share some important values. First, they apply primarily to the needs of support service professionals who practice in school settings, specifically those who focus on the academic and social–emotional needs of at-risk students: school counselors, school psychologists, school social workers, school nurses, special education consultants, and so forth. These books may also be useful for classroom teachers, administrators, and mental health professionals who work with youth in settings other than schools, but the specific audience for whom these books are intended is educational support service professionals. Second, the books in this series are aimed at providing practical solutions to real problems. Although every book in the series will be based on sound scientific principles, empirical evidence, and current theory, these foundational aspects are not emphasized in the series books to the extent that they would be in academic or reference texts. Rather, the specific focus of these books is on practical solutions for everyday problem situations in the schools. Third, all books in the series will be designed to be used by practitioners in their day-to-day work. They are meant to be used directly and frequently in planning, delivering, and monitoring effective assessment and intervention services. As such, all books in the series will contain easy-to-use tools such as reproducible handouts, checklists, step-by-step directions, and illustrative case studies.

If the past half-century is any indication, we can anticipate that the demands placed on our educational systems will continue to change in response to external pressures, changing legal mandates, new findings, and more importantly, the specific problems and needs of students. As circumstances change, so will the approaches used for providing educational support services. However, it is unlikely that the need for practical and effective tools for use by educational professionals in solving day-to-day problems will ever change. The books in *The Guilford Practical Intervention in the Schools Series* will provide educational support service professionals with practical tools that will be valuable not only now, but well into the future.

KENNETH W. MERRELL, PhD
*Series Editor*

# About This Book

This book is intended for day-to-day use by school counselors, school psychologists, school social workers, special education consultants, mental health specialists, and other support service professionals in their work with at-risk students in school settings. The intervention techniques for depression, anxiety, and related internalizing problems that are emphasized in this book are eclectic, but are most influenced by the cognitive-behavioral and psychoeducational approaches to prevention and treatment. None of the chapters in this book contain scripted treatment packages, although such programs are discussed. The guidelines for intervention and prevention that are provided here are easy to use and readily adaptable for work with children and youth in a variety of settings. This book should not be considered an "empirically validated treatment" in the strict sense of the term. However, *all* of the intervention techniques that are included have at least a moderate amount of empirical support behind them, and several of these techniques have a great deal of empirical support for their efficacy. Thus, all of the techniques presented in this book are "evidenced-based" to varying degrees.

The first two chapters of the book provide a foundation for understanding how depression, anxiety, and related problems are manifested in children, and how these problems develop and are maintained. Chapter 3 provides a practical guide to assessing depression and anxiety in children and adolescents, and emphasizes a suggested model for effective assessment, as well as how to link assessment to intervention. Chapters 4 through 7 cover a wide range of intervention strategies for depression, including cognitive treatment techniques, interpersonal therapy, behavioral treatment strategies, emotional education, interpersonal problem-solving and conflict resolution training, social skills training, and comprehensive, cognitive-behavioral treatment approaches. Chapters 8 and 9 cover the most widely used psychological and psychoeducational treatment approaches for anxiety and related problems, including systematic desensitization, modeling, reinforcement, and various cognitive-behavioral intervention methods such as self-control training, self-instructional training, the "transfer of control" approach, and social skills training. The final chapter of this book, Chapter 10, provides guidelines for making referrals for outside mental health counseling services and psychiatric medications, and includes an overview of psychiatric medications that are used for treating depression and anxiety in children and adolescents.

This book is intended for use by professionals who have received basic training in delivering psychoeducational interventions to students in school settings. It is not intended to be a replacement for specific treatment services needed by seriously troubled students, which should be provided by specialists. Although the focus of this book and most of the examples are specific to working with children and youth in school settings, many of the principles and techniques are relevant to work in other settings as well, such as clinics and community-based programs for at-risk youth.

More than 40 specific psychoeducational and psychosocial intervention techniques are detailed in this book. These techniques were selected for inclusion on the basis of their broad applicability, empirical support, practicality, and potential ease of implementation in school settings. This large number of potential intervention techniques is obviously more than you will ever be able to implement with one individual student or one group of students. It is not my intention that these techniques be viewed as individual components of one massive intervention that you should use in a rigid manner, or that they should be pitted against each other in a "which one is the best?" manner. Each of them will be useful for various specific purposes. Rather, you are encouraged to select among the various intervention techniques presented in this book based on the specific needs of the students with whom you are working, the time and resource availability to conduct an intervention, and your own practical and theoretical preferences for working with children and adolescents.

The chapters in this book contain tables, figures, and worksheets that were designed to make the theories and techniques easier to understand and apply. Most of the chapters that deal specifically with intervention contain reproducible worksheets for use in applying specific intervention techniques with individuals and groups of students. Individuals who purchase this book are granted permission to photocopy these reproducible worksheets for use in their own educational and clinical work with children and adolescents (see copyright page for details).

# Index of Intervention Programs and General Intervention Strategies, with Descriptions of Purpose and Developmental Level

## Comprehensive Intervention Programs for Depression

| Program | Purpose | Developmental level |
|---|---|---|
| The Adolescent Coping with Depression Course | A comprehensive cognitive-behavioral program (16 2-hour sessions) for treatment of depression in small groups, using a psychoeducational approach for teaching skills | Primarily for adolescents ages 14–18, but may be used with younger adolescents and older children with sufficient cognitive maturity |
| The Taking ACTION Program | A comprehensive cognitive-behavioral program (30 1-hour sessions) for group and individual treatment of depression | Intermediate-elementary-school age (ages 9 or 10) through late adolescence |
| Interpersonal family therapy for childhood depression | A comprehensive family-centered program (16 sessions) for treatment of depression in children and adolescents, including cognitive, behavioral, affective, and interpersonal treatment components | May be used with families of elementary- and secondary-grade students |
| Interpersonal psychotherapy for adolescents with depression | A comprehensive intervention program (12 sessions) aimed at decreasing symptoms of depression and improving interpersonal functioning | Adolescents with average or higher intellectual ability |

## Intervention Strategies for Depression

| Technique | Purpose | Developmental level |
|---|---|---|
| Cognitive therapy (Ch. 5) | A comprehensive method for treating depression by helping students identify, monitor, and change their patterns of thinking and believing | Older children and adolescents |
| The Emotional Thermometer (Ch. 5) | To teach that emotions vary in intensity | All ages, but keep emotional gradations simple for younger children |
| The Emotional Pie (Ch. 5) | To identify the overall composition of mood states, or which moods/ emotions are experienced more frequently than others | Older children and adolescents |
| Thought Chart (Ch. 5) | To identify automatic thoughts and the situations and feelings that elicit those thoughts | Older children and adolescents |
| The Cognitive Replay Technique (Ch. 5) | To identify automatic thoughts | All ages, but younger and less sophisticated children will need more structure and feedback |

*(continued)*

## Index of Intervention Programs and Strategies (*continued*)

| Technique | Purpose | Developmental level |
|---|---|---|
| Thought forecasting (Ch. 5) | To identify automatic thoughts | Older children and adolescents |
| Hypothesizing/guessing (Ch. 5) | To detect automatic thoughts and beliefs | All ages |
| The Down-Arrow Technique (Ch. 5) | To identify underlying beliefs associated with negative thoughts | Cognitively mature older children and adolescents |
| Identifying cognitive distortions or thinking errors (Ch. 5) | Identification of basic errors in thinking or distorted cognitions | Older children and adolescents who are cognitively mature |
| Examining the evidence (Ch. 5) | Evaluation of whether automatic thoughts and underlying beliefs are realistic | Older children and adolescents |
| Evaluation of positives and negatives (Ch. 5) | Evaluation of whether automatic thoughts and underlying beliefs are realistic | Older children and adolescents |
| Daily Record of Thoughts (Ch. 5) | To substitute appropriate and realistic thoughts for automatic negative and distorted thoughts | Older children and adolescents |
| The Triple-Column Technique (Ch. 5) | Identification and substitution of automatic negative thoughts and thinking errors | Older children and adolescents |
| Reframing and relabeling (Ch. 5) | To substitute adaptive beliefs or thoughts for dysfunctional ones | Older children and adolescents |
| Cognitive rehearsal (Ch. 5) | To rehearse appropriate and adaptive thoughts and beliefs | All ages |
| Increasing positive statements (Ch. 5) | To practice making positive self-statements or affirmations that are realistic and personal | All ages |
| Rational-emotive therapy (Ch. 6) | To dispute irrational maladaptive thoughts and replace them with more realistic and productive thoughts | Older children and adolescents |
| Self-monitoring and self-control training (Ch. 6) | To train students to adequately monitor their thoughts, activities, and feelings, and to attend to the results of these circumstances in a realistic and effective manner | Older children and adolescents |
| Attribution Retraining (Ch. 6) | To reduce cognitions that may lead to depression, by using a combination of environmental enrichment, personal control training, resignation training, and attribution retraining | All ages |

(*continued*)

| Technique | Purpose | Developmental level |
|---|---|---|
| Learned optimism training (Ch. 6) | To retrain pessimistic patterns of thinking into more optimistic and productive patterns | Older children and adolescents |
| Journal writing (Ch. 6) | To keep track of thoughts, activities, and feelings in a structured way that allows for monitoring and reflection | All ages |
| Activity scheduling (Ch. 7) | To increase the amount of time that is spent in purposeful, positive, and potentially reinforcing activities | All ages |
| Positive reinforcment, extinction (Ch. 7) | To reduce symptoms of depression and anxiety by increasing behavioral responses that are incompatible with those symptoms | All ages, but especially useful for younger children |
| Identifying comfortable and uncomfortable feelings (Ch. 7) | To increase awareness of one's emotions in general, and to evaluate "feeling words" based on whether they are linked to feelings of comfort or discomfort | All ages, but younger children will require simplified lists of feelings |
| Incomplete sentences techniques (Ch. 7) | To increase self-identification of one's patterns of emotionality | All ages |
| The Feeling Menu Technique (Ch. 7) | To increase one's emotional vocabulary and to enhance awareness of emotional states that accompany specific events or circumstances | All ages |
| The Reacting to Emotional Situations Technique (Ch. 7) | To practice or rehearse reactions to common emotionally charged situations | Older children and adolescents |
| Self-Rating for communicating feelings (Ch. 7) | Self-appraisal of one's confidence and ability at communicating feelings | Older children and adolescents |
| Interpersonal problem-solving and conflict resolution training (Ch. 7) | To increase skills in solving interpersonal problems and conflict | All ages, but younger children will require higher levels of structure and support |
| Social skills training (Chs.7 and 9) | To increase skills for interacting appropriately and effectively with other people | All ages |
| Relaxation training (Ch. 8) | To produce states of relaxation and calmness that are incompatible with depression, anxiety, and related social–emotional problems | All ages |

(*continued*)

## Comprehensive Intervention Programs for Anxiety

| Program | Purpose | Developmental level |
| --- | --- | --- |
| The "Coping Cat" Program (Ch. 9) | A comprehensive cognitive-behavioral program for group and individual treatment of anxiety | Older children and adolescents |
| The Transfer of Control Approach (Ch. 9) | To reduce anxiety and phobia symptoms through gradually increasing exposure to the problem stimuli and gradually transferring control over the treatment techniques from practitioner to student | Cognitively mature older children and adolescents |

## Intervention Strategies for Anxiety

| Technique | Purpose | Developmental level |
| --- | --- | --- |
| Systematic desensitization (Ch. 8) | To reduce and inhibit fear responses to specific stimuli, by teaching relaxation responses in the presence of the feared stimuli | All ages, but particularly students in grades 3 and older |
| Relaxation training (Ch. 8) | To produce states of relaxation and calmness that are incompatible with depression, anxiety, and related social–emotional problems | All ages |
| Differential positive reinforcement, shaping, and extinction (Ch. 8) | To reduce anxious behavioral responses and increase behaviors that are incompatible with anxiety | All ages |
| Modeling (Ch. 8) | To reduce anxiety and fear responses by observing and modeling another individual who deals appropriately with the anxiety-provoking stimuli | All ages |
| Self-control training for anxiety (Ch. 9) | To train students to adequately monitor their thoughts, activities, and feelings, and to attend to the results of these circumstances in a realistic and effective manner | Older children and adolescents |
| Self-instructional training (Ch. 9) | To learn to appropriately alter maladaptive thoughts and behavior through the use of carefully scripted self-talk | All ages, but scripts for younger children must be very simple |
| Social skills training (Chs. 7 and 9) | To increase skills for interacting appropriately and effectively with other people | All ages |

## List of Specific Treatment Techniques for Depression and Anxiety, Grouped by Program Component

### Treatment Techniques for Depression

*Initial Screening and Intervention Planning*
    Social–Emotional Assessment Worksheet (Worksheet 3.1)

*Mood and Activity Ratings*
    Daily and Weekly Mood Log (Worksheet 5.1)
    Weekly Journal Entry Form (Worksheet 6.4)
    Weekly Journal Entry Form with Mood Rating (Worksheet 6.5)
    Baseline Record for Positive Activities (Worksheet 7.2)

*Emotional Education*
    The Emotional Thermometer (Ch. 5)
    The Emotional Pie (Ch. 5)
    Feelings Identification (Worksheet 7.3)
    Incomplete Sentences (Worksheets 7.4, 7.5)
    The Feeling Menu Technique (Worksheets 7.6, 7.7)
    Reacting to Emotional Situations (Worksheet 7.8)
    Expressing Feelings Inventory (Worksheet 7.9)

*Changing Behavior (Behavioral Interventions)*
    Activity Scheduling (Ch. 7)
    Reinforcement (Differential, Positive) of Desired Behavior (Ch. 7)
    Extinction of Undesired Behavior (Ch. 7)
    Relaxation Training (Ch. 8)
    Social Skills Training (Chs. 7 and 9)

*Detecting Automatic Thoughts and Identifying Beliefs*
    Thought Charts (Ch. 5)
    The Cognitive Replay Technique (Ch. 5)
    Thought Forecasting (Ch. 5)
    Hypothesizing/Guessing (Ch. 5)
    The Down-Arrow Technique (Ch. 5)
    Identifying RET's Common Irrational Thoughts (Ch. 6)

*Evaluating Automatic Thoughts and Beliefs*
    Identifying Thinking Errors (Ch. 5)
    Examining the Evidence: Three Questions (Ch. 5)
    Evaluating Positives and Negatives (Ch. 5)
    Disputing Common Irrational Thoughts (Ch. 6)

*Changing Negative Automatic Thoughts and Maladaptive Beliefs*
    The Daily Record of Thoughts (Ch. 5)
    The Triple-Column Technique (Ch. 5)
    Reframing and Relabeling (Ch. 5)
    Cognitive Rehearsal (Ch. 5)
    Increasing Positive Self-Statements (Ch. 5)
    Changing Irrational and Negative Thinking the RET Way (Worksheet 6.1)
    Attribution Retraining (Ch. 6)
    Learned Optimism Training (Ch. 6)

*(continued)*

## List of Specific Treatment Techniques (*continued*)

*Relaxation Training*
    Progressive Muscle Relaxation (Ch. 8; Table 8.1)
    The Abbreviated Relaxation Technique (Ch. 8; Table 8.2)

*Interpersonal Problem Solving and Conflict Resolution*
    Four Maladaptive Styles of Dealing with Conflict (Ch. 7; Table 7.2)
    Five Steps for Solving Conflicts (Worksheet 7.10)


## Treatment Techniques for Anxiety

*Systematic Desensitization*
    Progressive Relaxation Training (Ch. 8; Table 8.1)
    Abbreviated Relaxation Training (Ch. 8; Table 8.2)
    Development of an Anxiety Hierarchy (Ch. 8; Worksheet 8.1)
    Desensitization Proper (graded exposure) (Ch. 8)

*Changing Behavior*
    Modeling (Ch. 8)
    Differential Positive Reinforcement (Ch. 8)
    Shaping and Extinction (Ch. 8)
    Social Skills Training (Ch. 9)

*Cognitive Change Strategies*
    Self-Control Training for Anxiety (Chs. 6 and 9)
    Self-Instructional Training (Ch. 9)
    See also Chapters 5 and 6

# 1

# Understanding Depression and Anxiety in Children and Adolescents

## INTRODUCTION AND OVERVIEW

Depression, anxiety, and related "internalizing" problems of children and adolescents have been the focus of increased professional concern during the past two or three decades. During the majority of the 20th century, relatively little attention was given to these problems. In some cases, there was widespread denial that certain types of internalizing disorders, such as depression, could even exist in children. Fortunately, clinicians and researchers alike now understand that these problems are serious, complex, real, and most importantly, treatable.

This class of disorders, particularly depression and anxiety, is the focus of this handbook for school-based practitioners. Although there are several excellent, scholarly books available in this area, there are surprisingly few practical guides available to assist in understanding, evaluating, and treating depression, anxiety, and related problems of children and youth. Even fewer available resources are designed specifically to be applicable to intervention in school settings. This book is specifically designed to be such a practical handbook. This introductory chapter is designed to provide a foundation for understanding internalizing disorders in straightforward and practical terms.

The specific purpose of this introductory chapter is to help you develop a general understanding of depression, anxiety, and related internalizing disorders and problems, by defining, describing, and analyzing this area in some detail, particularly as it relates to children and youth. The first sections of this chapter provides some very specific descriptions and definitions of internalizing problems and the four specific clusters of disorders, syndromes, and symptoms that constitute this area. A brief overview of the major characteristics, prevalence rates, and related problems is provided for depression, anxiety, social with-

1

drawal, and somatic problems. Next, the issue of overlap and similarity among various internalizing symptoms is discussed. Finally, the information in this chapter is tied together by three case studies that help to set the stage for the development of interventions, which is the major focus of this book.

## WHAT ARE INTERNALIZING DISORDERS?

### Definition

Often misunderstood and frequently overlooked, internalizing disorders constitute a specific type of emotional and behavioral problem. In general terms, internalizing disorders consist of problems that are based on *overcontrolled* symptoms (Cicchetti & Toth, 1991). The term "overcontrolled" is used to denote that these problems in part are manifest when individuals attempt to maintain too much or inappropriate control or regulation of their internal emotional and cognitive state—in other words, the way they think about the way they feel. The term "internalizing" also indicates that these problems are developed and maintained to a great extent *within* the individual. For this reason, internalizing disorders have been referred to as *secret illnesses* (Reynolds, 1992), meaning that they are difficult to detect through external observation.

### Relation to Externalizing Disorders

Internalizing disorders contrast with *externalizing disorders* such as aggressive conduct problems, hyperactivity, antisocial behavior, and the like. These externalizing problems are thought to result in part from *undercontrol* or poor self-regulation. In other words, children who exhibit serious conduct problems such as fighting, stealing, assaulting, threatening, and other behaviors, tend to have serious difficulties in regulating their behaviors and emotional expressions. These problems are typically anything but secret, and they are generally easy to identify because they can be observed directly. Of course, although it has been well established that internalizing and externalizing disorders are indeed distinct domains, it is possible for children to exhibit *both* types of problems at the same time. In other words, a child or adolescent could be depressed and anxious, while at the same time engaging in hostile antisocial behaviors as a gang member. Therefore, it is important to consider that the presence of depression, anxiety, or related internalizing problems does not necessarily mean that the existence of externalizing problems is not a possibility as well.

### Terminology: Symptoms, Syndromes, and Disorders

Several key related terms have been introduced thus far or will be introduced later in this book. Specifically, the terms "symptom," "syndrome," and "disorder" are of interest and need to be fully understood to best comprehend the general area of internalizing disorders. These terms are sometimes used interchangeably, which can be confusing.

A *symptom* is a specific behavioral or emotional characteristic that is associated with particular types of problems or disorders. For example, depressed mood is a symptom of depression. In contrast, a *syndrome* is a collection of common symptoms. For example, the combination of depressed mood, sleep problems, fatigue, and feelings of low self-esteem would indicate depression as a syndrome. At this point, there are enough symptoms present to indicate a problem, and the affected person is in some distress. However, this problem or syndrome may not necessarily be formally diagnosable as a disorder. A *disorder* exists when a collection of symptoms or a syndrome meets specific diagnostic criteria, according to standard classification systems such as the fourth edition of the *Diagnostic and Statistical Manual of Mental Disorders* (DSM-IV; American Psychiatric Association, 1994), or the Individuals with Disabilities Education Act. For example, the syndrome of depression, as listed earlier, when accompanied by other symptoms, when exhibited over a common 2-week period, and when representing a change from previous functioning, would meet the criteria for *major depressive disorder* in DSM-IV. *A disorder always includes a syndrome and symptoms, and a syndrome always includes symptoms; however, symptoms do not always constitute a syndrome or disorder, and a syndrome is not always formally diagnosable as a disorder.* In this book, the general term "problem" is often used, instead of symptom, syndrome, or disorder. This term may indicate any or all of the three specific terms. An *internalizing problem* simply means an internalizing symptom, syndrome, or disorder that affects an individual to the point of causing distress.

For intervention purposes, it is usually not necessary to differentiate among the terms "symptom," "syndrome," and "disorder." However, for conducting effective assessments and for communicating information regarding a student to other professionals, such differentiation is very important.

## FOUR TYPES OF INTERNALIZING DISORDERS

Although the symptoms of internalizing disorders are numerous and complex, researchers have shown that there are four main types of specific disorders within this general category (Quay, 1986). These problems include *depression, anxiety, social withdrawal,* and *somatic or physical problems.* Of course, depression and anxiety are the best known of the four types of internalizing disorders and constitute the major focus of this book. However, to promote the complete understanding of internalizing disorders of children and youth, these four types are described briefly in this section.

### Depression

#### Characteristics

Probably the most recognized and best understood of the internalizing disorders, depression in both children and adults is primarily characterized by the following symptoms (see Table 1.1): depressed mood or excessive sadness; loss of interest in activities; sleeping problems (either sleeping too much or not enough); psychomotor retardation or slowing of

**TABLE 1.1. Main Characteristics of Depression in Children and Youth**

- Depressed mood or excessive sadness
- Loss of interest in activities
- Failure to make expected weight gains
- Sleep problems
- Psychomotor retardation (or agitation)
- Fatigue or lack of energy
- Feelings of worthlessness or excessive guilt
- Difficulty thinking or making decisions
- Preoccupation with death
- Irritability
- Physical/somatic complaints

physical movement (or in some cases, physical agitation); fatigue or lack of energy; feelings of worthlessness or excessive guilt; difficulty in thinking, concentrating, or making decisions; and a preoccupation with death. With adults, loss of weight is often associated with depression, but with children and adolescents, this symptom is sometimes manifest as a failure to make expected weight gains. The preoccupation with death that is often seen with adults and older children may not be seen in young children, for whom the concept of death is often too vague and abstract. Two additional symptoms often characterize the presentation of depression in children and adolescents: *irritability* and *complaints about physical symptoms*, such as stomach pain, headaches, and so forth. Of course, not all of these symptoms need be present for significant depression to exist. The general criterion for a diagnosis of depression is that at least five of these symptoms are present most of the time for the same 2-week period, and at least one of the symptoms is depressed mood or loss of interest.

## Prevalence

It is difficult to estimate with much certainty how many children and youth suffer from depression. The few large-scale studies that have been conducted to determine the proportions of the population that suffer from psychological or psychiatric disorders have often overlooked children and youth. Of the even fewer studies that have focused on children and youth, most have been designed to identify those individuals who exhibit symptoms to a great enough extent that they are diagnosed with a specific disorder, according to a formal criterion such as the DSM-IV. Such studies do not usually take into account cases in which there are enough symptoms present that the person is in significant distress and may benefit from intervention, but not enough symptoms present to be formally diagnosed with a disorder. Again, this type of symptom presentation is referred to as a *syndrome*.

Despite the limitations in our understanding of how many children suffer from depression, there are some general estimates that we can use as a guideline. I have previously reviewed the available studies on depression in children and adolescents (Merrell, 1999), and concluded that 4–6% would be a conservative estimate of the percentage of children who suffer from the symptoms of depression to a great enough extent to constitute a syndrome or disorder, and would benefit from further assessment and intervention. In practical terms, this estimate represents at least one or two students out of a classroom of 30.

Girls seem to report the presence of depression to a greater extent than boys. During and after adolescence (by ages 13–14), this difference between the sexes becomes particularly noticeable, with about twice as many girls as boys experiencing the symptoms of depression at a significant level. Before adolescence, there is more similarity in reported levels of depression, but even then, girls seem to report somewhat more symptoms than boys. There are many potential explanations for this gender difference, some of which are explored in Chapter 2.

## Disorders That Include Depression as a Major Feature

When we think of serious or "clinical" cases of depression, we are usually thinking in terms of what DSM-IV refers to as *major depressive disorder*, or a *major depressive episode*. However, it is important to realize that several other mood or adjustment disorders include depression as a major feature. Table 1.2 includes a list of disorders from DSM-IV in which depression is a key element of the symptom presentation. Although these classification categories were developed primarily from research with adults, they may also apply to children and adolescents in many cases.

Dysthymic disorder (or dysthymia) is a condition in which an individual has exhibited mild or moderate symptoms of depression for a long period of time (at least 2 years for adults, at least 1 year for children and adolescents). In this case, depression is less a temporary state and has become a more stable trait. In effect, being depressed becomes part of one's personality or general way of being. *Depressive disorder, not otherwise specified* is a general classification category used to diagnose depression when it is serious enough to interfere with one's life functioning but is not clearly diagnosable as one

---

**TABLE 1.2. DSM-IV Disorders with Depression as a Major Feature**

- Major depressive disorder
- Dysthymic disorder
- Depressive disorder, not otherwise specified
- Bipolar disorders
- Cyclothymic disorder
- Mood disorder due to medical condition or substance abuse
- Adjustment disorder with depressed mood

---

of the other disorders in Table 1.2. *Bipolar disorders* (commonly referred to as *manic–depression*) include serious levels of depression, or major depressive episodes, that alternate with *manic or hypomanic episodes*, which are periods of time when one feels a great deal of energy, invincibility, exhilaration, and a flood of ideas, all of which may lead to poor decision making. Bipolar disorders may include depression as the predominant symptom and occasionally alternate with manic episodes, or the reverse situation may be true. *Cyclothymia* has some similarity to bipolar disorders but lacks the intense severity of symptoms and tends to be longer lasting (at least 1 year). Individuals with cyclothymia tend to experience unpleasant mood swings that may alternate with varying degrees of depression, energy and exhilaration, and agitation or irritability. Parents of children and youth who exhibit cyclothymia tend to feel that their child is on an "emotional rollercoaster" that never ends. *Mood disorders due to medical condition or substance abuse* occur when individuals manifest significant symptoms of depression (or other mood problems) as a result of medical conditions (such as hypothyroidism—an underactive thyroid gland) or substance abuse (such as abuse of alcohol, barbiturates, or other depressants). Finally, *adjustment disorder with depressed mood* is a presentation of depressive symptoms that accompanies serious and long-lasting (6 months or longer) problems in adjusting to a major life event, such as a move, death of a loved one, or significant change in circumstances.

More specifics regarding depression in children and youth are discussed in Chapter 2, and some of the major issues presented in this section are summarized in Table 1.3. The mental health and human behavior professions have made a great deal of progress in understanding childhood depression in recent years. As unbelievable as it may seem to those professionals who received their training in the past decade or two, it was not many years ago that the existence of depression during childhood was seriously questioned in some circles. Today, it is generally understood that childhood depression does indeed exist and, fortunately, we are now much better equipped to provide effective assessment and intervention techniques. However, there is still much to learn about this perplexing problem and how best to deal with it.

---

**TABLE 1.3. Important Points in Understanding Depression in Children and Youth**

- Includes several possible symptoms, but *depressed mood or loss of interest is a hallmark characteristic.*

- May sometimes be differentiated from adult presentation of depression by *irritability, physical complaints, and lack of making expected weight gains.*

- *Approximately 4–6% of children and youth may exhibit depression as a syndrome or disorder.*

- Girls tend to exhibit more symptoms than boys, particularly after onset of adolescence.

- May be exhibited in several other mood or adjustment disorders besides major depressive disorder.

---

# Anxiety

## *Characteristics*

Anxiety disorders are an extremely broad category of problems, and the specific symptoms involved may vary considerably from one type of anxiety disorder to another. However, anxiety disorders do share some common elements. First, these disorders tend to involve three areas of symptoms: *subjective feelings* (such as discomfort, fear, or dread), *overt behaviors* (such as avoidance and withdrawal), and *physiological responses* (such as sweating, nausea, shaking, and general arousal). This particular way of explaining the presentation of anxiety symptoms has been referred to as the *tripartite model* because of the three main routes that are involved. Some of the more common presentations of anxiety symptoms (see Table 1.4) include negative and unrealistic thoughts, misinterpretation of symptoms and events, panic attacks, obsessions or compulsive behavior, physiological arousal, oversensitivity to physical cues, fears, or anxiety regarding specific situations or events, and excessive worry in general.

Two other terms are closely related to anxiety: *fears* and *phobias*. There is actually a great deal of similarity in the meaning of these terms but important differences as well. Fears are usually considered to differ from anxiety because fears involve *specific reactions to very specific situations* (such as a perceived threat), whereas anxiety usually involves a more *general type of reaction* (such as apprehension or discomfort) to a more *vague situation or stimulus*. Phobias are similar to fears in that they involve a reaction to a specific threat, but they differ because they are more intense, persistent, and maladaptive. For example, being accosted by a couple of large, tough, bullies after school would be a good reason for a student to show a fear response, but developing a debilitating fear of birds or bugs is less understandable and more maladaptive.

## *Prevalence*

Because anxiety is such a broad category, and because so many of its characteristics are common, it has been quite difficult to develop an accurate estimate of how many children and youth have anxiety disorders. The problem is further compounded by the same com-

---

**TABLE 1.4. Major Characteristics of Anxiety Disorders in Children and Youth**

- Negative and unrealistic thoughts
- Misinterpretation of symptoms and events
- Panic attacks
- Obsessions and/or compulsive behavior
- Physiological arousal
- Hypersensitivity to physical cues
- Fears and anxieties regarding specific situations or events
- Excessive worries in general

---

plications that have made it difficult to develop a good estimate of depression among children and youth. However, it is known that anxiety symptoms are quite common, and that anxiety disorders are not uncommon. In fact, anxiety disorders may be the largest category of internalizing disorders. It has been estimated that anxiety problems constitute about 8% or less of referrals to clinicians or of behavioral–emotional problems among the general child population (Morris & Kratochwill, 1998). However, the percentage of children and youth who have diagnosable anxiety disorders is probably somewhat less than this figure, perhaps somewhere in the range of 3–4%. Although the evidence is not as convincing as the evidence for depression, girls may have a somewhat higher risk than boys for developing anxiety disorders or problems.

## Disorders That Include Anxiety as a Major Feature

As Table 1.5 indicates, there are a large number of diagnosable disorders in the DSM system that include anxiety symptoms as a key feature. Some of these disorders, such as *obsessive–compulsive disorder*, are a bit peripheral to the aims of this book, whereas others, such as phobias, may be very specific to particular children and their circumstances. A couple of these disorders are particularly important when working with children. *Separation disorder*, a condition in which one shows excessive and continued distress when separated from a parent or primary caregiver, is particularly common in younger children. Often related to separation disorder is a problem commonly referred to as *school phobia*, in which children exhibit unusual fear, anxiety, and panic symptoms in response to going to school. *Generalized anxiety disorder* (formerly referred to as *overanxious disorder of childhood*) is a broad category indicating severe anxiety symptoms that are not necessarily tied to specific events or situations. A child or youth with this disorder will typically show significant "free-floating" anxiety characteristics across a variety of situations and across time. The particular symptoms that may be seen with generalized anxiety disorder include restlessness, fatigue, difficulty concentrating, irritability, muscle tension, and sleep disturbances. Obviously, some of these characteristics are quite similar to what might be exhibited with depression. And like depression, anxiety symptoms may also be caused by medical conditions or substance abuse. For example, use of amphetamines and marijuana may provoke general anxiety symptoms.

As is true with depression, for diagnostic purposes (but not necessarily for intervention purposes), it is important to understand the difference between anxiety symptoms, syndromes, and disorders. As has already been mentioned, anxiety symptoms are very common among children and youth but in most cases do not cause any significant or lasting problems. When symptoms of anxiety are abundant and severe enough to cause such problems, we would say that an anxiety syndrome is present. If the characteristics of an anxiety syndrome meet specific diagnostic criteria, say, from DSM-IV, then one would also have an anxiety disorder. However, one of the main points of this book is that the overlap between depression, anxiety, and other internalizing problems is so great that it is not unusual for someone to have a combination of co-occurring symptoms that may not be diagnosable as a specific disorder in DSM-IV, but for all practical purposes constitutes a "general internalizing disorder."

**TABLE 1.5. DSM-IV Disorders with Anxiety as a Major Feature**

- Separation disorder
- Panic disorders
- Agoraphobia
- Specific phobias
- Social phobia
- Obsessive–compulsive disorder
- Posttraumatic stress disorder
- Acute stress disorder
- Generalized anxiety disorder (overanxious disorder)
- Anxiety disorder due to medical condition or substance inducement

## Social Withdrawal

### Characteristics

Social withdrawal is usually not thought of as a specific type of internalizing problem or disorder but is generally considered to be something that often goes along with or is a part of these problems, specifically, depression and anxiety. However, some of the previous research on classification has shown that social withdrawal is often identified as a specific cluster of internalizing problems (Quay, 1986). Social withdrawal usually includes several key characteristics (see Table 1.6). Children and youth who are socially withdrawn actively avoid the companionship of others. They may lack responsiveness to the social initiations of other children and have behavioral deficits in the particular skills required to make and keep friends. Social withdrawal may be a temporary characteristic or be a long-term concern or trait. For example, a youth with a former pattern of many social interactions may withdraw from the companionship of his or her friends during a bout of severe depression and return to the pattern of frequent social interaction at a later time. Or a child may have a long-standing pattern of social withdrawal because of excessive shyness and social immaturity. In some cases, a socially withdrawn student may actually have reasonably good social skills but avoid getting involved in social interactions because of an unrealistically negative view of his or her social ability. For example, a high school student who consistently thinks, "*I am such an idiot when I try to talk to other people,*" may actively avoid getting involved with others, even though he or she might like to and may actually have the skills to do it effectively.

### Prevalence

Because social withdrawal is not traditionally thought of as a specific disorder, it is impossible to estimate the percentage of children and youth who have significant problems in this

**TABLE 1.6. Major Characteristics of Social Withdrawal in Children and Youth**

- Not usually considered a separate disorder, but is a main component of several disorders.
- May involve unrealistic self-appraisal of social performance.
- May involve a lack of interest in social interaction.
- May be complicated by excessive fear.
- May involve a deficit in *social approach behaviors*.

area. However, this is not a rare problem, and many children exhibit and suffer from the characteristics of social withdrawal.

## Somatic Problems

### Characteristics

Somatic problems, by definition, are complaints of physical discomfort, pain, or illness that have no known medical or physical basis. It is presumed that such symptoms are caused by emotional distress and are *psychological rather than physical in nature*. However, it is important to realize that just because a somatic symptom may have no known medical or physical cause does not mean that the discomfort is not very real to the person who is experiencing it, just as real as if the cause were an injury, infection, or structural problem. It is also important to consider that we must always emphasize the word "known" when we say that a somatic symptom has no known medical or physical basis. It is quite possible that there may be an injury, infection, structural problem, or allergic reaction of some kind that is causing the physical discomfort, but it simply is not detectable within the limits of current medical assessment technology.

Like social withdrawal, somatic problems are usually viewed as an ancillary part of internalizing disorders such as depression and anxiety rather than a separate internalizing disorder. But like social withdrawal, the classification research has often shown somatic problems to be a unique component of the broad domain of internalizing disorders. Because they are not usually viewed as a distinct disorder, exact prevalence data are difficult to find. However, it is widely understood that somatic problems are extremely common in children and youth.

The most common somatic complaints of children and youth (see Table 1.7) seem to be *stomachaches, pains, or nausea; headache; pain in the eyes; pain in the limbs or joints;* and *tingling sensations or numbness in the extremities.* It is not uncommon for children who exhibit somatic problems to report feeling dizzy or faint. In some cases, somatic complaints may be inconvenient and uncomfortable but not debilitating. In other cases, the severity with which these symptoms are experienced results in a major obstacle to adaptive functioning in life. It has been theorized that many individuals with significant and long-lasting somatic problems may have an *oversensitivity to physiological cues*; that is, they have a

TABLE 1.7. Major Characteristics of Somatic Problems in Children and Youth

- Often a key component of depression and anxiety disorders.
- May involve *oversensitivity to physiological cues*.
- Common complaints in children include *stomachache or nausea, headache, pain in eyes, pain in limbs or joints, tingling sensations or numbness*.

heightened ability or tendency to focus on and become aware of physiological sensations that many persons would not be aware of or simply pass off as being unimportant. Obviously, the way one thinks about such unpleasant sensations plays an important role in how distracting and problematic they may be.

## OVERLAP OF INTERNALIZING PROBLEMS

It has long been known that internalizing problems—whether they be symptoms, syndromes, or disorders—have a strong tendency to overlap or occur together. In the medical field, the term "comorbid" indicates the simultaneous existence of two separate diseases processes, each having a separate pattern of development. For example, one could at the same time have a sinus infection and a skin rash; the two conditions exist in the same person and at the same time, but might be presumed to be unrelated in terms of their causes. In psychology, the term "comorbidity" has been used to indicate similar relationships. For example, a child could exhibit depression and panic attacks at the same time.

The use of the term "comorbidity" to describe the relationship among various internalizing problems is perhaps unfortunate. This term implies that the two problems have separately occurring processes of development and maintenance. However, in reality, it is understood that internalizing problems, like many psychological disorders, may exist in a kind of symbiotic relationship; that is, they may nurture and sustain each other, and may have developed through similar events, predispositions, and patterns of responding.

Regardless of the language used to describe this phenomenon, it is widely known that depression, anxiety, social withdrawal, and somatic complaints often occur in unison. In some cases, the symptoms are the same. For example, irritability, fatigue, difficulty concentrating, and sleep problems are key diagnostic features of both major depressive disorder and generalized anxiety disorder in DSM-IV. Also, children with significant depression and those with significant anxiety may both develop somatic problems such as stomach pain, headaches, and so forth. Additionally, social withdrawal may be both a cause and effect of depression and is in many cases also linked with anxiety disorders. This similarity among core symptoms has made it difficult for researchers statistically to separate internalizing disorders in the manner that they are distinguished in DSM-IV.

The overlap or co-occurrence of internalizing problems is not limited only to symptoms shared by depression and anxiety, or common consequences of the two problems. In fact, it is known that in a surprisingly large number of cases—as many as one out of three—anxiety and depressive disorders are formally diagnosed in the same individual at the same time. This fact should not be surprising given that several of the symptoms are the same. You will also note in later chapters of this book—those that focus exclusively on intervention—that some of the effective interventions for one internalizing problem are also effective for others, such as relaxation training, social skills training, and cognitive restructuring. However, in some cases, very specific and somewhat narrow intervention strategies may be effective for one type of internalizing problem but not for related types of internalizing problems. As is shown in Chapter 2 in the discussion of development of internalizing problems, much is still unknown regarding the similar or separate processes of internalizing problems.

## STUDENTS WITH INTERNALIZING PROBLEMS: THREE CASE STUDIES

In this section, three case studies or stories are presented. These true stories (with names and certain other facts changed to ensure confidentiality) are all from my own clinical experience as a psychologist and educator. Any other practitioner or educator of at-risk students has or will have many similar stories. These stories are not unusual or remarkable; they are quite commonplace. They all differ according to the situation, the background, the details, and the outcome, but they share a common thread. Each of these three children or adolescents was suffering greatly from depression, anxiety, and related symptoms of *internalizing disorders,* such as social withdrawal and physical symptoms. These case studies are presented to illustrate the challenges and complexities of internalizing disorders, along with the exciting possibilities available to school-based practitioners for helping troubled students.

### Emma

Emma was 8 years old and in second grade when her mother brought her in to the university training clinic where I supervised the work of psychology graduate students. Our intake meeting revealed a family history of severe depression, and Emma seemed destined to continue this history with a vengeance. A precocious girl, Emma's verbal and cognitive skills were more like those of a fifth grader than a second grader. But she also talked frequently of wanting to die. She had difficulty sleeping at night because of feelings of anxiety, hopelessness, and panic. She had to be physically removed from her bed in the morning and literally taken to school. Although she had previously been a gregarious girl, Emma's peer relations had deteriorated significantly that year, and most other kids actively avoided her. At school and at home, Emma would engage in "crying jags" that sometimes lasted for an hour or more. Although from my point of view Emma had many things going for her, she seemed convinced otherwise, and her self-esteem and desire to engage in life had plummeted to an alarmingly low level.

Emma's father—convinced that counseling was futile—maintained that "drugs are the only thing that work." But Emma's mother first wanted to give counseling a try. After a careful intake assessment, we designed a basic treatment plan that focused on behavioral and cognitive change strategies, as well as affective education. Individual counseling sessions would be carried out by a second-year graduate student working under my supervision. This student was highly competent but voiced doubts that such a serious case of depression could be treated adequately without first making a referral to explore the use of antidepressant medication. We all agreed to implement the individual counseling plan and reevaluate our progress after four sessions.

The following 10 weeks were nothing short of amazing. Following a carefully developed treatment plan that included 1 hour per week of individual counseling, follow-up meetings, phone checks with Emma's parents, and weekly data collection to gauge progress, we observed a steady improvement over the first 4 weeks, to the point that our concerns about Emma being a danger to herself, and the possibility of considering medication evaluation or even hospitalization, diminished and then vanished. By 7 weeks into the intervention, it was hardly noticeable—across settings—that Emma was depressed, anxious, or had any social concerns. By 9 weeks into the intervention, all of our indicators showed that Emma was not only functioning normally in all respects but that she was also thriving. During the 10th session, when termination of counseling was being considered, the student therapist asked Emma why she thought she was doing so much better. Emma replied, "I think I'm doing better because I think about my problems in a different way than I used to, and I do different things than I used to, and then I usually feel okay even if things aren't going okay." Follow-up meetings at 2 and 4 months after the termination of individual counseling sessions showed us that Emma had maintained all, or almost all, of the progress she had made during treatment.

## Brandon

Brandon was 17 years old and beginning his senior year in high school when I began to work with him through my consulting contract with a rural school district. He had been a concern of the high school staff since his first year there, but these concerns had increased substantially over time. Brandon had become heavily involved in the local drug culture and was currently serving probation for an incident that resulted in arrest and 1 week in a juvenile detention facility. According to school board policy, any illegal drug use at school would result in an automatic expulsion, as well as a call to the local sheriff's department. It seemed likely to many staff members that this result was inevitable for Brandon. He had formerly been a B student, but his grades had plummeted dramatically, and he was in serious danger of not earning enough credits to graduate from high school that year. Brandon's English teacher had been alarmed by the overtly suicidal content of his essays and journal entries. Brandon had told more than one peer and teacher that he thought constantly of dying, and that he might even try to take his own life.

Brandon agreed to meet with me one time, with no obligation to continue in counseling. Although he refused to make eye contact with me for the first 30 minutes of our meeting, by the end of an hour, we had established reasonably good rapport, and he agreed to see me one more time. That "one more time" turned into Brandon's agreement to have weekly sessions with me and to make an effort to get better. And getting better was not easy in this case. Brandon was living, as he described it, "in a black hole." Every day was a struggle for him to go on, as he had very little energy and seldom desired to go on. Hardly a day went by that his thoughts were not preoccupied with death, dying, and feeling alienated "from the entire universe." He was also angry, resentful, and seemed to have a unique talent for simultaneously getting teachers in his corner pulling for him and getting them so angry that they wanted him out of their classes.

Progress, not easy in this case, did emerge. I had decided to go with an intervention plan that focused on identifying and disputing irrational and unrealistic thoughts, coupled with lots of modeling and role playing on more productive ways to think and react. My plan also included a heavy emphasis on keeping daily journals, confronting him when necessary, and helping him explore his feelings about his life in general. Week to week, there would be some progress, but it was often followed by regression and falling into old habits. There was the Friday night at 11:30, when I received a call at home from Brandon, who said he was at a phone booth "a long way from here," during a suicidal urge that was so serious I had to call the sheriff's office for possible backup support. After Brandon terminated our conversation abruptly, I was not sure where he was and wondered if I would be reading about him in the paper the next day. There were also the times when his descriptions to me of his involvement in the drug culture pushed my desire to keep confidentiality to the very limits of law and ethics.

But progress did occur. Within a few weeks, Brandon and I both began to notice an upturn in the way he was feeling, accompanied by a downturn in his school problems. Brandon began to incorporate the strategies he learned in our sessions into his everyday challenges and gradually noticed how much they helped. Within about 4 months, it was clear that his depression was at a manageable level, and our more serious concerns diminished. At our termination session, 1 week before he graduated from high school, Brandon spoke with enthusiasm and confidence about what he would do in the future, if and when the depression and suicidal thoughts returned.

## Marcus

A highly athletic and physically strong seventh-grade boy, Marcus seemed to be perpetually consumed in a chain reaction of anger and rage. He and his older brother, when they were younger, had been seriously physically abused by their father, a man for whom violence was the first approach to solving problems and conflicts. For the past 6 years, Marcus's mother had been divorced from his father, after years of domestic abuse and brutal control. A gentle and well-meaning woman, Marcus's mother was simply at her wits end with parenting two sons who seemed to perpetuate their father's disrespect toward this woman, which they had witnessed as young boys. Her view was that the best way to get Marcus's behavior under control was weekly karate lessons, to teach him self-discipline.

At school, Marcus was in a self-contained classroom for students with behavioral disorders because of his generally out-of-control behavior and extreme aggressiveness. On the surface, Marcus seemed to be a vicious, even dangerous boy, with an extremely serious case of conduct disorder. And his overt behavior at school only emphasized this one-dimensional view of him. He frequently assaulted other students, threatened to teachers, and exploded in uncontrollable episodes of rage. On one occasion, he caused another student to break a leg, by deliberately shaking him off of a 20-foot-high climbing rope in the gymnasium. Another time, he spit in the Vice Principal's face while he was being confronted for fighting, in full view of 10 or so other students.

But underneath Marcus's overt aggression, anger, and antisocial behavior was another dimension, that few people saw or understood. He often seemed to sink into a state of despair and hopelessness, sometimes refusing to remove his head from his desktop for an hour or two at a time. His journal entries revealed a scared and confused boy, who, because of his own hostility and anger, exhibited a desire to die, to end the perpetual torment he felt. Paradoxically to some, he was also consumed by fears and anxieties, and frequently awoke during the night in a sweaty state of panic. My own efforts to work with Marcus individually were uniformly unsuccessful. Referral to a psychiatrist resulted in two or three medication trials that tended to make him drowsy and "spaced out" but did not improve any of the major symptoms. The only person who seemed to make any impact with Marcus was his special education teacher, a remarkable veteran educator in her early 60s. This slightly built woman was barely 5 feet tall but showed no fear toward Marcus, even when he was confronting her during an explosion of rage. Through individual attention, group affective exercises, and interpersonal educational techniques, she had a knack for helping Marcus express his feelings, redirect his anger, and regain composure and calm when he was most upset. Although this was not a case in which we saw a quick turnaround, the progress that this teacher made with Marcus was remarkable and certainly helped to keep him in school many times when suspension or even expulsion might have otherwise been a certain outcome.

## The Common Thread

These three case studies share some common threads. First, it is important to note that symptoms of depression, anxiety, and other internalizing problems, although clearly present and prevalent, were often intermixed with other problems. Particularly in the cases of Brandon and Marcus, treatment of their internalizing problems had to take place within the context of many other problems, such as substance abuse, aggression, and overt hostility. Second, these cases illustrate how challenging, even daunting, treatment of children and youth with serious internalizing problems can be. With each case, there were some initially good reasons for hesitation, even skepticism, regarding how well the intervention might be expected to go. Third, and most importantly, these cases all show that the common intervention techniques illustrated in this book have tremendous potential for improving the lives of students who are in real pain. Although there will not always be a happy ending, you should proceed through this book, encouraged that the intervention techniques that are available to you offer *real possibilities*.

## CONCLUDING COMMENTS

A great deal of progress has been made during the past two or three decades in our understanding of depression, anxiety, and related internalizing problems of children and youth. Having clearly defined the general concept of internalizing disorders, there is now a relatively good understanding of the components and symptoms of these disorders. Defining and describing clearly the overlap of internalizing symptoms, syndromes, and disorders has been an important recent development. Despite the impressive progress in this area, we still have a long way to go. One issue that still needs some definitive clarification is the incidence and prevalence of the various internalizing disorders. At the present time, we can only estimate or approximate the percentages of children and youth who suffer from these problems. Additional comprehensive prevalence studies would be very useful in this regard. Another issue that is still not well understood is the overlap or co-occurrence of internalizing symptoms and disorders. Sometimes, classification or diagnostic labels such as "depression" or "anxiety" simply do not provide an accurate description of the problem, or do not fit particular children who experience many distressing symptoms, but not enough in any one category to justify a formal diagnosis.

This introductory chapter provides an initial foundation for understanding internalizing problems but is certainly not exhaustive or all-encompassing. Additional, helpful details for understanding this area are presented in Chapter 2, which provides additional practical insight into understanding internalizing problems, particularly regarding how these problems develop and emerge in children, what factors may cause or influence them, and the consequences to which they tend to lead. Additionally, Chapter 2 provides some practical guidelines for sorting out internalizing disorders from other common behavioral and emotional problems of children and youth.

# 2

# How Depression and Anxiety Develop and Are Maintained

## INTRODUCTION AND OVERVIEW

The previous chapter presented a basic description of depression, anxiety, and related concerns. Effective assessment, classification, and intervention practices, however, require a more comprehensive understanding of the development, course, and complications of internalizing problems. In recent decades, there has been a vast accumulation of evidence regarding depression and anxiety among children and youth. Although there is a great deal yet to be learned, accumulating evidence is beginning to provide a solid basis upon which to deal with these problems. The purpose of this chapter is to highlight some of the major developmental and outcome information regarding depression and anxiety among school-age youth, and to provide a solid foundation for selecting appropriate assessment techniques in particular situations.

The chapter begins with an overview of factors that influence the development of depression, anxiety, and related problems among young persons, especially biological, family, cognitive, behavioral, and life events influences. Next, a few comments on the stability and persistence of internalizing problems are presented. Some of the more direct possible consequences that internalizing problems pose are discussed, including diminished self-esteem, academic problems, peer problems, mental health problems, substance abuse, and suicide. Because internalizing problems are often complex and difficult to sort from other types of behavioral and emotional problems, extensive information and practical guidelines or keys are provided to help practitioners differentiate depression and anxiety from some of the other problems that are most commonly confused with them, including bipolar disorders, attention-deficit hyperactivity disorder (ADHD), conduct disorders, eating disorders, substance abuse, and Tourette's disorder.

17

# DEVELOPMENT OF INTERNALIZING PROBLEMS

To work effectively with depressed or anxious children, practitioners should have at least a basic understanding of how these problems develop, as well as some of the basic developmental complications they present. This section provides a brief and very basic overview of how internalizing problems are likely to develop. In particular, the influences of biology, family, psychological stress and life events, cognition, and behavior on the development and maintenance of depression and anxiety in children and youth are discussed briefly. The information in this section has been simplified greatly. It is not comprehensive and many potentially important aspects of development have intentionally been excluded. The focus here is on factors most commonly identified.

## Biological Influences

Most of the evidence for biological influences on depression and anxiety has been gathered through research with adults. Relatively little evidence specific to children and youth is available in this area. Given this state of affairs, readers should interpret the generalizations in this section with some caution. It is obvious that there are important differences in biological–neurological functioning of children and adults, but it may be some time before there is clear evidence in the role these factors play in emotional problems of young persons.

### Neurotransmitters

Abnormalities in neurotransmission (sending and receiving of brain chemicals) have been implicated in depression, particularly in the neurotransmitters acetylcholine, norepinephrine, serotonin, and neuropeptide (Harrington, 1993). Although it is extremely difficult actually to observe the workings of neurotransmitters in the brain, problems in this area have been connected to depression through secondary means. For example, medications such as fluoxetine (Prozac) and paroxetine (Paxil) are known to block the reuptake of serotonin (thus increasing its availability and transmission) and are also known to impact positively the symptoms of depression. Therefore, abnormalities in serotonin transmission are linked to depression. It has been presumed that some of the vulnerability to depression through neurotransmitter abnormalities may be genetically inherited in many cases. In fact, the available evidence indicates that genetic inheritance of vulnerability to depression, particularly severe depression and bipolar disorder, is quite likely.

### Temperament

Although neurotransmitter abnormalities may also play a role in anxiety, there is probably better evidence for biologically based temperament characteristics as an influence. Temperament, which is thought to be based in one's neurobiology, involves the unique way of reacting and responding with which each person is born and further unfolds during the first few months of life. Temperament in infants serves as a sort of template for later personality development. Researchers have noted that infants whose temperamental characteristics make them easily excitable, highly alert, and very reactive to new and different stimuli are more likely than other infants to become anxious, shy, and socially withdrawn during childhood (Kagan, Reznick, & Snidman, 1990). Although learning plays a very clear role in the development of anxiety problems, biological risk factors undoubtedly have a hand in shaping them.

## Endocrine System

The *endocrine system* is a series of glands throughout the body that release specific substances called *hormones* into the bloodstream. Each of the various hormones plays a particular role in regulating the body. For example, hormones assist in regulating growth, metabolism, body temperature, levels of blood sugar, sex drive, and other important functions. Although the parts of the endocrine system function somewhat independently, they are linked together as a system because they are all controlled and regulated by chemical messengers from the pituitary gland (also called the "master gland"), the endocrine gland that is closest to the brain, as well as the hypothalamus of the brain.

Medical researchers have found that abnormalities in the functioning of particular endocrine glands may promote the symptoms of depression (Harrington, 1993). For example, abnormalities in the functioning of the thyroid gland, which releases hormones that regulate body metabolism and temperature, among other things, have been shown to produce symptoms such as depressed mood, poor concentration, and a slowing of speech and movement. Overactivity or underactivity of the adrenal gland may also produce mood disturbances, ranging from symptoms of depression to the pressured speech, overactivity, and abnormal mood elevation that is typical of the manic state in bipolar disorders. Abnormalities in the release of sex hormones have also been implicated in mood disturbances and other internalizing problems in older children and adolescents.

## Family Influences

Family influences have a potentially powerful impact on the development and maintenance of depression in children and youth. Strained family relationships, extensive family conflict, poor family conflict resolution skills, and poor family communication patterns all increase the risk of depression in children. Having a family history of mood disorders or other psychological problems also heightens a child's or youth's vulnerability to depression. Even though vulnerability to depression within a family might be partially transmitted genetically, the role of modeling and social learning within family systems should not be underestimated. Children raised by parents who are themselves depressed have as their primary social and emotional role model a person who is struggling to cope with life, and they may model behaviors, emotional symptoms, and cognitive patterns that are part of the vicious cycle of depression. Certain family structure variables, such as divorced and single-parent families, also may increase vulnerability to depression.

Family influences for anxiety disorders have also been noted. Insecure attachment patterns between children and their parents have been linked to anxiety problems. Parents who are themselves highly anxious model the types of behavioral patterns that may perpetuate anxiety symptoms in the children. Parents who are depressed may become withdrawn and unresponsive to their children for periods of time, and thus unknowingly elicit clingy behavior, fear of separation, and anxious tantrums in their children. As in the case of depression, a family history of mood disorders increases the risk of anxiety problems among children. Development of fears by children is part of a normal pattern of emotional growth, and certain fears tend to be more prevalent at certain ages. However, if children live in a family where there are unusual or intense fears, they are much more vulnerable to developing a fearful, insecure, and anxious way of responding to normal situations in life.

Family influences on internalizing problems are not limited only to increased risk for depression and anxiety. Salvador Minuchin and his associates developed a comprehensive family–systems model and demonstrated that certain family functioning characteristics, such as rigidity in rules and expectations, inflexibility, and poor conflict resolution skills may serve to increase a wide range of somatic or physical symptoms of various family members (Minuchin, Baker, Liebman, Milman, & Todd, 1975; Minuchin, Rosman, & Baker, 1978). In this model, the somatic problems are presumed to serve the function of distracting family members from dealing with significant family problems. In such cases, the somatic problem becomes the focus of family attention, and excessive and inappropriate overprotectiveness toward particular family members may result.

## Psychological Stress and Life Events

A high degree of psychological stress and exposure to unusual or highly stressful events clearly increase the risk for depression, anxiety, and related internalizing problems for persons of all ages. Stressful life events such as death of a family member or other loved one, traumatic separation from parents, divorce of parents, exposure to disasters, hospitalization, chronic medical problems of a family member, and physical or sexual abuse heighten vulnerability to internalizing problems of all kinds. For example, a child or adolescent who becomes overwhelmed by stress and losses may become withdrawn and depressed. A child who loses a loved one or is exposed to a disaster may become clingy, anxious, fearful, and panicky. Additionally, it is well known that high rates of stress have a direct impact on the development of somatic symptoms such as headaches, abdominal pain or nausea, sweating, accelerated breathing and heart rate, numbness or tingling sensations, and dizziness (Siegel, 1998). Whether exposure to particular stresses and unusually difficult life events result in depression, anxiety, or other problems seems to depend on several factors, including other vulnerabilities and risk factors, a child's resiliency, and the amount of available social support.

## Cognitive Influences

The manner in which children develop particular styles of thinking about their world can have a strong influence in the development of depression and anxiety. Regarding depression, three very influential models of cognitive influence have been developed. The first model involves the attributions children make about their world. If persons perceive that they are helpless to influence or change events in their life, then they may become hopeless and depressed. This way of thinking is referred to as *learned helplessness*. Children who have developed learned helplessness feel that they have no power to make any positive changes in life; therefore, they see no use in trying. This way of thinking is particularly likely to lead to depression when children believe that they may be responsible for their failures and problems but that successes and positive events are totally beyond their control (Seligman, Reivich, Jaycox, & Gillham, 1995).

The second model involves cognitive distortions, or systematic negative biases in the way one thinks. Specifically, this model proposes that *persons who become depressed tend to have developed a negative view of themselves, the world, and the future* (Beck, Rush, Shaw, & Emery, 1979). They might also interpret their experiences and evaluate their own behavior in dysfunctional ways. This style of thinking results in a general negative view of things, as well as low self-esteem.

The third influential model is based on the idea that persons who are depressed have developed *a dysfunctional way of monitoring the events in their lives*. Also called the *self-control model* (Rehm, 1977, 1990), this notion proposes that depressed persons tend to (1) pay more attention to negative events than to positive events (thus distorting the prominence of negative events), (2) pay more attention to immediate as opposed to future consequences of their behavior, (3) evaluate themselves using unrealistic and overly strict standards, (4) make negative attributions about responsibilities for their behavior, and (5) punish themselves ("I did such a bad job on that assignment") more than they reward themselves ("I did a good job on that assignment") in the way they think (Rehm, 1977). Each of these cognitive styles are dealt with in more detail in the chapters on cognitive and cognitive-behavioral interventions.

Anxiety problems may also be influenced by the way in which children think about their world. Like depressed children, anxious children and youth tend to have developed a general pattern of negative and often unrealistic thinking about things. They often worry excessively about many things—they may fret, worry, or be overly concerned with things that most other people regard as being unimportant or would not even consider. Children and youth with anxiety disorders tend to misinterpret symptoms and events in a negative way that continues to provoke their anxiety (Albano & Barlow, 1996). For example, a simple glance by a teacher might be misinterpreted by anxious children as meaning that the teacher is upset with them, might get them in trouble, or is disappointed with them. In the case of children who experience panic attacks, the misinterpretation of events can be particularly serious or even "catastrophic." For example, anxious children who begin to panic when they experience mild sweating and some difficulty breathing might think that they are going to die, or that they are "going crazy." Additionally, highly anxious children and youth may selectively pay attention to physical symptoms that most children would simply ignore or pass off as being unimportant. Some mild abdominal distress after eating lunch would probably be dismissed by most teenagers without further thought, but a highly sensitive and anxious teen might pay very close attention to the sensations, and worry about whether he or she might become ill.

## Behavioral Influences

The particular patterns of behavior in which children and youth engage may strongly influence both the development and maintenance of depression and anxiety. Self-isolation or withdrawal from the company of others may be a characteristic of depression as well as social anxiety. Not getting involved and doing things with other children tends to lead to a lack of social reinforcement and can both cause and maintain feelings of depression, loneliness, and low self-esteem (Lewinsohn, Clarke, Hops, & Andrews, 1990). Another behavioral characteristic that often accompanies depression is not engaging in fun or positive activities. In some cases, children's depression might cause them to want to quit doing things they formerly enjoyed, such as bike riding, playing sports or games, or engaging in personal hobbies. Again, the loss of reinforcement that accompanies such behavioral changes may serve to cause as well as to maintain depressive symptoms. This pattern can then turn into a vicious cycle in which the child avoids doing the very things that might help him or her begin to feel better (Lewinsohn et al., 1990).

Behavioral influences on anxiety problems can also take other forms. For example, children and youth who have severe fears and anxieties about specific situations or events might be likely to escape or avoid those things. For instance, a child with severe social anxiety might want to approach another child on the playground, but as he or she thinks about it and gets closer to doing it, the anxiety symptoms become overwhelming, so he or she decides to avoid the situation altogether. The subsequent reduction in anxiety symptoms that follows the avoidance behavior serves as a strong source of negative reinforcement. Essentially, the child has terminated an aversive stimulus (approaching a social situation) by engaging in a specific behavior (social avoidance and withdrawal), and the result is that he or she is more likely to engage in avoidance and withdrawal behaviors in the future.

Children who have severe school phobia symptoms serve as a good example of this negative reinforcement process. When they awake in the morning on a school day, they may immediately begin to feel the arousal, distress, and panic that accompanies going to school. If they protest seriously enough (sometimes by developing severe symptoms such as vomiting, panic attacks, or shaking) and their parent decides to not send them to school that day, then the serious anxiety symptoms will eventually diminish, because the perceived threat has temporarily been removed. The relief that accompanies this lessening of symptoms is likely to serve as a powerful reinforcer to both the children and their parent, and they will likely continue the process of school avoidance in the future. This behavioral reinforcement can also serve to maintain other types of anxiety problems, such as obsessive–compulsive behavior.

# DO SPECIFIC INFLUENCES REQUIRE SPECIFIC INTERVENTIONS?

After reading about the five main categories of influences (biological, familial, psychological stress and life events, cognitive, behavioral) on the development of depression and anxiety, you might wonder whether a problem that is influenced primarily by one source or another requires a specific type of intervention. For example, if it can be determined that the primary influence on the development of depression with a particular student is biological in nature, then should an intervention be selected that is primarily biological in nature (such as psychiatric medication?).

Although such an automatic link between developmental influence on the problem and the indicated type of treatment might seem natural, my recommendation is to be very cautious about making such attributions. Certainly, there are some cases in which such a link is useful. For example, if you can determine clearly that the primary influence on a student's depression is cognitive in nature, then it makes good sense to emphasize cognitive interventions in order to change his or her maladaptive thought, belief, and attribution processes. Or if the best explanation for a young person's serious anxiety symptoms seems to be a combination of psychological stress and life events, it would make sense to try and help this student by using some stress reduction and life management techniques. But the reality of this matter is that such a direct automatic connection is seldom possible or essential.

There are two primary reasons why I urge you to be cautious about developing such influence–treatment connections. First, it is seldom possible to identify clearly one specific primary cause for depression or anxiety. Because behavioral, personal, and environmental factors are known to influence one another in a reciprocal manner (for a more detailed explanation of what is referred to as "reciprocal determinism," see Merrell, 1999), there are usually multiple causes, even though one type of influence may have come first. Second, many intervention techniques seem to work effectively regardless of the specific etiology or origin of the problem. For example, an individual with a diminished ability to produce or transmit serotonin may ultimately develop depression, but a cognitive-behavioral intervention may be just as effective (or even more effective) in reducing the depressive symptoms as a biological intervention. As a practitioner, it is useful to understand the developmental influences on depression and anxiety for a number of good reasons, but the design of interventions is probably best informed by the basic steps of linking assessment to intervention (Chapter 3), and by a solid foundation in knowing which intervention tactics are known to be useful, regardless of the foundation from which they spring.

## THE COURSE OF INTERNALIZING PROBLEMS: STABILITY AND PERSISTENCE

Until recently, it was generally thought that depression and anxiety in children and youth were usually just brief and transient. In other words, it was commonly thought that particular episodes of such problems did not last very long, and that these problems might "come and go" but not carry over into adulthood.

Current thinking in this area, bolstered by an increasing body of research on the topic, has evolved considerably. Although most researchers who study behavioral and emotional disorders of childhood would agree that internalizing problems are not as persistent as externalizing problems such as conduct disorder and ADHD, it is now understood that internalizing problems are often more than just "brief and transient" occurrences. For example, Silverman and Ginsburg (1998) reviewed several recent studies on this topic and concluded that serious internalizing symptoms of childhood may persist for perhaps as long as 2 to 5 years.

But just because a serious internalizing problem during childhood may last for several years does not mean that it will necessarily carry over into adulthood. In this regard, there is simply not much evidence, and the evidence we do have is complex and perhaps difficult to interpret clearly. Some earlier studies on this problem (e.g., Robbins, 1966) indicate that internalizing problems in childhood do not accurately predict internalizing problems in adulthood. Later, researchers began to look at the long-term persistence of internalizing problems in childhood with more precision and detail, and found that, in certain cases, there is a very strong likelihood of carryover of persistence in adulthood. For instance, serious depression during adolescence may be a very strong predictor of depression during adulthood (Cantwell, 1990).

An interesting aspect of childhood emotional and behavioral disorders to consider in general is that there is a *probabilistic relationship* between the occurrence of one episode and future episodes. Stated simply, such probabilistic relationships mean that each occurrence of a particular problem episode or disorder increases the probability of future occurrences. So a child or youth who has one major episode of depression, anxiety, or some related internalizing problem now faces an increased chance of a second occurrence, which in turn increases the chance of a third occurrence even more dramatically. As a general rule, behavioral and emotional problems of childhood that have an earlier onset and more severe symptoms are more predictive of future problems than problems with later initial onset and milder symptoms (Merrell, 1996).

# CONSEQUENCES OF INTERNALIZING PROBLEMS

Even if internalizing problems did not have any additional consequences other than the immediate distress and difficulties in functioning that accompany their symptoms, they would still be serious concerns. Unfortunately, the problems caused by various internalizing disorders are not limited to their immediate symptoms and deficits. Instead, there is ample evidence that the consequences of internalizing problems may be extensive. Some of these possible consequences are discussed briefly in this section and listed in Table 2.1. This information is presented not only to provide an increased informational perspective into this area but also to emphasize the seriousness of these problems and that they often require early identification and treatment to prevent some of their more damaging consequences.

## Diminished Self-Esteem

*Self-concept* is a term used to refer to the specific perceptions that individuals hold regarding themselves. These perceptions might include how persons evaluate various aspects of

TABLE 2.1. Possible Consequences
of Internalizing Problems

- Diminished self-esteem
- Academic problems
- Poor social relationships
- Chronic mental health problems
- Substance abuse
- Suicidal thoughts, attempts, completion

their abilities to perform a variety of tasks, as well as how they feel about themselves in general. This latter aspect of self-concept, how we feel about ourselves in general, is commonly referred to as self-esteem. Poor self-esteem is a common symptom of depression in children and adults alike. Persons who are depressed often feel that they are not worthy, good, or valuable. They are likely to underestimate their abilities and assets, and not seek out opportunities that might be good for them. Their distorted view of themselves and the world convinces them that they are bound to fail, so there is no use in even trying.

Having a poor self-concept or low self-esteem is not limited only to children and youth who suffer from depression. It is widely understood that there is a negative relationship between self-esteem and internalizing symptoms in general. In other words, as children's internalizing symptoms increase, their self-esteem is likely to diminish. And as internalizing symptoms decrease, self-esteem is likely to increase. Although diminished self-esteem is not necessarily a defining symptom of anxiety disorders, social withdrawal, or somatic problems, it is certainly likely to accompany these problems, particularly as they become more severe.

For example, consider the situation of a 12-year-old girl, Catherine, who does not suffer greatly from depression but does have serious struggles with anxiety and other related problems. Let us say that she suffers from a generalized anxiety disorder, a tendency to experience serious anxious arousal in a wide variety of situations, and with a considerable variety of precipitating events. Along with her feelings of fear, dread, and panic, she experiences certain somatic or physical symptoms, including accelerated breathing and heart rate, stomach pain, and sweaty hands and feet. Catherine is a very shy girl, and her anxiety and physical symptoms seem to get worse when she is the center of attention, or when she has to interact with other kids she does not know well. As a result, although she is lonely and would like to have some friends, she withdraws from the company of other kids at school and in her neighborhood. Although Catherine is a good student and actually has a number of other positive things going for her, the internalizing symptoms she experiences on a daily basis overwhelm her, and she constantly berates herself as being "stupid, ugly, boring, and no fun to be with anyway." Her negative view of herself keeps her from taking chances and trying new and potentially rewarding things in life. In summary, her self-esteem plummets as her anxiety-related symptoms worsen. Catherine's case illustrates how diminished self-esteem may accompany a range of internalizing symptoms even when depression is not the major problem.

## Academic Problems

Children and adolescents who suffer from moderate or severe depression, anxiety, or related internalizing problems may experience a decline in their school achievement or academic performance. As depression symptoms increase, students' abilities to concentrate, focus, and maintain the physical and mental energy needed to complete school assignments typically decrease, as does their motivation. The lethargy, sleep problems, diminished self-esteem, and negative self-evaluation that often accompany depression also complicate academic performance. As symptoms of depression become increasingly severe, a student may struggle simply to get to school and attend class, and the thought of facing difficult schoolwork may be perceived as being more than one can handle.

Although it is true that mild levels of *performance anxiety* (worry about the ability to perform on particular tasks) might not negatively impact students' performance, and in some cases, might even motivate them to improve their performance slightly, there are "diminishing returns" as anxiety increases. As anxiety regarding performance of school tasks becomes more severe, students' ability to adequately perform these tasks gradually declines, and even plummets as the anxiety becomes extreme. Students in such a predicament may feel so overwhelmed by the tasks facing them, and their ability to perform these tasks, that they simply cannot complete these tasks effectively. Nearly everyone has had the experience of becoming nervous about having to speak or make a presentation or perform in front of a group, and most people can relate to how such nervousness can frustrate people's ability to perform as they would like. Multiply this problem severalfold and you can get an idea of how debilitating performance anxiety can be for students.

Performance anxiety is not the only type of anxiety-related problem that can create academic difficulties or negatively impact school performance. Severe generalized anxiety can negatively affect many aspects of life, including academic adjustment and performance. Children who are overwhelmed by anxiety symptoms will likely not perform up to their potential in school, even if the anxiety is not specifically related to school performance. Specific fears and phobias may produce the same negative effects on school adjustment and academic performance. Obviously, a child who develops *school phobia*, or refuses to attend school because of severe fears about it, will experience a significant decline in his or her academic performance.

Little is known about the effects of social withdrawal and somatic problems on school performance and academic problems because these issues are seldom studied as separate syndromes or disorders. However, it takes no stretch of the imagination to understand that as symptoms in these areas become more troublesome, a student's schoolwork is likely to suffer.

## Poor Social Relationships

Difficulties with peers can be both a cause and effect of depression (see Table 2.2). Several years ago, Lewinsohn and colleagues theorized that the lack of social reinforcement that accompanies peer relationship problems can lead to depression (e.g., Lewinsohn & Graf, 1973; Lewinsohn, Mischel, Chaplin, & Barton, 1980). More recently, this theory about

**TABLE 2.2. Interpersonal Problems as a Cause and Consequence of Depression**

**A cause**

Interpersonal relationship problems, and the loss of social reinforcement that accompanies these problems, lead to depressed mood and related symptoms of depression.

**A consequence**

As symptoms of depression worsen, the withdrawal, negativity, lethargy, and irritability may produce interpersonal relationship conflicts, even when such conflicts did not previously exist.

**An insidious process**

As depression and the interpersonal relationship problems that accompany it become pronounced, the depression is likely to be maintained by the lack of social reinforcement.

depression and social relationship problems has also been adapted by those who advocate *interpersonal psychotherapy* (e.g., Mufson, Moreau, & Weissman, 1996). The interpersonal psychotherapy approach is based on the idea that depression often occurs in the context of interpersonal relationship problems. Both of these ways of thinking about depression are based on the idea that problems in the domain of social or interpersonal relations may lead to depression. However, it is also clear that, in many cases, depression might actually precipitate an increase in social–interpersonal relationship problems, even when there were not significant problems in this area beforehand. For example, take the case of a 12-year-old boy who, for a variety of reasons unrelated to peer problems, develops moderate to severe symptoms of depression. As his depression symptoms worsen, he becomes more irritable, negative, and withdrawn. Some of his friends find that he is now more difficult to get along with and just not as fun as he was before. So they are likely to spend less time with him. As this boy's friends become less available to him, he becomes angry with them, and when he is around them, he is not as friendly toward them as he used to be. So what was a result of the depression now also serves as a way of maintaining the depression, because the boy is less likely to receive the social reinforcement that might help improve his symptoms.

Children and youth who have significant anxiety problems may also experience peer social problems, particularly if the anxiety symptoms are centered on social relationships. Children who are socially anxious, or who develop strong fears of social situations, are likely to not develop adequate social skills, and their emotional growth and ability to evaluate their social competence will likewise suffer (Albano & Barlow, 1996). As outlined in Chapters 8 and 9, there are some very promising treatment approaches for anxious children and youth who suffer specifically from social problems, anxiety, and fears.

It almost goes without saying that children who are socially withdrawn will have few friends and may experience other social relationship problems with peers. They might be excluded, overlooked, and teased by their peers because they are so isolated. Socially withdrawn children who also exhibit high levels of aggressive behavior—sort of a combination of internalizing and externalizing problems—are especially vulnerable to serious social relationship problems with peers. Children with these combined characteristics may not only be excluded and teased but may also be actively avoided, disliked, and feared. In short, this combination of internalizing and externalizing characteristics is particularly bad.

## Chronic Mental Health Problems

Although internalizing problems in children and youth may not necessarily lead to more severe mental health problems, they certainly increase the risk. Particular characteristics seem to increase the risk of developing chronic and debilitating mental health problems: severe symptoms, multiple episodes, and early onset of problems all may serve as increased risk factors. Of course, when these three risk characteristics occur together—early onset, severe symptoms, followed by multiple episodes of severe symptoms—the risk for developing chronic and more debilitating problems is even greater. Also, a lack of family support and other social support will increase such risk, as will a lack of appropriate intervention.

There are several possible ways that chronic mental health problems may follow internalizing problems when there are sufficient risk factors present. Severe depression can be a chronic and debilitating illness in and of itself, whether or not it leads to other disorders. In the most serious cases of depression, individuals may experience "psychotic" symptoms such as delusional thinking and auditory hallucinations. In addition, chronic, serious depression may make even the basic tasks of life—going to school, work, and caring for self and family—nearly impossible. Prolonged serious cases of depression early in life may also increase the risk for development of schizophrenia or related psychotic disorders, provided that the other necessary risk factors for those serious disorders are in place.

Serious anxiety disorders may also become debilitating if they are untreated and prolonged. Particularly, obsessive–compulsive disorder, panic disorder, posttraumatic stress disorder, and phobias can make the most basic functions of daily living extremely difficult if these disorders occur across settings and the symptoms are severe.

Social withdrawal is usually not thought of as a something that may lead to chronic mental health problems, but when it is severe and prolonged, this possibility is certainly present. Children who actively avoid others, either because of a desire to be alone or because of social anxiety, may sometimes develop odd or unusual interpersonal characteristics and ways of presenting themselves. Over a long period of time, such peculiar behavior, in the extreme, may lead to the development of such serious problems as schizoid personality disorder and schizoptypal personality disorder. Most persons who experience social withdrawal in such a prolonged and serious manner end up with severely impaired personal and social judgment throughout their lives.

## Substance Abuse

It has been understood for many years that depression, especially as it becomes more severe, may be accompanied by alcohol abuse and other substance abuse problems. The relationship between depression and substance abuse is complicated because the problems may be both causes and effects of each other. For example, a previously normally functioning teenager who begins to experiment with alcohol, and gradually begins to increase alcohol use to the point where it becomes an impediment to school functioning and interpersonal relationships, may likely become depressed as a result. Likewise, young persons who become depressed may turn to alcohol or other drugs as an attempt to diminish the pain they feel. In either case, the depression and substance abuse tend to complicate each other. Alcohol in particular is a serious problem in this regard because it is so widely used and easily available, and because it ultimately worsens symptoms through its depressant effects on the body and brain.

Anxiety disorders are not linked to substance abuse quite as clearly as depression, but they certainly may act as a risk factor for substance abuse. When using a class of drugs referred to as *benzodiazepines* to treat anxiety symptoms, you must be particularly careful to ensure that serious substance abuse problems do not develop. This class of drugs, which includes widely used and highly effective compounds such as Xanax, Valium, Librium, and Atavan, is quite habit forming and potentially addictive. Additionally, the effects of benzodiazepines, like many other sedatives and tranquilizers, may be heightened when they are used in conjunction with alcohol. It does not take a great deal of these types of drugs in combination with alcohol to produce death, and they are sometimes used together as a way of committing suicide.

## Suicidal Thoughts, Attempts, Completions

Clearly, suicide is the most serious problem that may accompany or follow internalizing problems. In recent years, the number of self-inflicted intentional deaths among youth in the United States has risen dramatically, which is cause for serious concern among educators, mental health professionals, and parents (Brock & Sandoval, 1997). A few basic facts about suicide among youth, particularly teenagers, include the following:

- Suicide attempts are often preceded by a number of signals or warning signs, such as suicide notes, suicidal threats and statements, preoccupation with death, making "final arrangements," feelings of helplessness and hopelessness, losses and severe stressors, loss of interest in activities that were once important, heavy substance abuse, and marked changed in temperament and behavior.
- Girls are more likely than boys to make suicide attempts, but boys are more likely to actually complete attempts (commit suicide), because boys tend to use more lethal means of suicide than girls.
- A family history of suicide or severe psychiatric illness increases the risk for suicide.
- The highest rates of suicide among youth in the United States are found in the white (Caucasian, non-Hispanic) and Native American ethnic groups.

Certain behavioral and emotional disorders are particularly linked to suicide among youth, especially depression and conduct disorder. Therefore, where internalizing problems are concerned, depression is the most serious risk factor for suicide. There is also some thinking that youth with panic disorders may be at increased risk for suicide. In either case, it is important to understand that most children and youth who have internalizing problems (even serious disorders) *do not* attempt or commit suicide. Depression should be thought of as a risk factor that in combination with other circumstances and risk factors increases the likelihood that a person may attempt to commit suicide.

This book is intended to be a practical guide to depression and anxiety for school-based practitioners who work with students for prevention and basic intervention purposes. It is not intended to be a crisis intervention manual or a handbook for clinical or psychiatric treatment. However, no book on this topic would be complete without at least a basic set of guidelines for dealing with children and youth with whom there are concerns regarding suicidal ideation, gestures, or attempts. Table 2.3 provides a very basic list of recommended steps for dealing with students who may consider harming or killing themselves. You are encouraged to refer to this table to develop a basic framework for dealing with suicidal students and to consult more specific and detailed sources for more comprehensive information on suicide assessment, intervention, and postvention.

## TABLE 2.3.  Basic Steps in Responding to Students Who May Be Suicidal

1. **Thinking about suicide.** If there is any reasonable concern about the possibility of suicide, ask the student directly. Keep your questions simple and appropriate for his or her developmental level. Simply ask, "Have you been thinking about hurting or killing yourself?," or "Have you been thinking about wanting to be dead?"

2. **Suicide plan.** If there is enough evidence to indicate that the student has been having suicidal thoughts, try to find out if he or she has made a particular plan for a suicide attempt. Questions such as "Do you have a plan?" or "Have you thought about how you might do it?" might be useful. Note how specific or detailed the plans, if any, are. The more detailed or specific the plan, the more likely there will be an attempt.

3. **Means and preparations.** If students indicate that they have a plan, find out if they have made preparations to carry the plan out, or if they have the means available to do so. If the students indicate that they do have a plan or specific preparations, find out the exact location of any lethal means, such as guns, ammunition, drugs, and so forth.

4. **Intended place or setting.** If a suicide plan is in place, find out where the student might intend to commit the act. Ask if he or she has written a suicide note, and if so, what it says.

5. **Immediate protective action.** If, after going through steps 1–4, there is reasonable evidence that a student is seriously considering the possibility of a suicide attempt, immediate protective action must be taken. At this point, there is clearly an obligation to protect students from harming themselves. If there is a risk of imminent danger, notify parents, local law enforcement officials, and the local crisis center or mental health center, depending on the circumstances and laws in your locale. Never leave a clearly suicidal student alone, even for a short time.

6. **Suicide contract and follow-up planning.** If there is no reasonable evidence of imminent danger but still concern about the possibility of suicide, obtain a promise or written contact with students that they will not engage in any self-harmful behavior and that they will call an appropriate person or center if they feel inclined to do so. Provide names and phone numbers as needed. Make plans for ongoing counseling or consultation. Consider the confidentiality issues involved. Meet with the student's parent(s) and your supervisor, if the situation warrants it.

## COMPLICATIONS: SORTING OUT RELATED PROBLEMS

In addition to the potentially severe and long-lasting consequences posed by internalizing problems, another area of complication is sorting out these from other types of problems. Young people who are referred for assessment or counseling because of behavioral, social, and emotional problems often present a perplexing picture of characteristics. In many cases, it is extremely difficult to identify accurately the major problem because so many types of problems are present, or because the symptoms that are clearly present overlap with more than one type of disorder.

This section provides a basic guide to sorting out or differentiating depression and anxiety from the other types of problems that most frequently involve overlapping symptoms or are otherwise confusing to practitioners. Although there are a great many types of specific disorders that potentially could involve symptoms that overlap to some extent with depression and anxiety, only the most common types of other problems are dealt with here; specifically, bipolar mood disorders, ADHD, conduct disorders, substance abuse problems, eating disorders, and Tourette's disorder are discussed briefly in this section. These six problem areas are the most common situations in which depression and anxiety may either be confused or overlap. Tables 2.4 through 2.10 provide brief summary information regarding sorting out depression or anxiety from each of these other problems.

### Bipolar Disorders

As is indicated in Chapter 1, there is a considerable amount of overlap between the symptoms of regular (unipolar) depression and certain bipolar mood disorders ("manic–depression"). See Table 2.4. What is referred to as bipolar disorder I in DSM-IV is typified by the *occurrence of a manic or hypomanic episode*, or a *distinct and uncharacteristic period of elevated, expansive, or irritable mood*. The difference between a manic and hypomanic episode is one of severity. Both types involve the elevated, expansive, or irritable mood, but a manic episode is stronger in severity, of longer duration, and creates more significant distress in functioning. Certain subtypes of bipolar disorder I can occur within the context of a recent or previous major depressive episode. In other words, a manic or hypomanic episode is the key characteristic, but in some cases, it may be linked to depression.

What is referred to as bipolar disorder II in DSM-IV is typified by the occurrence of a hypomanic episode that is *secondary to the presence or history of a major depressive episode*. In other words, the key characteristic of the disorder is the presence or relatively recent history of depression, and the hypomanic episode(s) seem to play a secondary role. With either type of bipolar disorder, it is important not to confuse a hypomanic episode with a return to normal mood that may follow a remission of depressive symptoms. This is sometimes an easy mistake to make, because after someone has been seriously depressed for a long period of time, any change back to a "normal" mood can seem dramatic. It is important to evaluate the possible hypomanic symptoms within the context of what is normal for that person over a long period of time, not just since he or she became depressed. It may also be valuable to evaluate the characteristics of a sudden mood elevation in comparison to typical peers within the same developmental age group.

**TABLE 2.4. Keys to Differentiating Depression and Bipolar Mood Disorders**

Potential similarities

- Significantly depressed mood or notable irritability.

Differentiating characteristics

- Bipolar mood disorders always include at least one manic or hypomanic episode: a period of elevated, expansive, or irritable mood that may be severe and may cause significant impairment in functioning.

To summarize, the key feature in differentiating typical depression from a bipolar disorder is *the presence of a manic or hypomanic episode* or a marked and unusual period of mood elevation, expansiveness, or irritability that may become problematic in its own right. When such mood swings are long-lasting (at least 1 year for children or adolescents) but are not quite as intense (e.g., hypomanic symptoms and depressive symptoms without the presence of a major depressive disorder), the savvy practitioner will also consider the possibility of *cyclothymia*, which a less intense type of alternating mood disturbance (discussed briefly in Chapter 1). Because mood swings are not uncommon in children or adolescents, great care must be exercised to differentiate bipolar disorders or cyclothymia from the normal ups and downs that children and youth experience. Again, the keys to successfully understanding these problems include symptom intensity and duration, whether or not the mood swings cause difficulties in functioning, and how normal or abnormal the symptoms are in comparison with typical children or youth of similar age.

## Attention-Deficit/Hyperactivity Disorder

Although ADHD clearly falls within the externalizing domain, some of its symptoms are frequently confused with both depression and anxiety (see Table 2.5). The major feature of ADHD is a persistent pattern of inattention and/or hyperactivity–impulsivity that is more frequent and severe than that of most other persons at a comparable level of development. For example, it is not unusual for preschool and primary school-age children to display symptoms of inattentiveness, motor overactivity, or impulsiveness, but a young child whose characteristics in these areas or noticeably more severe than those of his or her peers might potentially be diagnosed as having ADHD. There are several ways that the common symptoms of ADHD might superficially overlap with internalizing symptoms and in some cases be mistaken for them (or vice versa).

Depressed children whose most noticeable presenting symptom is irritability often act in an agitated manner. They might pace, shuffle objects, break or scratch things, or otherwise exhibit what is referred to as *psychomotor agitation*. These symptoms may appear to be similar to the fidgeting, squirming, and restlessness that is so often seen in the hyperactive–impulsive or mixed type of ADHD. In cases such as this, it is important to

**TABLE 2.5. Keys to Differentiating Depression and ADHD**

Potential similarities

- Psychomotor agitation, restlessness, fidgeting
- Difficulty thinking, paying attention, or concentrating

Differentiating characteristics

- With ADHD, *inattentiveness or hyperactivity–impulsivity* are typically the primary problem areas.
- With depression, *depressed mood (or irritability)* or loss of interest or pleasure is typically the primary problem area.

focus on the *most essential feature* of the child's behavior. With depression, the hallmark feature to look for is either *depressed mood* or *irritability*, or *loss of interest or pleasure*. Although children with ADHD certainly can exhibit irritability, it is very unlikely that the irritability will be the most noticeable feature of their behavior. It is also very unlikely that loss of interest or pleasure, or depressed mood, will be the most noticeable and continuous feature for children with ADHD. Rather, extreme difficulty concentrating, excessive motor activity, or intense impulsivity will be the hallmark characteristics.

Another feature of depression that may be confused with ADHD, especially with older children and adolescents, is the *diminished ability to think or concentrate* that often accompanies depression. Depressed children and youth sometimes act as though they are "in a fog" or "zoned out." They may have a difficult time concentrating or making decisions. In some cases, they may simply put their head down on their arms or the table and not respond. This feature of depression is strikingly similar to the symptoms of inattentiveness that are exhibited with mixed or primarily inattentive type ADHD. Children and youth with this manifestation of ADHD will often have difficulty sustaining attention to tasks, following directions and instructions, listening, and staying organized, and they may also easily forget or lose things. How does one sort out these similarities? The best way to differentiate between these types of depression and ADHD characteristics is first to identify the primary feature (the one that is most bothersome) of the presenting behavioral or emotional problems and then to determine how many manifestations of inattentiveness are present. If the primary feature is inattentiveness, it is likely that ADHD is the sole or primary problem. If there are many different manifestations of inattentiveness rather than a simple difficulty concentrating, then ADHD is likely the sole or primary problem. On the other hand, if irritability, depressed mood, or loss of interest or pleasure are the primary concern, then depression is the most likely scenario.

Anxiety symptoms may also be mistaken for or confused with ADHD, and vice versa. Because there are several specific types of anxiety disorders, some of them bearing only a slight similarity to each other, generalizations are not easy to make. However, some guidelines can be very useful in particular situations. One of the most common manifestations of anxiety in children and youth is generalized anxiety disorder, which has also been referred to as overanxious disorder of childhood. Some of the symptoms that frequently accompany this disorder are *restlessness*, *difficulty concentrating*, and *muscle tension*. Of course, restlessness and muscle tension might appear similar to the hyperactive–impulsive symptoms of ADHD, and difficulty concentrating might appear similar to the inattentive symptoms of ADHD. Again, the primary feature of the presenting problems will provide the key for appropriate classification and understanding. With generalized anxiety disorder, the key feature is *excessive worry and anxiety*, occurring most days for at least 6 months. The child or youth afflicted with these symptoms finds them extremely difficult to control. Although someone with ADHD can certainly experience worry and anxiety, these symptoms are not marked or long-lasting. Additionally, difficulty concentrating and restlessness are not the major characteristic of anxiety disorders—they are simply important related features. With ADHD, these and similar symptoms will occur to a more marked degree and constitute the primary concern.

The previous examples of the similarities of some internalizing symptoms with ADHD symptoms are based on situations in which one disorder exists and might be mistaken for another disorder. In many cases, perhaps most cases, sorting out ADHD from internalizing disorders will involve this type of selection process to determine which problem should be clearly identified. It is important to consider that there is also the possibility that ADHD and various internalizing disorders can both be present at the same time, with the same individual. Although such co-occurrence is not nearly as common as one individual having two internalizing disorders (e.g., depression and anxiety), it probably occurs at a rate higher than seen in the general population of children and youth. In fact, the frustrations and peer difficulties associated with ADHD may increase the risk of other problems (Hinshaw, 1994).

In cases where there appears to be a mixture of ADHD and internalizing symptoms, the wise practitioner will evaluate the possibility that there may be co-occurring problems or disorders. In many (but not all) cases where ADHD and an internalizing disorder coexist, one or the other will probably be considered the "primary" problem, because the symptoms associated with it are more pronounced and are causing the most difficulty. Making a determination of coexisting or co-occurring problems should involve a careful evaluation of the presenting problems and assessment data using DSM-IV and other appropriate criteria.

---

### TABLE 2.6.  Keys to Differentiating Anxiety and ADHD

Potential similarities
- Restlessness
- Difficulty concentrating
- Muscle tension

Differentiating characteristics
- With ADHD, *inattentiveness or hyperactivity–impulsivity* is typically the primary problem area.
- With anxiety (generalized anxiety disorder) *excessive worry* is typically the primary problem area.

---

## Conduct Disorders

The symptoms of conduct disorder are for the most part quite distinct from those of depression or anxiety (see Table 2.7). The four major symptoms areas of conduct disorder from DSM-IV include aggression toward people and animals, destruction of property, deceitfulness or theft, and serious violations of rules. It is generally very unlikely that skilled practitioners will have a difficult time differentiating these types of symptoms from the symptoms of various internalizing problems.

Perhaps the only symptom area where there may be confusion with conduct disorder would be the irritability that is often seen (instead of or with depressed mood) in childhood depression. In cases where the irritability is intense and prolonged, adults might overlook the other symptoms of depression and focus on the seemingly surly, hostile, and angry displays that might be part of the irritability. Children with milder forms of disruptive behavioral disorders (particularly oppositional defiant disorder) often exhibit similar surly, hostile, and angry affective and behavioral characteristics. Again, the key to distinguishing the problem accurately is to avoid focusing only on the overt symptoms of intense irritability and to identify the overall characteristics or symptoms. With depression, loss of interest or pleasure is likely to be a key feature; it is also quite likely that sleep problems, failure to make expected weight gains, low self-esteem, and fatigue or listlessness will accompany the irritability. These symptoms are not likely to be a prominent feature of disruptive behavior disorders such as conduct disorder and oppositional defiant disorder. In addition to exhibiting the angry, surly, and hostile demeanor that is so often seen with these disorders, children and youth with disruptive behavioral disorders will likely exhibit a pattern of antisocial behavior and violation of school, family, and community rules that is not at all typical of depression or anxiety.

Despite the general distinctiveness of symptoms of internalizing disorders and disruptive behavioral disorders, there is always the possibility of co-occurrence. In fact, it is known that children and youth with conduct disorder are at greater risk than the general population of young people for developing emotional and psychiatric problems (Kazdin, 1995, 1998). A careful evaluation of the general presenting problems will usually be helpful in determining whether both types of problems are occurring simultaneously. In cases of such a co-occurrence of problems, interventions for both types of problems should also occur. Because the interventions that have been shown to be most effective for disruptive behavior disorders and internalizing disorders generally differ greatly, effective treatment

---

**TABLE 2.7. Keys to Differentiating Depression and Conduct Disorders**

Potential similarities
- Irritability; sullen, hostile, or angry mood

Differentiating characteristics
- The defining feature of conduct disorders is typically antisocial behavior or violation of rules.

---

should first target whatever problems are thought to be primary but also include provisions for treating other problems.

## Substance Abuse

Children and adolescents who develop substance abuse problems may also display characteristics that are similar to some of the characteristics of either depression or anxiety (see Table 2.8). For example, young people who develop serious substance abuse problems often become withdrawn, irritable, and exhibit a change in their eating and sleeping habits, which may lead you to confuse their symptoms with depression. Additionally, youth who use hallucinogenic drugs (particularly marijuana and LSD) sometimes display intense anxiety symptoms, even panic attacks. Adding to the confusion, youth who become heavily involved in using alcohol or other drugs may also be depressed and may be maintaining their substance abuse as a way of "self-medicating" the emotional or mental pain and hopelessness that they feel. When there is confusion regarding the differentiation of internalizing symptoms and potential substance abuse, or in cases where co-occurring substance abuse and internalizing problems are suspected, it is important to look at the "big picture" and try to assess the more overt signs of substance abuse. Indicators such as new and questionable friends, secretive behavior, heavy use of eye drops, breath fresheners, incense or fragrant oils; deterioration in school performance, missing money or presence of large sums of money that cannot be accounted for, and presence of stems, seeds, or other unusual substances in clothing pockets might all raise concern that there is a substance abuse problem. And, of course, determining the existence of a serious internalizing disorder and a serious substance abuse problem should lead to treatment for both problems.

## Eating Disorders

The most common eating disorders, anorexia nervosa and bulimia nervosa, often include symptoms that overlap with depression and anxiety. In many cases, there is a co-occurrence of these disorders with anxiety or depressive disorders (see Table 2.9). The typical onset for both anorexia and bulimia is during adolescence, and these disorders are

**TABLE 2.8. Keys to Differentiating Depression or Anxiety and Substance Abuse Problems**

Potential similarities
- Substance abuse and depression: social withdrawal, mood swings, changes in sleeping and/or eating patterns
- Substance abuse and anxiety: intensive anxiety symptoms, panic attacks, social withdrawal

Differentiating characteristics
- Specific signs associated with substance abuse: secretive and erratic behavior, new friends, presence of unusual substances or paraphernalia, missing money, use of "masking" tools (eye drops, breath fresheners, incense, or fragrant oils)

**TABLE 2.9. Keys to Differentiating Depression or Anxiety and Eating Disorders**

Potential similarities

- Eating disorders and depression: mood disturbances, low self-esteem, weight loss or failure to make expected weight gains
- Eating disorders and anxiety: obsessive–compulsive behavior, excessive worry
- In general: somatic complaints, social withdrawal

Differentiating characteristics

- Specific signs of eating disorders: refusal to eat, binge-eating, fasting, excessive exercise, preoccupation with body size or shape, self-induced vomiting, misuse of laxatives, diuretics, or enemas

much more likely to be seen in girls than with boys. Anxiety symptoms, depressive symptoms, and social withdrawal frequently are associated features with both types of eating disorders. Additionally, it is not uncommon for individuals with eating disorders to have frequent and continual somatic complaints. With anorexia nervosa, obsessive–compulsive disorder is also frequently a co-occurring problem.

In cases where there is not a clear co-occurrence of eating disorders with depressive or anxiety disorders, but there is some symptom overlap, it will be useful to determine which set of problems is primary and which is secondary in importance. Because anorexia nervosa is characterized by refusal to maintain minimally normal body weight, intense fear of gaining weight, and a major disturbance in perception of the shape or size of her (or his) body, these characteristics should be evaluated carefully. Anorexia may take the form of a restricting type, where the individual accomplishes weight loss through dieting, fasting, or excessive exercise; or a binge-eating–purging type, where the individual may engage in binge-eating episodes and resort to self-induced vomiting or misuse of laxatives, diuretics, or enemas to accomplish weight loss. Bulmia nervosa involves binge eating accompanied by inappropriate compensatory methods to prevent weight gain. Self-induced vomiting or misuse of laxatives, diuretics, or enemas are the most common compensatory methods. Therefore, a careful evaluation of the possibility of these symptoms should occur in cases where eating disorders are suspected along with depression, anxiety, or other internalizing symptoms.

Because some of the treatment procedures that are used with eating disorders (use of serotonin-blocking medications, cognitive, behavioral, and family therapy) are very compatible with treatment procedures for depression or anxiety, overlapping symptoms or a co-occurrence of eating and internalizing disorders can often be dealt with together in a comprehensive intervention.

## Tourette's Disorder

Tourette's disorder, a specific type of tic disorder, has received a great deal of attention during the past two decades. Although it occurs much less frequently than internalizing problems (only about 4 or 5 persons out of 10,000), Tourette's is frequently misunderstood and misdiagnosed, especially in its early stages with children. Some of the characteristics that tend to accompany Tourette's disorder are easily mistaken for internalizing disorders: Depressed mood, social discomfort, shame, self-consciousness, and obsessive–compulsive behaviors are all common (see Table 2.10). Although it is possible simultaneously to have Tourette's disorder and a specific internalizing disorder, this scenario is usually not the case. Rather, there are usually just some overlapping symptoms.

The hallmark diagnostic characteristic of Tourette's disorder is the presence of multiple motor tics, as well as vocal tics, that occur several or more times a day for a long period of time—usually 1 year or longer. Therefore, practitioners who work with children need to be aware of the various manifestations of motor and vocal tics that are exhibited with Tourette's. The dramatic manifestations of these symptoms (such as barking, growling, severe motor tics, and uncontrollable, continuous use of obscene language) that are often shown on clinician training tapes and informational television programs as being characteristic of Tourette's are sometimes deceiving. Children and youth afflicted with this disorder may often exhibit less stereotypical and dramatic manifestations of both motor tics (such as eye blinking, making faces, or continually tapping with the hands or feet) and vocal tics (such as coughing, repeating words, or making unusual noises with the mouth). Accurate identification of the problem is critical for effective treatment, whether Tourette's disorder occurs separately or along with an internalizing disorder.

## CONCLUDING COMMENTS

The recent gains in our understanding of depression, anxiety, and other internalizing problems among children and youth presented in this chapter should not be viewed as a comprehensive or cutting-edge approach to these concerns. Rather, this chapter provides a practical summary of some of the more clear-cut and important aspects of understanding the development and course of internalizing problems among young people. Readers who are interested in developing a more precise and full understanding of these issues should refer to the many excellent scholarly works on the topic, some of which have been referenced in this chapter. Our knowledge of the biological influences of depression, and anxiety in particular, has increased substantially in recent years. With these impressive

---

**TABLE 2.10. Keys to Differentiating Internalizing Disorders and Tourette's Disorder**

Potential similarities
- Depressed mood, irritability, social discomfort, shame, self-consciousness, obsessive or compulsive behavior

Differentiating characteristics
- Specific signs associated with Tourette's: presence of notable multiple motor tics and vocal tics

advances, it is understandable that some researchers and practitioners might end up simplifying these problems in their own minds, reducing them to an explanation that is almost entirely biological in origin. This type of thinking would be a mistake. It is important to recognize continually that our knowledge base regarding child psychopathology is in a constant state of flux, and we must not become too confident about reducing complex problems to simple or one-dimensional explanations.

In my own view, the best explanation for nearly all childhood behavioral and emotional problems is a model that takes into account multiple influences and also assumes that various influences may not only shape the problem but also may shape and be shaped by other influences. Noted social learning theorist Albert Bandura (1986) referred to this concept as "reciprocal determinism," a theory that has been very influential among broad-minded researchers and scholars working in this area. Whether you are a practitioner, a scholar, or the parent of a child with emotional or behavioral problems, I urge you reject one-dimensional or simplistic explanations (or solutions) for these problems and adopt the type of inclusive thinking that is supported by the notion of reciprocal determinism.

# 3

## Guidelines for Assessment and Intervention Planning

### INTRODUCTION AND OVERVIEW

Before effective interventions for depression and anxiety can be implemented, these problems must first be assessed accurately. The process of assessment is more complex than simply making a determination regarding whether a particular problem exists. Rather, effective assessment should provide a strong foundation for understanding the problems that have been identified and developing an appropriate plan for intervention. Assessing depression, anxiety, and related internalizing problems of children and youth can be particularly challenging. In addition to the problems of co-occurrence and sorting out depression and anxiety from other problems, which are discussed in Chapters 1 and 2, there are other challenges to consider. One of the persistent challenges in assessing internalizing problems is that so many of the symptoms are not easily observed through external means. Therefore, obtaining the child's self-report through interviewing and using self-report instruments is more important with internalizing problems than with externalizing problems such as conduct disorders or ADHD, which are much easier to evaluate through direct behavioral observation and behavioral rating scales. The focus of this chapter is on practical strategies for assessing depression and anxiety in children and youth. Readers who are interested in a more in-depth, technical, and theoretical treatment of the process of assessing behavioral, social, and emotional problems of children and youth are referred to more comprehensive sources on this topic (e.g., Merrell, 1999).

This chapter begins with a discussion of the purposes of assessment, as well as an introduction to models of social–emotional assessment of children and youth as a problem-solving and information-gathering process in multiple settings, from multiple sources, and using multiple methods. Three specific methods of assessing internalizing problems are emphasized in this chapter, including behavior rating scales, self-report instruments, and interviewing techniques. Each of these three methods is discussed in some detail, with

40

particular examples of how they might be used for assessing depression and anxiety. Because the most important purpose of assessment is to provide information that might be useful in developing effective interventions, the latter part of this chapter is devoted to the topic of linking assessment to intervention, and describes several methods that may be useful for internalizing problems.

## WHAT ARE THE PURPOSES OF ASSESSMENT?

### General Purposes of Assessment

Assessment of children's emotional and behavioral problems can serve several purposes. A thorough assessment is often necessary for identifying problems accurately. Assessment is usually essential for formal classification of behavioral and emotional problems or disorders. Although formal classification (using DSM-IV or special education classification categories) is not always necessary, it often serves valuable purposes, such as opening the door for access to services and providing a means for remuneration or third-party payment for services and a common framework for professionals to use in communicating and understanding the problem. Moreover, a thorough assessment should provide many of the details needed to develop an intervention plan that is targeted specifically at the areas of greatest concern. Additionally, assessment information can provide a baseline with which to gauge treatment progress or evaluate the effectiveness of particular interventions.

### Assessment as a Problem-Solving Process

In recent years, the potential purposes of assessment have been expanded well beyond identification and classification of problems. In a more comprehensive treatment of this topic (Merrell, 1999), I proposed a four-phase model of assessment as a *problem-solving process*. This model, which is detailed in Table 3.1, includes four phases. *Phase I, Identification and Clarification*, involves questions that may need to be answered before any assessment data are actually gathered, such as who is the client, what is the problem, and what is the purpose of the assessment? *Phase II, Data Collection*, involves actually designing the assessment and determining which means should be used to obtain information. *Phase III, Analysis*, occurs after assessment data are collected and involves specific questions regarding interpretation of the data and responding to the assessment questions. *Phase IV, Solution and Evaluation*, which is often overlooked in assessing children and youth but may be the most important phase, involves using the assessment data and the hypotheses developed using these data to plan an appropriate intervention and evaluate its effectiveness. Whether one subscribes to a particular model such as this one is not particularly important. Rather, the important thing to consider is that assessment, if planned and implemented with care, can serve many important purposes other than those traditionally considered. The end result of a carefully considered and orchestrated assessment can be a solution-focused approach that links the problems a particular child or adolescent is exhibiting to the tools for addressing these problems.

**TABLE 3.1. Four Phases of Assessment as a Problem-Solving Process**

Phase I: Identification and Clarification

- Who is the client (or who are the clients)?
- From the client's perspective, what is the problem?
- What is the intended purpose of the assessment?

Phase II: Data Collection

- What information is needed?
- What assessment methods, procedures, and tests will best provide this information?
- Which of the potential means of gathering information are most appropriate for this specific client, problem, and situation?

Phase III: Analysis

- Does the assessment information confirm the problem?
- What other information do the assessment data provide regarding the problem?
- How can the assessment information be used to answer specific referral questions?
- What are the factors that appear to contribute to the problem?
- Is there any missing assessment information that is needed to help analyze this problem? If so, how can it be obtained?

Phase IV: Solution and Evaluation

- Based on all the available information, what should be the target for intervention?
- What appear to be the most appropriate types of intervention?
- What resources are available to implement the intervention?
- Which means of assessment can be used to collect data continuously during intervention?
- Which means of assessment can be used to evaluate the effectiveness of the solution?

# A MODEL FOR DESIGNING ASSESSMENTS

In other sources I have written on the topic of assessment (Merrell, 1999; Merrell & Gimpel, 1998), I have recommended a model for designing social–emotional assessments that will provide a thorough and detailed portrait of the child or adolescent. I have referred to this model as the *multimethod, multisource, multisetting assessment design*. Because depression, anxiety, and related internalizing problems of children and youth present some unique challenges for assessment, this model may be particularly useful.

The essential feature of the model is that assessment should be *broad-based*, so that an aggregated, comprehensive portrait of the child's functioning is obtained. Because each particular instrument, method, or source from which assessment data may be gathered is subject to some unique types of error, a comprehensive and aggregated assessment design may overcome the limitations of any particular method of assessment and therefore reduce the amount of error go in the interpretation of results. Figure 3.1 provides an overview of the major components of social–emotional assessment, which are discussed in the following sections.

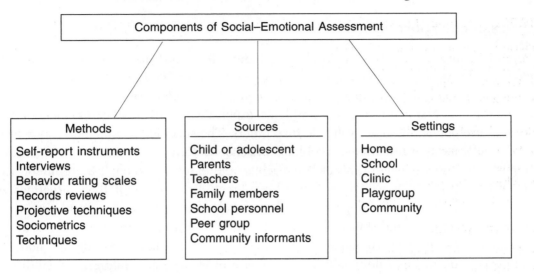

**FIGURE 3.1.** Possible components of a multimethod, multisource, multisetting assessment design.

## Assessment Methods

The methods of assessment might potentially include *direct observation, behavior rating scales, interviews, records reviews, sociometric techniques, self-report measures,* and *projective–expressive techniques.* Of course, not all of these methods will be equally useful for assessing internalizing problems. Because the symptoms of depression and anxiety are often not easily measurable through "external" means during limited time intervals, direct behavioral observation may be particularly limited in usefulness for this purpose. Peer sociometric techniques are potentially useful for assessing internalizing problems, but the amount of time and effort required to obtain such information is typically greater than can be justified for obtaining information on individual students in school settings. Projective–expressive techniques such as drawing tests, sentence completion tests, and thematic approaches may be helpful in obtaining a holistic picture of the child's perceptions and particularly valuable for establishing rapport. However, such methods are often unreliable and of questionable validity for making classification and intervention decisions. Although projective–expressive assessment techniques certainly have their place in assessment, they should not be considered a main assessment method for decision-making purposes because of the questionable technical properties and lack of specific validity evidence. Records reviews may be a very useful means of gathering assessment information for social–emotional problems, but this method does not require a great deal of specific comment or training information within this chapter. Therefore, the focus in this chapter for methods of assessing internalizing problems is primarily on behavior rating scales, self-report instruments, and interviewing techniques. These three methods have been proven over time to be the most reliable, valid, and practical methods for assessing depression, anxiety, and related concerns.

## Assessment Sources

Potential sources of social–emotional assessment information are varied and include *the student* who is being evaluated, his or her *parents*, other *family members*, *teachers*, and *school personnel*, the *peer group*, and *community-based informants* such as youth group leaders. For assessing internalizing problems, especially in individual cases, some of these sources are potentially more valuable than others. The specific recommended sources for assessing these types of student problems in school settings include, in general order of importance, the student and his or her teachers and parents. Although there might occasionally be situations in which other possible sources might be useful, these situations will not be the norm. Because depression, anxiety, and other internalizing problems involve internal perceptions and states, obtaining the child's self-report (through interviews and objective self-report instruments) is critical and usually the most essential method. The only exception to this rule would be in the case of very young children, or children or youth who otherwise have limited cognitive and verbal skills. Because children's parents have the most opportunity to observe their social and emotional behavior, a parent report (through interviews and behavior rating scales) is also usually essential to the assessment. Teachers also can provide useful information through similar methods.

## Assessment Settings

Assessment settings refer to the particular places in which the assessment information is based rather than the actual physical setting where meetings take place. For example, parents might meet with a practitioner in a school office to provide information about their child's emotional problems, but the setting on which this information is based will generally be the home, where parents have the opportunity for day-to-day observation and interaction with the child. Potential settings for obtaining assessment information include school, home, clinic, playgroup, or other community settings. In most situations, the school and home settings will be the primary focus for social–emotional assessment information on students.

## Best Practices

Given the many possible combinations of assessment methods, sources, and settings, where should the most attention be placed? After all, practitioners are limited by available time and other constraints, and it is seldom possible to obtain assessment information using all the possible or preferred methods, sources, or settings. My recommendation in this regard for best practice in comprehensive assessments is to *use a minimum of two methods, sources, and settings*. This type of assessment design would actually be fairly easy to implement with some careful planning. For example, an assessment involving an interview and a self-report instrument from the student, an interview and behavior rating scale from the parent(s), and an interview and behavior rating scale from a teacher would include three methods, three sources, and at least two settings. In some cases of school-based assessment, it may be difficult to obtain information from parents, but every effort should be made to involve them to whatever extent they are willing and capable. For screening purposes, it is generally considered acceptable to administer one assessment tool, such as a self-report instrument or a teacher behavior rating scale. Table 3.2 provides an outline of the recommended minimum components assessment that should be used for screening and assessment of depression and anxiety in children and youth, and the preferred alternatives within these components. It is important here recognize the emphasis on the term "minimum"; where possible, more methods, sources, and settings will almost always yield a more comprehensive portrait of the student's functioning.

# RECOMMENDED ASSESSMENT METHODS

As mentioned earlier, this chapter focuses on three specific methods recommended as best to use for evaluating depression, anxiety, and related internalizing problems with children and youth. These three methods include behavior rating scales, self-report instruments, and interviewing techniques, each of which is discussed in some detail in this section.

## Behavior Rating Scales

Behavior rating scales have become immensely popular in recent years as a method for assessing social–emotional behavior of students. Rating scales are sometimes referred to as "third-party" evaluation instruments because they are completed by neither the practitio-

---

**TABLE 3.2. Recommended Minimum Design Components for Screening and Assessment of Depression and Anxiety in Children and Youth**

For screening purposes, use a minimum of one method
- For screening from classrooms or other large groups, use an appropriate self-report instrument for older and more intellectually mature students, and use an appropriate parent or teacher behavior rating scale for younger or less sophisticated students.
- For screening individual students, use either self-report instruments or a brief interview. Ideally, use a self-report instrument followed up with a brief interview.

For assessment purposes, use a minimum of two methods, two sources, and two settings
- Methods: emphasize self-report instruments and interviews (with the student and with a parent or teacher) for older and more mature students, and emphasize parent or teacher behavior rating scales and interviews (with parents or teachers) for younger and less sophisticated students.
- Sources: emphasize obtaining information directly from the student whenever possible, as well as from an adult informant (parent or teacher) who knows the child well.
- Settings: whenever possible, obtain information on the child's functioning in both school and home settings. If the assessment must be exclusively school-based, attempt to obtain information from at least two school settings (classrooms).

ner or the child whose behavior is being assessed. Rather, they are completed by other persons ("third parties") who know the child well and have had the opportunity to observe him or her under varied conditions for a period of time. The rating scale design provides a standard format for evaluating the frequency or intensity of specified behavioral problems and competencies. The raters, most typically a parent or teacher of the child, rate the frequency or intensity of specified behavioral characteristics that they have observed the child to exhibit during a particular time interval (e.g., the previous 3 months or 6 months), according to an anchored rating format such as *Never, Sometimes,* and *Very often.* Because almost all published behavior rating scales are norm-referenced instruments that utilize subscales and total scale scores, the obtained raw scores are typically converted to standard scores, *T*-scores, or percentile ranks using score conversion tables based on the instrument standardization group. The use of norm-referenced scores in this manner allows for comparisons between the target child's scores and those of a nationwide reference group of same-age (and in many cases, same-gender) youth. For example, a *T*-score of 70 on the *Internalizing Problems* broadband score of the Child Behavior Checklist would allow a practitioner to note that the parent of 10-year-old girl rated this child's general internalizing symptoms in the highest 2% in comparison with the national standardization sample of similar-age girls.

The advantages, uses, and potential problems of behavior rating scales are widely known and have been discussed extensively in other sources (e.g., Merrell, 1999). It is not essential to discuss these technical matters in detail in this chapter. However, it is important to recognize that behavior rating scales do not necessarily assess specific behaviors, per se. Rather, they are designed to assess *perceptions of behavioral and emotional characteristics* of children and youth that have been formed over time through observation and experience of the rater. Also, it is important to recognize that assessing internalizing symptoms such as the characteristics of depression and anxiety through the use of third-party rating scales presents particular challenges. The primary challenge in this regard is that many internalizing characteristics (such as low self-esteem, distorted thinking, and depressed mood) are not easily observed through external means, unlike most externalizing characteristics. Therefore, extra caution and care should be taken when using behavior rating scales for assessing internalizing problems. Despite some of the limitations of rating scales, they offer many advantages, even for assessing internalizing problems.

Table 3.3 presents a sampling of some of the more widely used "general purpose" child behavior rating scales (or rating scale systems) that include at least one scale for internalizing problems. These scales are referred to as "general purpose" (or "broadband") because they are designed to be used to evaluate a broad range of problems and competencies, and not just one type of problem. For example, the Child Behavior Checklist and Teacher's Report Form (for ages 4–18), which are parent and teacher counterpart forms of the same rating scale system and include similar items, each have 120 problem behavior items. These items are designed to describe a wide range of problems, ranging from withdrawn and anxious behavior to acting-out and antisocial–aggressive behavior. Both of these instruments include an *Internalizing Problems* broadband score, an empirically derived collection of items that describe problems that are clearly in the internalizing domain. Within the *Internalizing Problems* items are three empirically derived subscales: *Anxious/Depressed, Somatic Com-*

*plaints*, and *Withdrawn*. Likewise, the Preschool and Kindergarten Behavior Scales (for ages 3–6) include an *Internalizing Problems* broadband score, as well as *Social Withdrawal* and *Anxiety/Somatic Problems* subscales within the internalizing domain.

The instruments and rating systems that are overviewed in Table 3.3 are not an exhaustive, all-inclusive listing. Rather, this collection reflects some of the more popular and widely used commercially published instruments that have internalizing problems items and scales as part of a comprehensive collection of items and scales. Other technically adequate and potentially useful instruments in this regard are also available.

## Self-Report Instruments

Like behavior rating scales, self-report instruments designed for use with children and adolescents have experienced a strong increase in popularity as well as dramatic improvements in technical characteristics since the early 1980s. Prior to that time, there were many popular and psychometrically strong personality tests and self-report inventories available for use with adults but very few that could be recommended for use with children and youth. Additionally, most of the instruments that were available for young persons were simply downward extensions of adult instruments for use with adolescents, and there were almost no instruments that could be used with elementary-school-age children. Of the few instruments that were available, most had sparse or questionable validity evidence and were lacking in psychometric quality in other ways as well.

Fortunately, this poor state of affairs has changed dramatically. During the latter two decades of the 20th century, there were tremendous advances in the development and refinement of self-report instruments for assessing social–emotional concerns of children and youth. Currently, there are many excellent self-report instruments available for use with students in school settings. Some of these instruments are personality inventories or general purpose problem inventories that include internalizing symptom items and subscales, but there have also been a surprisingly large number of self-report instruments developed specifically for the purpose of evaluating depression and anxiety.

Self-report instruments are not just an acceptable means for assessing internalizing problems with young people; in many cases, they are now considered to be an essential method or even the preferred method (Merrell, 1999). The desirability of using self-report instruments for assessing these problems is due to more than the increased availability and technical adequacy of these instruments. Because many of the symptoms of depression, anxiety, and other internalizing problems are difficult (if not impossible) to detect through external methods of assessing (such as observation and third-party rating scales), and because a carefully designed self-report instrument provides a structured and norm-referenced way to evaluate these problems, self-report instruments are uniquely suited for internalizing problems.

Despite the obvious advantages of using self-report instruments in this manner, some concerns should also be considered. One concern involves the cognitive maturity that is required for a child to understand the demands of various self-report tests and to make accurate differentiations on response choices. Most experts agree that for typical children, it is very difficult for those younger than the age of 8 years to comprehend accurately and

TABLE 3.3. A Sampling of General Purpose Child Behavior Rating Scales That Include Items and Subscales for Internalizing Problems

| Instrument | Publisher | Purpose | Norm sample | Items and subscales |
|---|---|---|---|---|
| Behavior Assessment System for Children | American Guidance Service 4201 Woodland Rd. Circle Pines, MN 55014-1796 800-328-2560 | Assessment of child and adolescent behavioral, emotional, and adaptive problems and competencies; includes teacher, parent and self-report forms | Parent and teacher ratings of over 2,000 students ages 6–18 | 126 to 148 items, 20 scales and subscales |
| Behavior Evaluation Scale, 2nd Edition | Hawthorne Educational Services 800 Gray Oak Dr. Columbia, MO 65201 800-542-1673 | Evaluation of youth with behavior problems for eligibility, placement, and programming; based on IDEA definition of behavior disorders/emotional disturbance; includes parent and teacher versions | Parent and teacher ratings of 2,272 students ages 5–18 | 76 items, 5 subscales |
| Behavior Rating Profile, 2nd Edition | PRO-ED 8700 Shoal Creek Blvd. Austin, TX 78757-6869 800-897-3202 | Evaluation of problem behaviors, adaptive skills, and interpersonal relationships; includes parent, teacher, student, and peer report forms | Parent and teacher ratings of over 2,000 youth ages 6–18 | 30 items, no subscales |
| Child Behavior Checklist and Teacher's Report Form | University Associates in Psychiatry 1 S. Prospect St. Burlington, VT 05401-3456 802-656-8313 | Evaluation of behavioral and emotional problems in children and adolescents; includes comprehensive "broadband" internalizing problem scales | Ratings of over 2,000 youth ages 4–18 | 120 problem behavior items, 8 subscales |
| Devereux Behavior Rating Scale | The Psychological Corporation 555 Academic Court San Antonio, TX 78204-2498 800-211-8378 | Evaluation of behavioral characteristics that may indicate severe emotional disturbances in children and adolescents; includes school and home versions | Teacher and parent ratings of more than 3,000 students ages 5–18 | 40 items, 4 subscales |
| Preschool and Kindergarten Behavior Scales | PRO-ED 8700 Shoal Creek Blvd. Austin, TX 78757-6869 800-897-3202 | Evaluation of social skills and emotional–behavioral problems of young children (ages 3–6); includes comprehensive internalizing problems broadband scale | 2,855 parent and teacher ratings of children ages 3–6 | 34 social skills items, 3 subscales; 42 problem behavior items, 5 subscales |

complete self-report instruments, and the lower age limit may be higher for children and youth who are below average in their intellectual functioning or have serious learning problems. Another concern in using self-report instruments is the various types of *response bias* that may occur, such as endorsing items in a socially desirable manner, faking, acquiescence, and deviation. Instruments that contain items with obvious "correct" or "deviant" choices are particularly prone to the effects of response bias. The problems of response bias and error variance in self-report social–emotional assessment of children and youth are discussed in more detail in other sources (e.g., Merrell, 1999).

Despite some of the practical and measurement problems that are inherent in using self-report assessment instruments with children and adolescents, this method clearly has many advantages for use in assessing depression, anxiety, and other internalizing problems and symptoms. Table 3.4 provides a listing of some of the more widely used general purpose or broadband self-report instruments for children and adolescents that contain specific scales for various internalizing problems. These instruments are not designed specifically for assessing internalizing problems but assess depression, anxiety, and other internalizing syndromes as part of a broad evaluation of concerns. For example, The Minnesota Multiphasic Personality Inventory for Adolescents (MMPI-A), perhaps the best known of these instruments, contains 10 basic clinical scales, of which four (*Hypochondriasis, Depression, Conversion Hysteria, Social Introversion*) appear to specifically target internalizing problems. Additionally, of the 15 adolescent "content" scales of the MMPI-A, five (*Anxiety, Obsessiveness, Depression, Low Self-Esteem, Social Discomfort*) appear specifically relevant to internalizing problems.

Table 3.5 provides a sampling of some of the more widely used self-report instruments for children and youth that are designed specifically for evaluating internalizing symptoms and concerns. Unlike the general purpose instruments overviewed in Table 3.4, these instruments are designed to evaluate internalizing problems specifically and in detail rather than as part of a broader screening process. Some of these instruments (such as the Reynolds Adolescent and Child Depression Scales, and the Children's Depression Inventory) are focused specifically on the symptoms of depression. Other of these instruments (such as the Revised Manifest Anxiety Scale, and the State–Trait Anxiety Inventory for Children) focus specifically on the symptoms of anxiety. One of these measures, the Internalizing Symptoms Scale for Children, is designed to provide a broader assessment of internalizing symptoms in general. All of these narrowband self-report instruments listed in Table 3.5 have adequate to excellent psychometric properties, and several of these have impressive validity evidence for clinical assessment of internalizing problems. For example, the Internalizing Symptoms Scale for Children, the Reynolds Child Depression Scale, and the Reynolds Adolescent Depression Scale all have clinical "cutoff" score levels that have been established through extensive research and are very likely to indicate that a particular child or youth may have an internalizing disorder.

## Interviews

Like self-report instruments, interviews are considered to be an essential technique for evaluating depression, anxiety, and other internalizing problems in children and youth.

**TABLE 3.4. A Sampling of General Purpose Self-Report Assessment Instruments for Children and Youth That Include Items and Subscales for Internalizing Problems**

| Instrument | Publisher | Purpose | Norm sample | Items and subscales |
|---|---|---|---|---|
| Behavior Assessment System for Children, Child and Adolescent Self-Reports | American Guidance Service 4201 Woodland Rd. Circle Pines, MN 55014-1796 800-328-2560 | Assessment of child and adolescent behavioral, emotional, and adaptive problems and competencies; separate forms for ages 8–11 and 12–18 | Over 4,000 cases for both the child and adolescent versions | 152 to 186 items, 5 composite score areas and 14 subscales |
| Millon Adolescent Clinical Inventory | National Computer Systems Assessment Services P.O. Box 1416 Minneapolis, MN 55440 800-627-7271 | Assessment of clinical problems and psychopathology in adolescents; designed for use in outpatient, inpatient, and residential settings | Over 1,000 clinical cases of youth ages 13–19 | 160 items, 30 scales within 5 dimensions |
| Minnesota Multiphasic Personality Inventory, Adolescent Version | National Computer Systems Assessment Services P.O. Box 1416 Minneapolis, MN 55440 800-627-7271 | Assessment of adolescent personality and psychopathology | Over 1,600 youth ages 14–18 | 478 items; 7 validity scales, 10 basic clinical scales, 15 adolescent "content" scales |
| Personality Inventory for Youth | Western Psychological Services 12031 Wilshire Blvd. Los Angeles, CA 90025-1251 310-478-2061 | Assessment of personality, behavior problems, and family difficulties of older children and adolescents | Over 2,000 children and youth ages 9–18 | 270 items, 9 clinical scales, 24 subscales |
| Youth Self-Report | University Associates in Psychiatry 1 S. Prospect St. Burlington, VT 05401-3456 802-656-8313 | Evaluation of behavioral characteristics that may indicate severe emotional disturbances in older children and adolescents | Over 1,000 youth ages 11–18 | 103 problem items, 2 broad-band scales, 8 narrowband scales |

Discussing concerns or symptoms with a client in an open-ended, unstructured format is probably the oldest form of assessment. Interviewing is easily adapted to a variety of situations, concerns, and settings. Interviews may be brief or lengthy, formal or informal, structured or unstructured. Perhaps more than any other assessment technique, interviews challenge the clinical skills of examiners, who are required to be simultaneously aware of many things and to rely on their interpersonal skills, observational skills, and knowledge of normal and abnormal child development. Because interviewing is such a complex process, it is necessary to consider several aspects of it to fully appreciate how interviews can be best used in assessing social–emotional problems of children and youth.

**TABLE 3.5. A Sampling of Self-Report Assessment Instruments for Children and Youth Designed Specifically to Measure Internalizing Symptoms and Problems**

| Instrument | Publisher | Purpose | Norm sample | Items and subscales |
|---|---|---|---|---|
| Children's Depression Inventory | Multi-Health Systems 908 Niagara Falls Blvd. North Tonowanda, NY 14120-2060 800-456-3003 | Screening and assessment of depression | Over 1,400 children ages 6–17 | 27 items, 5 subscale scores, and a total score |
| Internalizing Symptoms Scale for Children | PRO-ED 8700 Shoal Creek Blvd. Austin, TX 78757-6869 800-897-3202 | Screening and assessment of general internalizing problems and positive affect | Over 2,200 children ages 8-13 | 48 items, 2 subscale scores, and a total score |
| Revised Children's Manifest Anxiety Scale | Western Psychological Services 12031 Wilshire Blvd. Los Angeles, CA 90025-1251 310-478-2061 | Screening and assessment of "trait" anxiety | Over 5,000 children ages 6–17 | 37 items, 3 subscales |
| Reynolds Child Depression Scale | Psychological Assessment Resources P.O. Box 998 Odessa, FL 33556-9901 800-331-8378 | Screening and assessment of depression | Over 1,600 children ages 8–12 | 30 items with a total score, and 5 factor scores for research purposes |
| Reynolds Adolescent Depression Scale | Psychological Assessment Resources P.O. Box 998 Odessa, FL 33556-9901 800-331-8378 | Screening and assessment of depression | Over 2,400 adolescents ages 13–18 | 30 items with a total score, and 5 factor scores for research purposes |
| State–Trait Anxiety Inventory for Children | Consulting Psychologists Press P.O. Box 10096 Palo Alto, CA 94303 800-624-1765 | Screening, assessment, and differentiation of "state" anxiety and "trait" anxiety | Over 1,500 children ages 9–12 | A 20-item state anxiety scale, and a 20-item trait anxiety scale |

## Developmental Considerations

Age and developmental level of the student who is being assessed are important aspects to consider in conducting interviews. Young children, and older youth who have limited reading or verbal ability, may have difficulty understanding standardized assessment tasks such as those presented by self-report instruments. Similarly, the verbal skills and emotional development of children will have a strong influence on whether they can express their symptoms and concerns in an interview. Younger and less verbally sophisticated students will likely have a limited "emotional vocabulary." The characteristics and symptoms that might be identified by a mature student or adult as tension might be described as "feeling angry" by a younger or less sophisticated student. The nuances of emotional and cognitive expression are sometimes easily lost when interviewing younger and less sophisticated students: What might be described as disappointment by a more mature person might be referred to as "feeling sad" by a younger person; tension in the abdominal region might be described as a "stomachache" or symptoms of panic might probably be simplified as "feeling afraid." Because of these critical developmental issues, practitioners who intend to do extensive interviewing with students who have emotional problems must absolutely have developed background knowledge in normal and abnormal child development, including the verbal, intellectual, emotional, and social domains of development. Practitioners should also have received structured, supervised training in conducting interviews. Some potential readings for additional training in developmental aspects of interviewing include books by Hughes and Baker (1990), Merrell (1999), and Sattler (1998).

## Semistructured and Behavioral Interviews

For day-to-day use by school-based practitioners for interviewing students with emotional and behavioral problems, I particularly recommend the use of semistructured or behavioral interviewing techniques, or, preferably, some combination of the two techniques. These general methods of interviewing are potentially more reliable and less time intensive than unstructured, open-ended interviews, yet they are more flexible and adaptable than structured interviewing schedules. In short, they offer the possibility of reliable and valid assessment information that addresses the specific concerns of the child (and family or teacher) in a manner that can be modified easily for the particular circumstances and may be used for making classification and intervention decisions.

A semistructured interview is one in which the practitioner does not follow a set script or list of rote questions (as in a structured interview), yet still has a specific focus or aim for interview questions. For example, if there is concern that a particular student may be experiencing depression, the interviewer might ask him or her some specific questions regarding whether and to what extent he or she has experienced these symptoms. In this way, the interviewer attempts to maintain some structure in the interview, unlike the unstructured, open-ended type of interviewing. The interviewer might also ask specific questions regarding particular areas of the child's life experience. I have previously (Merrell, 1999) recommended five areas of questioning for semistructured interviewing with children: *interpersonal functioning, family relationships, peer relationships, school adjustment,* and *community involvement.* Table 3.6 provides some possible examples within these areas of questioning. These five areas and general examples can provide a template for conducting interviews with children and older youth. Of course, the interview questions will need to be tailored to the specific concerns and needs of the student and his or her circumstances.

Behavioral interviewing is a particular type of semistructured interview. Like general semistructured interviewing, behavioral interviewing has a particular aim or purpose, a general structure, yet it is still flexible and adaptable to individual circumstances. What sets behavioral interviewing apart as a specific kind of semistructured interviewing technique is the purpose of the interview. With behavioral interviewing, the objective is to obtain descriptive information about the problem(s), and the conditions under which the problems or concerns are elicited and maintained. Behavioral interviewing has roots in

**TABLE 3.6. Recommended Areas of Questioning and Examples for Semi-structured Interviews with Children and Youth**

Interpersonal functioning

- Eating/sleeping habits
- Unusual or strange perceptions or experiences
- Self-attributions
- Insight into own problems and circumstances
- Clarity or accuracy of thought processes
- Emotional status

Family relationships

- Quality of relations with parents/siblings
- Perceptions of family conflict and support
- Social support from extended family
- Responsibilities/chores/routines at home

Peer relationships

- Number of close friends
- Preferred activities and friends (by name)
- Perceived conflicts and rejection with peers

School adjustment

- General feelings about school
- Preferred and disliked classes, subjects, and teachers
- Extracurricular activities
- Perceived conflicts at school

Community involvement

- Involvement in clubs, organizations, church, sports, etc.
- Social support from others in community
- Level of physical mobility within community
- Part-time jobs (for teens)

behavioral psychology, particularly applied behavior analysis. However, it can be used by practitioners who identify with theoretical orientations other than behaviorism, although it does require a basic background in behavioral theory for maximum effectiveness. Behavioral interviewing is a process that may allow the interviewer to form hypotheses about the *functions* that the problem behaviors might serve, as well as to analyze the *antecedents* and *consequences* of the problem behaviors. Table 3.7 lists some basic steps in the behavioral interviewing process, including setting the stage for the interview, specifying the problem behaviors, and preparing to analyze the problem behaviors. As the third step in this process indicates, effective behavioral interviewing often requires the practitioner to go beyond the interview itself to gather information. It is often necessary to follow up the initial interview with observations in the settings in which the problem behaviors occur, and to use this additional information to form hypotheses about the problem behaviors and how they might be modified through interventions. More details on behavioral interviewing and observation can be found in other sources (e.g., Alberto & Troutman, 1999; Merrell, 1999; Shapiro & Kratochwill, 2000). Even with internalizing problems, which are often difficult to identify using external behavior methods of assessment, the behavioral interview offers many advantages and is recommended because of its flexibility and usefulness for intervention planning.

## Some Suggestions for Interviewing Parents

When using interviews to identify and evaluate internalizing symptoms and other social–emotional problems of children, it is almost always desirable, and usually necessary, to interview the child's parents (or one of the parents). Parents can be extremely valuable informants in the interview process because they are the ones who know the child best and are usually the only persons who can provide the practitioner with information about the student's developmental history, the unique ways in which the child manifests his or her strengths and problems, and the variety of situations in which the problems are manifest. I have previously (Merrell, 1999) identified five recommended areas of questioning for obtaining background information from parents regarding the child's assets and problems, including *medical history*, *developmental history*, *social–emotional functioning*, *educational progress*, and *community involvement*. Each of these areas is potentially important for assessing internalizing problems and should be addressed appropriately in interviewing parents. In addition, I recommend that practitioners ask parents about possible internalizing symptoms and problems in very concrete, specific ways and avoid using professional classification terminology. For example, rather than asking, "Has your daughter seemed depressed lately?", it is much better to ask the parents about their observations of specific symptoms or characteristics of depression, such as excessive sadness, poor self-esteem, irritability, changes in eating and sleeping patterns, and loss of interest. The labels that professionals often take for granted may not mean the same thing to parents and may actually complicate or inhibit the process of assessing the child's problems. In summary, interviewing parents can be a critical part of the assessment process, particularly if the interview is conducted in sufficient detail and with sensitivity to their specific concerns and circumstances.

## Recommendations

In summary, behavioral rating scales, self-report instruments, and interviewing techniques offer many advantages for assessing internalizing problems of children and youth. Although there are clearly times when other methods might be useful for assessing such problems, these three methods should be considered the "mainstay" methods for internalizing symptoms. The combination of advantages they offer, especially when considering how difficult it often is to assess internalizing symptoms using external methods of observation, makes rating scales, self-report instruments, and interviews (especially semistructured and behavioral interviews) essential methods. I recommend using these three methods in combination whenever possible for assessing students with internalizing social–emotional problems.

**TABLE 3.7. Suggested Steps in Conducting Behavioral Interviews**

Set the stage for the interview

- Build rapport with the person to be interviewed.
- Describe the purpose of the interview.
- Provide instructions on how to respond to questions (e.g., "be specific").

Identify the problem behaviors

- Specify the problem or problems.
- Get an objective description of the problems.
- Identify conditions in the environment that surround the problems.
- Estimate the how often, how intense, and how long the problem behaviors occur.

Prepare to analyze the problem behaviors

- Identify appropriate strategies for follow-up observation of the problem behaviors.
- Begin to form hypotheses about the functions the problem behaviors may be serving.
- Begin to form hypotheses about the antecedents that may be eliciting the problem behaviors.
- Begin to form hypotheses about the consequences that may be maintaining the problem behaviors.
- Determine times and places to collect additional data and to use these data to develop intervention strategies.

# LINKING ASSESSMENT TO INTERVENTION

Assessment practices that focus solely on diagnosis and placement are increasingly considered to be outdated, even archaic. In recent years, there have been many calls for reform in the practices of psychological and psychoeducational assessment. One of the primary aims of the assessment reform movement has been to develop assessment practices that will provide information that can be linked to intervention in an immediate and meaningful manner. However, linking social–emotional assessment information to effective intervention is not necessarily easy or simple.

One of the problems in linking social–emotional assessment to intervention is that historically, many assessment practices were developed to meet a different set of demands, such as diagnosis, placement, and prediction. Another problem in this area, particularly when children and youth are concerned, is that the evidence on treatment effectiveness has lagged well behind what is known regarding social–emotional interventions for adults. In addition, because the practitioners who conduct the actual assessments of children are not necessarily the same individuals who will be charged with implementing intervention efforts, they may not have a great deal of direct personal motivation to report the assessment results in a manner that can be easily linked to intervention. And finally, the practices that are believed to be useful in linking assessment to intervention are not necessarily taught uniformly in professional training programs, thus perpetuating the limited usefulness of assessment practices.

Despite these problems, there are many reasons to believe that it is possible to use social–emotional assessment information to develop effective interventions for students who are found to have depression, anxiety, and other types of social–emotional problems. This section provides a brief overview of some of the frameworks that might be used to link assessment to intervention for social and emotional problems. Specifically, the following procedures are presented briefly: *progress monitoring, template matching,* the *keystone behavior strategy,* and *functional assessment.* These four procedures are also illustrated in Table 3.8.

## Progress Monitoring

The emergence of curriculum-based measurement procedures (CBM) in the early 1980s for evaluating and monitoring academic progress has had a major impact on psychoeducational assessment practices (see Shapiro, 1996; Shinn, 1997). One of the main tenets of CBM is that frequent repeated measurement and monitoring of student academic performance will lead to continual modification of instructional procedures, as well as increases in student performance. A frequently cited study that illustrates this concept was a meta-analysis conducted by Fuchs and Fuchs (1986), who examined 21 investigations and found

**TABLE 3.8. Four Procedures for Linking Social–Emotional Assessment to Effective Intervention**

| Procedure | Description | Rationale |
|---|---|---|
| Progress monitoring | Frequent and repeated measurement of behavior, emotional symptoms, or other characteristics that are considered to be the major concerns. | During the course of intervention, the clinician will frequently gauge progress in the targeted characteristics and adjust the intervention to maximize treatment gains. |
| Template matching | Assessment data are first gathered on children or youth who have identified problems; these data are then compared to assessment profiles of youth who are higher functioning. | The discrepancy in the characteristics between the high and low functioning youth serves as a "template" for selecting appropriate intervention targets. |
| Keystone behavior strategy | Within each set of responses, one specific response is targeted as being the "keystone behavior," and it is hypothesized that altering this response may produce positive changes in the entire set of responses. | There is often a set of responses or characteristics that are linked to particular disorders, and some of these responses or characteristics may serve a controlling or eliciting function on other characteristics. |
| Functional assessment | A method of obtaining and integrating assessment data to identify the probable functions of the problem behavior, as well as environmental conditions that may be eliciting and maintaining these problems. | Hypotheses regarding probable functions that the problem characteristics serve are developed following assessment, and these hypotheses are tested by implementing specific interventions. |

that systematic evaluation procedures that employed frequent and repeated measurement and monitoring of student progress resulted in a net gain in performance of nearly three-fourths of a standard deviation (a weighted effect size of .70) in comparison with students who did not receive frequent monitoring. Considering that frequent measuring and monitoring was the only "intervention" that was specifically designated, these results are impressive! They indicate that educators who take specific steps to measure ongoing student progress are likely to modify their own instructional practices in a way that results in greater gains in student achievement.

Although the evidence in this area comes from the academic rather than the social–emotional domain of student performance, there is ample reason to believe that such procedures could be used successfully for linking assessment of internalizing and other social–emotional problems to effective intervention practices. In fact, many practitioners do utilize frequent measurement of depression, anxiety symptoms, social skills, and other social–emotional characteristics as part of their intervention.

It stands to reason that practitioners who monitor the social–emotional characteristics and intervention progress of students will adjust their intervention practices to maximize treatment gains. For example, a counselor conducting an individual or group intervention for high school students with depression could teach these students to conduct brief self-assessments of their depressive symptoms on a daily basis in their journals and could also administer a brief, modified depression symptoms scale to each participant on a weekly basis during the group sessions. Likewise, a practitioner who conducts weekly or twice-weekly social skills training sessions for depressed or socially anxious students could easily gather social behavior probes within the treatment session, or could ask parents or teachers to complete modified brief social behavior rating scales on a weekly basis during the intervention. This assessment information could then be graphed (in conjunction with phases of the intervention) to help determine the changes in social behavior that correspond to the intervention. Assumably, lack of sufficient behavioral change would facilitate changes in the intervention that might address the problems in a more effective manner.

## Template Matching

A procedure described by Hoier and colleagues (Hoier & Cone, 1987; Hoier, McConnell, & Pallay, 1987) as *template matching* seems to have strong implications for linking social-emotional assessment information to intervention. With this procedure, assessment data are first gathered on students who have identified problems and are thus targeted for intervention. These assessment data are then compared to the assessment profiles of higher functioning students in the problem areas, who do not need intervention. The profiles of the higher functioning students serve as "templates" for comparing the characteristics of the individual(s) targeted for intervention. The discrepancies between the characteristics of the higher and lower functioning students then serve as the basis for developing intervention targets.

For example, let us assume that a social–emotional screening procedure conducted in a middle school resulted in a group of five to eight students who were identified as being depressed and having social problems. Let us also assume that a practitioner intended to provide a group-based intervention for these students, who would meet as a group once a week for several weeks. After identifying the group, the practitioner would compare the assessment data (self-report instruments and behavior rating scales) gathered from this group with similar assessment data gathered on two or three high functioning students who were viewed as having excellent social skills and healthy emotional functioning. The data from the two groups would be compared, and the areas of most obvious common discrepancy would then serve as a preliminary basis for the direction of the intervention plan.

The template matching strategy has been described and analyzed in more detail by Shapiro (1996). Although most of the evidence for using this strategy for selecting intervention targets has been focused on behavioral and educational problems, there does not appear to be any reason why this strategy could not be used successfully for social–emotional concerns such as internalizing problems.

## Keystone Behavior Strategy

Another procedure for selecting intervention targets is the *keystone behavior strategy*, described by Nelson and Hayes (1986). This strategy is based on the notion that, often, a set of responses or characteristics is linked to particular disorders. Within each set of responses, one specific response is targeted as being the "keystone behavior," and it is hypothesized that altering this response may produce positive changes in the entire set of responses. Therefore, using this strategy requires a thorough identification of the problem through assessment, then selecting a particular behavior or characteristic that is viewed as being critical in the overall maintenance of the problem.

For example, let us assume that a practitioner receives a referral for assessment and treatment of a 14-year-old girl who appears to be experiencing significant emotional distress and social problems. After conducting a thorough assessment, the practitioner finds that she is socially withdrawn and has significant anxiety when engaging in social situations. Although she seems to have appropriate social skills, she fails to engage in social situations because of her debilitating anxiety, which is further fueled by her negative and unrealistic thought processes. As she considers approaching social situations, she thinks to herself, "I am going to be so embarrassed," "They are all going to laugh at me," "I cannot do this," and "None of them want me around." These thoughts then lead to increased anxiety and further social withdrawal. So the wise practitioner, upon considering this identified set of responses, chooses the negative and unrealistic self-statements as the target for intervention rather than focusing specifically on social skills training or behavioral methods of reducing anxiety. In other words, the negative and unrealistic self-statements are considered to be the "keystone" within the larger set of responses.

The keystone behavior strategy certainly has strong implications for linking assessment to intervention with internalizing problems. As Shapiro (1996) noted, previous research with adults has shown the strategy to be effective for designing interventions for depression, social skills problems, and stress. A skilled, school-based practitioner would undoubtedly be able to utilize this strategy for selecting specific intervention targets for students.

## Functional Assessment

In recent years, there has been a tremendous amount of interest in using *functional assessment* (related to, but not the same as, *functional analysis*) procedures to identify behavioral, social, emotional, and academic problems of students, and to link these problems to effective interventions. This increased interest has been particularly evident in the fields of special education and school psychology, primarily because of new requirements for assessment practice that were added to the Individuals with Disabilities Education Act in a mid-1990s reauthorization by Congress. Functional assessment procedures were initially developed as a way of linking assessment to intervention with students having severe disabilities (see Horner & Carr, 1997), but the applications of this assessment technology seem to be rather broad.

The basis for functional assessment is relatively straightforward, although certain types of implementation may require a great deal of time as well as expertise in using the tools of applied behavior analysis. In its most simple description, functional assessment is merely a way of assessing problems to identify the particular *functions* of these problems. In other words, it is assumed that virtually all problem behaviors serve some kind of a purpose in the student's environment, and that these purposes may sometimes maintain the problems. Functional assessment seeks to determine relationships between the problem behaviors or characteristics and any *antecedents* that may elicit or bring forth the problems. *The goal of functional assessment is to develop hypotheses about probable functions that the problem characteristics serve, and to test these hypotheses by implementing an intervention.* Thus, functional assessment is certainly a viable strategy for linking assessment to intervention.

Few case studies and reports of functional assessment practices tend to focus on internalizing problems. Rather, it is more typical to see functional assessment used with externalizing behavioral problems and other easily observable problems such as self-injurious behavior. However, there is little doubt that functional assessment practices could be used to link various internalizing problems to intervention. For example, consider the case of a 10-year-old boy who is considered to have school phobia. This student has developed a pattern of school avoidance behavior that is accompanied and perhaps precipitated by fears, anxious arousal, general panic symptoms, and severe somatic problems that at times include vomiting. A functional assessment of this situation could be done by gathering a wide range of information, ranging from interviews to self-report instruments, to direct observation of the problem situations. After a careful consideration of the antecedents, behaviors, and consequences of the problems that are manifest, the practitioner would generate hypotheses about the associations between the problem characteristics (such as school refusal, anxious arousal, somatic problems) and various environmental influences (such as parental responses, consequences of the problem behaviors, and events that precede school refusal episodes). Possible motivations for the problem behavior, such as attention, escape, or avoidance of unpleasant activities, access to reinforcing items (television and computer games), and internal reinforcement, are then considered. Drawing upon all of the evidence and considerations, one or more intervention strategies specifically linked to the presumed functions of the problem behavior are developed and implemented, and data are then gathered to determine the effectiveness of the interventions.

For instance, does removal of parental attention and reinforcing objects at home when the child refuses to go to school decrease his or her school refusal behavior? Does adding a mildly aversive task (household chores) during times of school refusal decrease the problems? Or is the problem being maintained by escape from aversive situations at school, such as being seated near another student who makes threats? Manipulation of these or similar associations will help both to answer the assessment and intervention questions and to determine the true "functions" of the problem behavior. Functional assessment can be a much more complex process than this brief description indicates, and there is still much left to learn regarding implementing it with internalizing problems of children and youth. However, it does seem to offer a great deal of promise as a technology for linking assessment to intervention.

## FROM ASSESSMENT TO TREATMENT PLANNING

Conducting an accurate and useful assessment of a student who has significant internalizing symptoms is a task that presents many challenges. The "secret" nature of many internalizing problems and symptoms is itself an issue that truly complicates this process. The stock methods and techniques of assessment that may work well for externalizing social–emotional problems such as conduct disorders and ADHD symptoms simply may not lend themselves well to the area of internalizing problems.

Fortunately, many significant advances in assessment theory and technology in recent years have greatly enhanced our ability to assess symptoms, problems, and disorders of the internalizing variety. Whether the presenting concerns involve depression, anxiety, social withdrawal, somatic problems, or some combination of the four areas, there are now many good choices of methods, instruments, and techniques that can help assess these problems in a reliable and valid manner. Worksheet 3.1 provides a framework for organizing social–emotional assessment information, generating hypotheses, and beginning the process of linking assessment results to intervention. This two-page worksheet is based on many of the premises of social–emotional assessment practices that are detailed in this chapter and may be a useful tool for assessing students who may be anxious, depressed, or have related social and emotional concerns. To use this worksheet most effectively, it will be necessary first to study the intervention techniques that are described in the remaining chapters of this book. The first section of this worksheet simply provides space for entering descriptive information about the referred student, as well as a summary of the concerns or problems for which the student was referred to your attention. The second section of this worksheet provides a space for summarizing the most important assessment information that has been gathered. In this section, list the most important test scores, observations, and information from interviews or other assessment sources. It is not necessary to list exhaustively each and every piece of assessment information; only the most relevant information is needed. The third part of this worksheet (at the top of page 2) provides a structured way to analyze the problem. First, describe any major problems, concerns, diagnostic indicators, and so forth, that are indicated and supported by the assessment information. Second, list your hypotheses regarding the possible origins and functions of any problems that are indicated. In addition, this is the space to describe briefly how these hypotheses might be tested. The fourth and final section of this worksheet, "Problem Solution and Evaluation," is for describing potential interventions that appear to be appropriate for identified problems. In this space, also describe or list any specific tools or methods that might be useful for monitoring intervention progress and evaluating the intervention outcome. Although the use of this worksheet is not essential for linking assessment to intervention, it provides a structured and very practical tool for this purpose. A sample completed assessment worksheet is provided in Figure 3.2.

## CONCLUDING COMMENTS

The current state of assessment technology in this area lends itself very well to the processes of diagnosis and classification. However, the frontier in assessing children's social–emotional symptoms is certainly the problem of linking these symptoms to effective intervention strategies in a useful and reasonable way. Some possible linking techniques, namely, progress monitoring, template matching, the keystone behavior strategy, and functional assessment, seem to offer a good deal of promise.

The balance of this book presents a broad range of specific intervention strategies and techniques that have been found effective in treatment of depression, anxiety, and related internalizing problems. Strategies for helping students overcome depression are covered in Chapters 4 through 7. Strategies for helping students overcome anxiety are covered in Chapters 8 and 9. A complete index of the intervention programs and strategies presented with their specific purposes and developmental levels can be found on pages xix–xxii. After you become familiar with these intervention options, you may choose from them to plan a treatment program. For example, you may choose a preplanned comprehensive treatment depression such as the "Taking Action" program described in Chapter 4. Although this book does not give you enough detail to implement such specific structured programs, it does tell you how to obtain what you need. On the other hand, this book does contain many individual techniques that are explained in full and often accompanied by student handouts or worksheets. These individual techniques can be used as building blocks for individualized intervention programs, including programs that need to target both depression and anxiety. The next chapter discusses the most effective, comprehensive treatments for depression and indicates the most important treatment components to include.

# Social–Emotional Assessment Worksheet

*Page 1*

## 1. Student information

Name: Jenny D.                    School: Central High School

Grade: 9                         Age: 14

Major concerns regarding student; reasons for assessment:

—poor adjustment to high school

—decline in academic performance during 9th grade (formerly
  an honor student in grade 8)

—seems withdrawn, may be depressed

—socially isolated, seems lonely

—poor self-concept

## 2. Summary of Assessment Information

Most important test scores, observations, and information from interviews
or other assessment sources:

BASC-Parent Rating Scale (from mother): internalizing problems composite is
elevated, bordering clinical range. Anxiety and depression subscales both elevated.
Possible deficits in social skills.

Reynolds Adolescent Depression Scale (self-report): total raw score = 75, just
below clinical cutoff of 77; item endorsement pattern includes evidence of
dysphoria, anxiousness, low self-esteem.

Interview with Jenny: seems both anxious and depressed. Is very shy—wants to
have friends but stays withdrawn. No evidence of suicidal ideation. Lots of
negative–distorted thinking.

School Social Behavior Scales (completed by 2 teachers): moderate deficit in
social competence overall, significant deficit in interpersonal skills area.

*(continued)*

FIGURE 3.2. A sample completed Social–Emotional Assessment Worksheet.

## 3. Problem Analysis

A. Major problems, concerns, diagnostic indicators, and so forth, that are indicated and supported by the assessment information.

—moderate depression, but not significant enough for formal DSM-IV diagnosis

—possible social phobia?

—social withdrawal, rumination about peer problems

B. Hypothesis regarding the possible origins and functions of any problems that are indicated. How might these hypotheses be tested?

—anxiety and negative self-statements appear to be fueling the social withdrawal

—social withdrawal appears to be contributing to feelings of alienation, loneliness, and depression

—"stuck" in a vicious cycle

## 4. Problem Solution and Evaluation

Potential interventions that appear to be appropriate for identified problems. Tools or methods that might be useful for monitoring intervention progress and evaluating the intervention outcome.

—individual counseling, with focus on the following:
  a. identifying and changing negative and distorted thought processes (from cognitive therapy)
  b. relaxation training
  c. goal setting, activity increase, behavior change

—social skills training: consider having Jenny join social skills group for 9th- and 10th-grade girls that will start next month. Focus on assertiveness, initiating social contacts.

—consult with Jenny's mother regarding activity scheduling and setting appropriate expectations.

# 4

# Comprehensive Intervention Programs for Depression

## INTRODUCTION AND OVERVIEW

Specific individual intervention techniques such as cognitive therapy, behavioral activity increase programs, emotional education, and others (which are detailed in Chapters 5–7) may be used individually as an intervention for depression in children and youth, often with a great deal of impact. However, the most prominent researchers in this area are increasingly finding that the most effective interventions for treating depressed children and youth are *comprehensive* intervention programs, particularly those that include a major focus on a combination of cognitive and behavioral intervention techniques (e.g., Lewinsohn, Clarke, Rohde, Hops, & Seeley, 1996; Harrington, 1993; Kaslow, Morris, & Rehm, 1998; Matson, 1989; Reynolds, 1992; Stark, 1990). Therefore, as the work in this area progresses, increased emphasis and attention are being placed on the use of comprehensive cognitive-behavioral treatment programs as the potentially most effective and systematic means of combating depression in children and adolescents. Although relatively few programs of this type have been developed and field-tested, several are now in existence and available in treatment manual format for use by practitioners. This chapter describes four of the best-known, most carefully designed and easily accessible of these comprehensive intervention programs that are currently available. These are model programs, and should be considered the "state of the art" for what is available at the present time. The first two programs reviewed are specifically grounded in cognitive-behavioral theory and techniques, whereas the last two are not, but they include many cognitive-behavioral elements. Following the discussion of these programs, some general issues regarding implementation of comprehensive treatment programs for depression are presented. Additionally, a recommended adaptation of the most common or essential elements of combined cognitive-behavioral intervention programs is provided for possible use in situations where there is insufficient time available for using one of these four model programs.

## FOUR COMPREHENSIVE INTERVENTION PROGRAMS

Although several comprehensive treatment programs for children and adolescents with depression have been described in the literature, only a few of these have been researched and field-tested very thoroughly. Of these programs, even fewer have been developed and refined to the point of being available to practitioners in the form of treatment manuals that provide specific directions, activity plans, student worksheets, or evaluation tools. This section provides brief descriptions and comments on four of the best of the comprehensive treatment programs that meet these criteria: the *Adolescent Coping with Depression Course* (CWD-A; Clarke, Lewinsohn, & Hops, 1990), the Taking ACTION Program (ACTION; Stark & Kendall, 1996), the *Interpersonal Family Therapy for Childhood Depression* (IFT) approach (Schwartz, Kaslow, Racusin, & Carton, 1998), and Interpersonal Psychotherapy for Adolescents with Depression (IPT-A; Mufson et al., 1996; Mufson, Moreau, Weissman, & Klerman, 1993). Each of these four programs has unique features but all share the commonality of being comprehensive and extensive intervention programs that include a substantial focus on cognitive and behavioral treatment methods. The first two programs reviewed, CWD-A and ACTION, are comprehensive cognitive-behavioral treatment programs that are designed primarily to be implemented with groups of students or individual students and also include some limited parent and family involvement components. In contrast, the IFT program is designed primarily to be implemented with depressed children and youth and their families, and IPT-A includes extensive family involvement as well. In my view, these four programs represent the best of the comprehensive treatment programs that are currently available. The intent of comparing and contrasting these four programs is not to determine which one is "best" but to illustrate how each has unique a unique focus and program components that may make it the best choice under certain circumstances.

## The Adolescent Coping with Depression Course

**Purpose:** A comprehensive cognitive-behavioral program for treatment of depression in small groups. Uses a psychoeducational-type program for teaching the essential skills to overcome depression. Includes 16 two-hour sessions and additional sessions for parents of group members.

**Developmental level:** Primarily intended for adolescents ages 14–18 but may be used with younger adolescents and older children with sufficient cognitive maturity to participate in the exercises.

The CWD-A (Clarke et al., 1990) is a carefully researched psychoeducational program designed to teach adolescents ages 14–18 the essential skills to overcome depression. Impressive research findings supporting the effectiveness of CWD-A as both a treatment and a prevention program have been documented (e.g., Lewinsohn et al., 1996). The CWD-A sessions are conducted like classes, with a recommended group size of four to eight students. The authors recommend delivering the CWD-A program in a classroom-type setting and as a psychoeducational intervention because they believe it will be less stigmatizing to the adolescent participants than participating in traditional psychotherapy. The specific goals, objectives, and activities in CWD-A are based on a combination of principles and techniques from cognitive therapy, behavioral interventions, emotional education, and relaxation and communication training.

The majority of cognitive, affective, and behavioral interventions for depression (including most that are covered in this book) provide a general set of principles for intervention goals and activities but do not require adherence to a specific routine. Unlike these, however, the activities in CWD-A are highly structured. In fact, the CWD-A leader's manual is actually scripted, meaning that the group leader is expected to read or closely paraphrase the set instructions in a very specific order to the participants. The advantage of such a carefully scripted program is that every detail has been painstakingly planned in advance, and presumably, treatment fidelity will be enhanced. Of course, the disadvantage is that some practitioners might consider such a carefully scripted intervention to be inflexible, rigid, and so forth. Obviously, there are some trade-offs in using a scripted intervention versus a general set of intervention principles and objectives to guide treatment, but the primary advantage in using CWD-A is that it is a painstakingly detailed in every respect and truly comprehensive intervention package.

CWD-A is designed as a set of 16 carefully sequenced 2-hour sessions. Table 4.1 describes the general content of the 16 sessions. Each session includes direct instruction from the group leader, modeling and practice of new skills, individual assignments designed to help master the skills that are taught, and homework assignments or home practice activities designed to generalize intervention gains outside of the classroom setting. The complete CWD-A package includes a the comprehensive scripted leader's manual; a student workbook filled with examples, activities, and homework assignments; and a similar but briefer workbook for parents, which is used in three optional but highly recommended joint parent–adolescent sessions.

Although CWD-A is designed to be used with groups of four to eight adolescents ages 14–18, it may also be adapted for use with individuals. The major modification for using CWD-A with individuals rather than small groups is that the numerous role-playing exercises, which are designed to be done with pairs of adolescents, would have to be modified and the practitioner/counselor would need to assume the role of the second adolescent. Other modifications of CWD-A are also possible. For example, the authors have stated that CWD-A could be used as a curriculum for high school health classes or "life skills" classes and in psychiatric hospitals or psychiatric day treatment settings.

Another possible modification would be to select and use only specific sessions or modules for the intervention rather than using all 16 two-hour sessions. For use as an intervention for students with depression in middle school or high school settings, this final modification is probably essential in most cases. Very few school-based practitioners who work in general school settings find that they have the luxury of conducting 2-hour intervention sessions or continuing the intervention for 16 sessions. CWD-A could be modified considerably to fit the time constraints that are likely within school settings. Of course, it is unclear whether any significant modification of the program would reduce its effectiveness, but there is no apparent reason why a shortened but carefully implemented

TABLE 4.1. Basic Outline of the Adolescent
Group Sessions in the Adolescent Coping
with Depression Course (CWD-A)

| Session | Title and content |
|---------|-------------------|
| 1 | Depression and social learning |
| 2 | Self-observation and change |
| 3 | Reducing tension |
| 4 | Learning how to change |
| 5 | Changing your thinking |
| 6 | The power of positive thinking |
| 7 | Disputing irrational thinking |
| 8 | Relaxation |
| 9 | Communication, part 1 |
| 10 | Communication, part 2 |
| 11 | Negotiation and problem solving, part 1 |
| 12 | Negotiation and problem solving, part 2 |
| 13 | Negotiation and problem solving, part 3 |
| 14 | Negotiation and problem solving, part 4 |
| 15 | Life goals |
| 16 | Prevention, planning, and ending |

version of CWD-A should not produce some beneficial gains for depressed students in terms of not only reducing current symptoms but also preventing or reducing the severity of future episodes of depression.

In summary, CWD-A is a highly structured teaching-based (psychoeducational) approach to helping depressed adolescents. The psychoeducational approach that is used in the carefully scripted session plans make it a natural fit for use in school settings. Although the extensive length and time requirements may make it difficult to implement in many school settings, it is a model program and is certainly worth considering for use by school-based practitioners.

## The Taking ACTION Program

**Purpose:** A comprehensive cognitive-behavioral program for group and individual treatment of depression that includes outlines and objectives for 30 one-hour sessions.

**Developmental level:** Adaptable for use with a wide age range of children and adolescents, presumably intermediate-elementary (ages 9 or 10) through late adolescence.

ACTION is another exceptionally comprehensive, detailed, and well-organized intervention package for treating depressed children and adolescents. Developed by Stark and Kendall (1996), it is described in detail in a chapter by Stark, Swearer, Kurowski, Sommer, and Bowen (1996). Like CWD-A, the ACTION program is a comprehensive intervention that includes not only cognitive and behavioral components but also affective education, relaxation training exercises, social skills training, and problem-solving training. Another similarity between CWD-A and the ACTION program is the availability of a student workbook or exercise manual (Stark et al., 1996). In addition, the ACTION program, like CWD-A, is based on the use of empirically proven treatment techniques, and was developed and refined based on a program of research by the authors over a period of several years.

Aside from the similarities, there are also a few areas where ACTION differs from CWD-A. Whereas CWD-A is designed specifically for use with adolescents ages 14–18, ACTION does not specify a strict age range for participation but is presented as being useful for wider age range of adolescents and older children who possess adequate cognitive maturity. Unlike the scripted and highly structured CWD-A treatment manual, the ACTION treatment manual provides a detailed list of materials, activities, and objectives but does not include a specifically worded script for the practitioner to follow. ACTION, like CWD-A is designed to target parents and families in the intervention as needed, but probably makes such involvement a stronger focus of the program. And although CWD-A is adaptable for use with individual adolescents rather than groups, ACTION makes such individually focused treatment a more specific part of the program:

> Experience in implementing the program has led to modifications in the delivery format. Initially, the intervention was delivered solely through a group format. Currently, a combination of individual and group therapy is used to teach youngsters the cognitive, behavioral, and affective coping skills. In this pilot work, the dual delivery format appears to be more efficacious for a variety of reasons. Depressed youngsters, because of the very nature of their disturbance, are especially difficult to engage in therapy. The relationship that develops between the youngster and the therapist during individual sessions can serve as leverage to get the child engaged in treatment and to comply with the treatment regimen, including therapeutic homework. By contrast, groups tend to take a longer time to develop a sense of cohesion and a demand characteristic that pushes for treatment compliance. Thus, the relationship that the youngster develops with an individual can serve as a motivation bridge until the group begins to develop an identity and motivational properties. (Stark et al., 1996, p. 210)

In short, the ACTION program is based on the assumption that it is both desirable and expected for the practitioner to work individually with students who are part of the intervention group, particularly during the early stages of the intervention. However, the group intervention format is viewed as being essential because of the opportunities for social learning and social support that are unique to groups. With this program, the determination of how often, when, and which skills should be addressed individually is left to the judgment of the practitioner rather than being a predetermined part of the intervention design.

Table 4.2 presents a brief overview of the major topics and activities in the 30 sessions of the ACTION program. Each of the sessions could presumably be completed in about 1 hour. In comparison with the 16 two-hour sessions of the CWD-A program, the 30 sessions in ACTION are comparable in terms of the total time that would be required to implement the complete intervention curriculum. Whereas CWD-A opts for longer sessions, ACTION covers many or most of the same topics but breaks sessions down into smaller components. However, the ACTION program, like CWD-A, may be modified according to the specific needs of the practitioner and the students. The parent training component of the ACTION program is not outlined in Table 4.2, but it is important to recognize that working with parents, and in some cases, other family members, is often an essential aspect of this program. The major objectives of the parent training component of ACTION include education on the use of positive behavioral management and interaction strategies, an emphasis on identifying and avoiding the use of coercive child-rearing strategies, training in effective communication with children, and practice in planning family activities that are positive, fun, and inexpensive.

The ACTION program is an exemplary intervention package that is comprehensive, easy to follow, and based on empirically supportable strategies. The manuals for ACTION include a variety of tools for interesting and fun activities, and the student-focused parts of the program materials are engaging and practical. This program is also quite flexible. For example, if it is not possible to conduct 30 treatment sessions, a practitioner could easily modify the program content to focus on the concerns and skills that are considered to be most important. Although the ACTION program has been field-tested primarily as an intervention for depressed students in general school settings, it seems to have the potential for use in a variety of other settings (such as inpatient treatment centers, day treatment programs, and self-contained special education settings). Like CWD-A, the ACTION program also appears to be potentially useful as a classwide (or schoolwide) prevention program, or as part of a mental health unit in high school health classes.

## IFT: A Comprehensive, Family-Centered Intervention

**Purpose:** A comprehensive family-centered program for treatment of depression in children and adolescents. Intervention is delivered primarily with entire families and includes various cognitive, behavioral, and interpersonal components implemented in 16 sessions.

**Developmental level:** May be used with families of elementary- and secondary-grade students.

Interpersonal family therapy for childhood depression (IFT) is an additional comprehensive intervention program for treating depressed children and youth, one that differs significantly in focus from the CWD-A and ACTION programs. This intervention has been described in detail by Schwartz et al. (1998). IFT differs from CWD-A and ACTION primarily in relation to the extent of family involvement or family focus in the intervention. Whereas CWD-A and ACTION are focused primarily on group-based treatment of older children and adolescents, and include parent and family involvement as a desirable additional component of the program, IFT is aimed specifically at treating depressed children and youth within the family context.

The rationale for focusing treatment of depressed children on the family rather than the individual is based on a large body of evidence indicating that the family context has a very powerful impact on childhood depression. Schwartz et al. (1998) reviewed a variety of

TABLE 4.2. Basic Outline of the ACTION Program for Depressed Youth

| Session | Content |
| --- | --- |
| 1 | Introductions; establishing appropriate expectations |
| 2 | Affective education; establishing a within-group incentive system; self-monitoring pleasant emotions |
| 3 | Affective education; introduction to coping orientation; self-monitoring pleasant emotions |
| 4 | Affective education; extend coping orientation; pleasant events scheduling; self-monitoring pleasant emotions |
| 5 | Affective education; introduction to problem-solving; self-monitoring pleasant emotions |
| 6 | Affective education; pleasant events scheduling and self-monitoring pleasant emotions; problem-solving game |
| 7 | Affective education; pleasant events scheduling; problem-solving game |
| 8 | Affective education; applications of problem solving to mood disturbance |
| 9 | Applications of problem solving to mood disturbance; missing solution activity |
| 10 | Introduction to relaxation; exercise and mood |
| 11 | Problem solving applied to interpersonal problems; pleasant events scheduling; relaxation as a coping strategy |
| 12 | Problem solving applied to interpersonal problems; self-evaluation of solution implementation; relaxation as a coping strategy |
| 13 | Spontaneous use of problem solving; relaxation and problem solving |
| 14 | Introduction to cognitive restructuring; identification of depressogenic thoughts |
| 15 | Practice catching negative thoughts; cognitive restructuring |
| 16 | Improve understanding of cognitive restructuring; practice catching negative thoughts; what is the evidence?; what to do when a negative thought is true |
| 17 | Alternative interpretation |
| 18 | Alternative interpretation; identifying negative expectations; introduce What If? |
| 19 | What If? |
| 20 | Review of cognitive restructuring procedures; assertiveness training; generate and rehearse coping statements |
| 21 | Positive assertiveness; generation of coping statements |
| 22 | Assertiveness training; generation of coping statements |
| 23 | Identify personal standards; introduction to self-evaluation training; identify areas for personal improvement |
| 24 | Set goals for self-improvement |
| 25–28 | Self-evaluation training; working toward self-improvement |
| 29–30 | Termination issues; programming for generalization |

studies demonstrating a family link to childhood depression in such diverse areas as genetic factors, family structure, family interactional processes, and parental depression or other forms of parental psychopathology. In particular, IFT was developed in response to evidence regarding the relationship between maladaptive parent–child and family interactional processes, and mood disorders and other forms of child maladjustment.

Although IFT has some similarities to interpersonal therapy and was developed in part based on the same premises as interpersonal therapy for adolescents with depression, detailed in the next section of this chapter, it clearly goes beyond the boundaries of the interpersonal therapy approach. A breakdown of session goals and tasks for IFT is presented in Table 4.3. A quick glance at the information in this table reveals that many of the treatment goals, objectives, and activities are essentially similar to much of what is found in the two previously reviewed comprehensive programs. For example, IFT is designed to include psychoeducation regarding depression, training regarding cognitive factors that maintain depression, behavior change strategies for increasing positive activities, affective education, problem-solving and communication training, and basic cognitive-behavioral methods of combating depressive symptoms. IFT differs from CWD-A and ACTION primarily in emphasizing treatment of the whole family and identifying and changing maladaptive family interaction patterns.

Although preliminary empirical evidence regarding IFT is encouraging, it is a treatment program that has been adapted primarily from established work with adults, and

**TABLE 4.3. Description of Sessions, Goals, and Tasks in IFT**

| Session | Title | Goals and tasks |
| --- | --- | --- |
| 1–2 | Joining and assessment | Development of a "working alliance" (therapeutic relationship) with each family member; comprehensive assessment of depressed child and family members |
| 3 | Feedback and disposition | Ascertain need for additional treatment resources; determine whether or not family treatment is intervention of choice; provide feedback from assessment to family; educate regarding depression |
| 4 | Psychological symptomatology | Teach strategies to alleviate depressive symptoms; identify precipitants of depressive reactions and education regarding adaptive methods of coping; reframe child's psychological symptoms to reflect family rather than individual dysfunction |
| 5–6 | Cognitive functioning | Educate regarding cognitive factors in depression (negative cognitive triad, attribution retraining, cognitive distortions); focus on identification of depressive cognitive patterns; challenge child and family's depressive cognitive patterns that maintain the problem |
| 7–8 | Affective functioning | Teach family members to label and verbalize both pleasant and unpleasant emotional or affective states; education regarding adaptive strategies for regulating affect |
| 9–10 | Interpersonal functioning | Increase interpersonal problem-solving skills and positive interpersonal communication within family; assist child in developing social relationship skills; increase participation in pleasurable activities with peers |
| 11 | Adaptive behavior | Educate regarding age-appropriate adaptive behaviors; focus on family members using "I" statements rather than "you" statements; help child increase appropriate daily living skills |
| 12–13 | Family functioning | Identification of dysfunctional family interaction patterns; promotion of changes in the structure of the family system |
| 14–16 | Review, synthesis, postassessment | Review goals and information from prior sessions, troubleshoot problems areas; evaluate progress with postassessment; address termination issues |

there is currently not as much research support for this program as for the other two comprehensive treatment programs highlighted in this chapter. As Schwartz et al. (1988) have stated, IFT should be viewed as a "work in progress" (p. 143), and more refinement and validation of the program is needed. However, IFT is built on sound principles, clearly articulated, and unique because of its intense family-centered focus. As school-based practitioners move increasingly into the realm of providing comprehensive, community-based mental health and social services within school settings, intervention programs such as IFT may provide the link to family and parental involvement that is often missing in traditional school-based interventions. However, school-based practitioners should also be realistic about the difficulties of obtaining high levels of parental and family involvement, particularly when highly dysfunctional families are involved. In commenting on this problem during the research and development of the ACTION program, Stark et al. (1996) stated:

> From our experience, it is difficult to obtain the desired level of parental and family involvement in the youngster's treatment. In fact, when we were conducting the school-based research, we were fortunate to have the parents in for treatment meetings once a month. They often were too busy working at multiple jobs or with other responsibilities to participate. In a related vein, the mental health of parents and other family members can limit the impact of intervention. In some instances, the parents were so seriously disturbed that they required simultaneous intense treatment. In other cases, parental substance abuse would be discovered late in the treatment and the parent would deny having a problem or refuse treatment, which undermined the overall effectiveness of the intervention. (p. 234)

In their description of IFT, Schwartz et al. (1998) do not specifically address the difficulty of engaging participation from parents and family members when treating a depressed student in a school setting, but this problem is so well known among school-based practitioners that it is simply taken for granted. Despite the potential difficulties, a family-based intervention such as IFT for depressed children and adolescents appears to have tremendous appeal and potential. "It is a growing conviction that given the family's primacy in the lives of children and adolescents, the association between dysfunctional family interactional patterns and depression in youth, and the demonstrated efficacy of family therapy for childhood disorders, family therapy may prove to be the treatment of choice for many depressed children and adolescents" (Schwartz et al., 1998, p. 143).

## Interpersonal Psychotherapy for Adolescents with Depression

**Purpose:** A comprehensive intervention program aimed at decreasing symptoms of depression and improving interpersonal functioning.

**Developmental level:** Adolescents with average or higher intellectual ability.

Interpersonal psychotherapy (IPT) was initially developed in the late 1960s as a brief psychotherapy for treatment of depression with adults. Several studies in the 1970s and 1980s produced evidence supporting its effectiveness. This unique treatment method does not fit neatly within the traditions of psychodynamic, behavioral, or cognitive theory or therapeutic techniques. There are two basic goals of IPT: (1) to decrease the symptoms of depression, and (2) to improve interpersonal functioning. IPT is somewhat unique among various methods of treating depression because of its strong focus on interpersonal relationships. Although IPT does not propose a specific theory of the etiology or development of depression, it is based on the assumption that depression usually has an interpersonal component; that is, depression occurs within the context of significant relationships. Therefore, the treatment focus for IPT is emphasis on the interpersonal nature of the problem as it occurs in current relationships.

In recent years, IPT has been adapted by Mufson and her colleagues (e.g., Mufson et al., 1993, 1996) for use with adolescents. This adaptation of IPT is referred to as interpersonal psychotherapy for adolescents, or IPT-A. This adolescent-focused version of IPT is similar to its predecessor in terms of focus, goals, and general methods. However, IPT-A differs from ITP to some extent because of the focus on specific issues related to adolescent development, such as relationships with parents and peers, and social problems at school and with teachers. IPT-A, unlike IPT, includes a strong focus on working with parents, and in some cases, the entire family. IPT-A is also comparatively brief and relatively structured. The definitive treatment manual for using IPT-A is the excellent book by Mufson and colleagues (1993), which provides a detailed discussion of IPT, illustrates how depression may be manifest in adolescents, covers the specific stages and steps of treatment, and also addresses some of the unique challenges in treating depressed youth, such as confidentiality, school problems, substance abuse problems, sexual abuse, homosexuality, and other issues. Because IPT-A requires the client to have a fair amount of interpersonal and intrapersonal insight, it is designed for use with nonpsychotic adolescents of average or higher intellectual ability.

As detailed in the treatment manual and in other sources (Mufson et al., 1993, 1996), IPT-A is designed for use with individuals in once-a-week sessions over the course of 12 weeks. Additional sessions may be scheduled if needed, such as in the event of crisis situations. IPT-A is divided into three phases of treatment. The initial phase of IPT-A, sessions 1–4, focuses on the symptoms of depression, identifies problem areas, and culminates in the establishment of a treatment contract. Six specific tasks that must be accomplished during the initial phase of IPT-A are detailed in Table 4.4. An interesting aspect of the first phase is that the adolescent is encouraged to think of him- or herself as being "in treatment" and is given a limited "sick" role. Parent(s) are brought into to some sessions for education regarding depression and how to be appropriately supportive of their adolescent while he or she is in treatment.

In the middle phase of treatment, sessions 5–8, one or two areas are targeted as a treatment focus. There is continued education about depression and interpersonal relationships. Although the four sessions in this phase are not broken down into a set of tasks or steps, there is a general guiding principle to be considered. First, adolescents are encouraged to "bring in their feelings" to the sessions. In other words, affect is addressed directly, within the process of tying this affect to situations involving important interpersonal relationships. By the end of the middle phase, the treatment focus gradually shifts to interpersonal situations outside of session. The practitioner may employ various tech-

**TABLE 4.4. Phases and Major Tasks of Interpersonal Psychotherapy for Adolescents (IPT-A)**

Initial phase (sessions 1–4)

- Conduct diagnostic assessment and evaluate possible need for medication
- Assess type and nature of social and family relationships, link to depression
- Identify problem areas
- Explain rationale and intent of treatment
- Make treatment contract with adolescent
- Explain adolescent's role in treatment

Middle phase (sessions 5–8)

- Direct work on one or two problem areas
- Therapist encourages client to "bring in feelings," monitors depressive symptoms, continues to work with family to support treatment
- Possible techniques: *exploratory questioning, encouraging affect, linking affect to events, clarifying conflicts, analyzing communication, role playing*
- Therapist gives continuous feedback to adolescent client
- Treatment focus gradually shifts to interpersonal events outside of session
- Continued education about depression and interpersonal functioning

Termination phase (sessions 9–12)

- Adolescent begins to give up relationship with therapist
- Adolescent establishes sense of competence about dealing with future problems
- Education regarding possible recurrence of symptoms
- Termination is discussed
- Planning for additional treatment sessions if needed
- Final meeting with entire family may be useful

niques during the middle phase, such as role-playing, exploratory questioning, encouraging affect, clarification, and so forth.

The final phase of IPT-A, referred to as the termination phase, includes sessions 9–12. In these four sessions, the issue of termination is addressed specifically. In this regard, the student is to establish a sense of competence in dealing with future problems and begins to "give up" his or her relationship with the practitioner. There is continued psychoeducation regarding depression and relationships and planning for possible recurrence of symptoms. It is recommended that the final session or two include the entire family. Again, the three phases of IPT-A, with the specific tasks and techniques for each phase, are detailed in Table 4.4.

IPT-A, a unique treatment among various interventions for depression, is based upon a therapeutic technique that is empirically supported and appears to be a potentially useful intervention. However, in comparison with the other intervention methods detailed in this book, IPT-A has a more narrow range of applicability. It seems to be ideal for use with mature and insightful adolescents but should not be the treatment of choice for use with younger or less mature youth, or with adolescents who are lacking in inter- and intrapersonal insight or have limited verbal mediation skills.

## WHICH PROGRAM IS BEST?

The four treatment programs discussed in this chapter are probably the best-known and most thoroughly field-tested comprehensive cognitive-behavioral interventions that exist at the present time for use with depressed children and youth. Information regarding how to obtain each of these programs is presented at the end of the chapter in Table 4.6. Each of these programs is exemplary in its own way, and potential users should consider which program might best meet their needs rather than which program is "best." CWD-A and the ACTION programs share many similarities but there are some key differences that might help determine which is best for use in specific situations. CWD-A may be the best choice in situations where longer treatment sessions (2 hours) are possible and desired, where a highly structured script for the group leader is desired, and where the primary treatment focus is a small groups of adolescents in a classroom-type situation. ACTION may be the better choice in instances when extensive individual counseling is a necessary or desired adjunct to the group sessions, when the sessions need to be shorter (1 hour), when the group leader desires more flexibility in how to implement the intervention, and when the parental education component of treatment needs to include a stronger focus on basic behavior management techniques for parents. If extensive family involvement is necessary and possible, then IFT may be the better choice. In IFT, family participation is not just an option, it is the basis of treatment. Thus, it requires a commitment from the entire family, as well as a group leader trained in working with families. IPT-A may be a good choice in situations when the causes of depression are clearly connected to problems in interpersonal relationships, and when working with more mature intellectually bright students who have good intrapersonal insight.

It is quite possible that for particular situations, none of these four comprehensive programs will be the best choice. In situations where a comprehensive cognitive-behavioral intervention is desired but there is not sufficient time to follow one of these manualized treatments, practitioners can simply develop their own programs, using the intervention principles and tools illustrated in this book in a manner that specifically suits their particular needs. The next section of this chapter provides a guide to the essential components that might be most important to include in a comprehensive intervention for depression, with cross-references to the individual chapters in which these techniques are detailed. Additionally, a recommended brief adaptation of a comprehensive cognitive-behavioral intervention program for depression is described.

## MODIFYING OR DESIGNING YOUR OWN COMPREHENSIVE TREATMENT PROGRAM FOR DEPRESSION

Implementing a comprehensive cognitive-behavioral treatment program for depressed students in schools or other settings requires much more than simply following a treatment manual or developing a list of activities and a schedule. In addition to the design and development of the intervention plan itself, there are several practical issues to consider, such as selecting the most appropriate treatment program, determining how many sessions should be scheduled, emphasizing the most important or critical components of the intervention program, and dealing with various issues related to group composition. This section provides some guidance with respect to these practical implementation issues.

## Which Components of the Program Are Most Important?

The only way really to answer this question is through experimental manipulation. To date, no such research has been done. However, one useful way to think about it is to identify the common elements of the four programs highlighted in this chapter. Because these programs are probably the most exemplary and carefully researched of the interventions currently available for depressed students, identifying their common elements is a good start toward determining which components are essential or critical. A careful review of the intervention components from these treatments indicates that the several elements are common to each of the four programs, meaning that they are found in at least three programs. These common elements and techniques, and cross-references for the chapters in which they are addressed, are as follows:

- Development of a therapeutic relationship of trust and respect
- Initial assessment of problem symptoms (Chapter 3)
- Education regarding depression (Chapters 1, 2, and 5)
- Activity scheduling: monitoring, recording, and increasing participation in pleasant activities or events (Chapter 7)
- Emotional or affective education: identifying and labeling pleasant and unpleasant emotions, identifying situations in which specific emotions are likely to occur, identifying the link between thoughts and emotions (Chapters 5 and 7)
- Identification of problem cognition patterns: automatic negative thoughts, cognitive distortions, maladaptive attribution styles, negative cognitive triad, irrational thinking (Chapters 5 and 6)
- Cognitive change strategies: challenging negative thoughts, disputing irrational thoughts, practicing appropriate attributions, increasing focus on positive thoughts and events (Chapters 5 and 6)
- Training in problem solving, negotiation, or conflict resolution (Chapter 7)
- Training in methods of relaxation (Chapter 8)
- Training in appropriate social skills (Chapter 7)
- Training in effective communication (Chapter 7)
- Cumulative review of concepts, skills, and techniques
- Goal setting, relapse prevention, planning strategies for dealing with future problems
- Posttreatment assessment and evaluation (Chapter 3)

As you can see, many components might be considered critical or essential to a comprehensive cognitive-behavioral intervention program for depressed students. If you are in a situation in which you are developing your own custom intervention program, try to incorporate as many of these 14 components as possible, allowing an appropriate amount of time for each one.

Another alternative is to use the recommended outline in Table 4.5 for a cognitive-behavioral intervention for depression that is less time intensive than any of the four comprehensive programs detailed in this chapter but still consistent with the use of the common elements from these programs. This recommended 10-session outline is a condensed version of some of the key elements of comprehensive cognitive-behavioral intervention programs. The content and specific techniques may be modified as necessary for specific problems, individuals, and groups. It is estimated that these sessions would require approximately 45 minutes each, as described in Table 4.5. Each of the 10 sessions in this recommended briefer intervention outline is cross-referenced with the chapter in this book that addresses the specific component.

In other cases, a comprehensive cognitive-behavioral intervention may not be possible or necessary, depending on such issues as students' availability for treatment, the types of symptoms they are exhibiting, and the amount of time available to the practitioner. In these cases, it may be best simply to implement one facet of an intervention, whether it be emotional education, behavioral activity contracting, cognitive techniques, or other specific components.

## What Is the Best Group Composition?

The question of what makes for an ideal group composition for conducting a group-based comprehensive intervention for depressed students cannot be unequivocally answered at the present time. But make no mistake about it: Groups are generally the preferred format for such interventions and may be a potentially powerful medium to effect change. "In a properly running group, the depressed child experiences safety, acceptance, support, and positive feedback that in and of itself leads to some restructuring of negative beliefs about social situations and about the self in a social context. With adolescents and pre-adolescents, it is often helpful for them to hear from a peer the same things that the therapist (an adult) has been saying" (Stark et al., 1996, p. 211). To construct a group in which such a climate is likely, several considerations are necessary.

### Group Size

Generally speaking, 4–10 students are considered to be best for a small intervention group, with 4–8 students being ideal. With fewer than four students, there are insufficient opportunities for modeling and providing feedback, and individual discomfort often increases. With more than 8 or 10 students, management issues become an increasing concern, and there are often insufficient opportunities for practice and feedback.

### Age or Grade Range

It is generally best to include students from no more than a common 2- or 3-year grade/age range. For example, it would make sense to have a group of students from grades 5–6 or

**TABLE 4.5. Recommended Outline for a Brief Version of a Combined Cognitive-Behavioral Intervention for Depression**

| Session | Major content and activity outline | Reference chapters |
|---------|-----------------------------------|--------------------|
| 1 | Introduction and overview<br>• Initial screening<br>• Mood and activity ratings (which will continue weekly)<br>• Psychoeducation: how thinking and behavior influence mood | 2, 3, 5 |
| 2 | Emotional education<br>• Awareness of emotional variability<br>• Identifying comfortable and uncomfortable feelings<br>• Learning to express feelings appropriately<br>• Reacting to emotional situations | 5, 7 |
| 3 | Changing behavior<br>• Activity scheduling<br>• Goal setting<br>• Review relationship between behavior and mood | 5, 6, 7 |
| 4 | Identifying and detecting maladaptive negative thoughts<br>• Selected exercises from steps II and II of cognitive therapy | 5 |
| 5 | Identifying and disputing irrational thoughts (RET)<br>• Overview of common irrational thoughts and beliefs from RET<br>• Education regarding "A-B-C" process<br>• Practice identifying and disputing irrational thoughts and beliefs | 6 |
| 6 | Attribution retraining and learning to be optimistic<br>• Self-monitoring and self-control training<br>• Practice in attribution retraining<br>• Practice in learned optimism techniques | 6 |
| 7 | Relaxation training<br>• Instruction and practice in active muscle relaxation<br>• Instruction and practice in passive muscle relaxation and imagery | 8 |
| 8 | Interpersonal problem-solving and conflict resolution<br>• Education about maladaptive styles of problem solving<br>• Training and practice in appropriate conflict resolution | 7 |
| 9 | Review<br>• Review, model, practice, and reinforce techniques learned<br>• Work on techniques and issues that appear to be the most important or problematic for the group | |
| 10 | Completion and planning for the future<br>• Self-assessment of progress<br>• Feedback from group leader<br>• Planning for relapse prevention, referral if necessary | 3, 4 |

*Note.* This recommended 10-session outline is a condensed version of some of the key elements of comprehensive cognitive-behavioral intervention programs. The content and specific techniques used may be modified as necessary for specific problems, individuals, and groups. It is estimated that these sessions would require approximately 45 minutes each as they are described here.

perhaps even grades 4–6, but mixing more than three grade levels by including students from grades 3–6 increases the possibility of too many developmental differences among students. Older students in such a situation might feel embarrassed that they are in a group with younger students, and the younger students may not be able to participate with as much cognitive or affective sophistication as the older students.

## Gender Composition

The issue of gender in intervention groups is important and sometimes difficult. Generally speaking, it is best to include both male and female students in intervention groups for youth, because a mixed-gender group more closely approximates the real world and provides opportunities for practice and feedback with both boys and girls (Merrell & Gimpel, 1998). It is also usually better to have relatively equal numbers and boys and girls in a group, to avoid having one gender be overly predominant. However, there may be some very specific situations in which single-gender groups are more appropriate. When forming a new intervention group, practitioners should appraise their particular situation and make a decision regarding gender composition that is best for their students and the treatment process.

## Range and Severity of Problems

Obviously, depression and related concerns should be the primary focus in a comprehensive cognitive-behavioral intervention group. But as all practitioners know only too well, it is the rule rather than the exception that student participants may have other troubles as well. For example, one student struggling with depression may also have serious acting-out behavior and a violent temper; another depressed student may be totally withdrawn and painfully shy; yet a student with depression may be heavily involved in substance abuse, and still another student may have co-occurring symptoms of ADHD or Tourette's disorder. Recommendations regarding group composition according to range and severity of problems are based on clinical experience rather than empirical evidence (there is little to none). It is generally acceptable to include in the group students with a range of depressive symptom severity. It is also generally acceptable to include in the group students with a variety of other problems, so long as the focus in the group stays on depression and closely related problems. If one participant has an intense concern with substance abuse, anger control, or some other externalizing problem, there is a good likelihood that the group will ultimately be distracted and the intervention will become less focused.

## How Many Sessions Are Enough?

Despite the growing research on comprehensive cognitive-behavioral interventions for depression, the question of the number of sessions sufficient for effective treatment is still an empirical one. The answer to this question is simply not known at this point in time. To implement one of the programs discussed in this chapter, practitioners should plan on a minimum of 12 sessions, and as many as 30 sessions. A minimum of about 1 hour, and up to

2 hours, is needed for conducting these programs. Realistically, it would be difficult to accomplish the goals of treatment if the sessions were delivered in much less than 1-hour blocks of time, although 45 or 50 minutes might be adequate and necessary in school settings. Other considerations regarding the number of sessions and how much time each session should consume include the age and attention span of the students and the severity of the depression they are experiencing. It is reasonable that younger students or those with co-occurring learning problems or ADHD characteristics will require shorter treatment sessions, and that students with more severe levels of depression will require more total time to benefit from the intervention. The typical format for treatment is weekly sessions, but in some cases in school settings, twice-weekly sessions of shorter duration may be helpful.

## CONCLUDING COMMENTS

Over the past several years, I have conducted numerous professional training workshops on school-based assessment and treatment of depression, anxiety, and general internalizing problems of children and youth. The participants in these workshops have for the most part been school psychologists, school counselors, and school social workers. Inevitably, when I have gotten to the part of the workshop in which I cover comprehensive cognitive-behavioral intervention programs for depressed youth, there has been more than a little concern regarding how realistic it would be to implement a comprehensive, group-based intervention program with as many as 16–30 sessions of 1–2 hours each. Regardless of their particular professional specialty, many school-based practitioners are under significant time and role constraints that may make it difficult to implement such a program. I recognize the reality of time demands and role constraints among practitioners in the schools. If you find yourself in a professional situation in which your ability to conduct a continuous group-based intervention on a weekly or twice-weekly basis for 3 or 4 months is compromised, here are some suggestions.

First, consider the possibility of conducting a comprehensive cognitive-behavioral intervention on a modified time-limited basis. Using one of the programs reviewed in this chapter, or designing your own, using the common elements of these programs (e.g., using Table 4.5 as an outline), determine a realistic number of sessions and select the particular skill or focus areas that you believe would be most important for your students. Second, consider lobbying your supervisor or administrator to allow you to attempt a comprehensive cognitive-behavioral intervention of several weeks' duration on an experimental basis. Carefully select the students who are most in need of intervention. Collect data that will help you to gauge treatment progress and overall benefits. Set a goal to expand your role, so that you can spend at least part of one morning or afternoon a week conducting a comprehensive intervention. For many students in your school who are struggling with depression, you may be the most likely person to provide the kind of intervention that is most likely to help them. If you do not, who will?

**TABLE 4.6. Sources for CWD-A, ACTION, IFT, and IPT-A Treatment Manuals and Workbooks**

*Adolescent Coping with Depression Course*
(Clark et al., 1990)
Castalia Publishing Company
P.O. Box 1587
Eugene, OR 97440
Phone: 541-343-4433

*Taking ACTION Program*
(Stark & Kendall, 1996)
Workbook Publishing, Inc.
208 Llanfair Rd.
Ardmore, PA 19003
Phone: 610-896-9797
Fax: 610-896-1955

*Interpersonal Family Therapy for Depressed Children*
Dr. Nadine Kaslow
Emory University School of Medicine
Department of Psychiatry and Behavioral Sciences
Grady Health System
80 Butler St., SE
Atlanta, GA 30335
Phone: 404-616-4757
E-mail: nkaslow@emory.edu

*Interpersonal Therapy for Adolescents with Depression*
(Mufson et al., 1993)
Guilford Publications
72 Spring Street
New York, NY 10012
Phone: 800-365-7006
Fax: 212-966-6708
Web site: www.guilford.com

# 5

# Changing Thoughts and Beliefs
## *Cognitive Therapy Techniques for Depression*

## INTRODUCTION AND OVERVIEW

Cognitive therapy has become one of the most popular specific methods for treating depression. Unlike behaviorally oriented interventions, which focus on externally observable behaviors, cognitive methods seek to impact depression by first identifying and then modifying the thought processes and beliefs that may be fueling the depression. Cognitive therapy requires that clients or students be integrally involved in identifying and monitoring their own maladaptive thoughts and beliefs. Additionally, cognitive treatments require a fair amount of intrapersonal insight and, to some extent, the ability to think in abstract terms. Therefore, most intervention methods that are based on cognitive theory and techniques are best used with normal- or high-functioning adolescents and, in some cases, older children (say, ages 9–12) who are intellectually bright and insightful. Cognitive therapy and other cognitive treatment methods should be considered for the intervention plan when assessment results indicate that the target student(s) have adopted maladaptive thoughts and beliefs that are likely contributing to the depression. This sort of information is best obtained through interviews and self-report assessment, which is detailed in Chapter 3. For example, if the assessment information indicates that students are thinking about present and future events in an overly pessimistic manner, or that they are focusing only on the negative aspects of things, then cognitive techniques may be an excellent choice for intervention.

This chapter provides a basic description of the four steps that comprise the main phase of cognitive therapy for treating depression in children and adolescents. Many practical exercises are illustrated, and several reproducible forms for use with individuals or groups of students in treatment are provided. This chapter focuses almost exclusively on the specific cognitive approach to treating depression that was developed by Aaron Beck and his colleagues, and modified for use with children and youth. In addition to this treat-

82

ment approach, several other cognitively based intervention methods have been developed that are potentially useful for dealing with depression. Several of these additional cognitive methods are illustrated in Chapter 6.

## COGNITIVE THERAPY FOR DEPRESSION: AN INTRODUCTION

The general collection of techniques upon which cognitive therapy for depression is built can be traced primarily to the work of Aaron Beck. He first articulated a comprehensive cognitive model for depression (1967) and, with his colleagues, developed an extensive intervention manual for use in treating depressed adults (Beck et al., 1979). The publication of this treatment manual stimulated widespread implementation and modification of the approach, as well as research that demonstrated its effectiveness. This approach to understanding and treating depression has made a major impact in the various fields of psychotherapy.

Beck's cognitive treatment approach for depression was later modified for use with adolescents (Wilkes, Belsher, Rush, Frank, & Associates, 1994), and with some additional modifications, it can be used with older children as well. The original premises and techniques of this approach have influenced the development of almost all cognitive and cognitive-behavioral treatment programs for children and youth. There are four primary ways that cognitive therapy is adapted for use with children and adolescents:

- There is a presumption that practitioners should already have been trained in general methods of child and adolescent psychotherapy, so that they possess the prerequisite skills and knowledge to be able to form an effective therapeutic alliance with children and adolescents.
- The parents and family of the depressed student who is in treatment should also be included in the assessment and treatment process because of possible family factors that contribute to the depression, as well as the potential help that the family can provide in treatment.
- There is an emphasis on taking into account and focusing on the student's cognitive developmental level. Because adolescents who have reached what Piaget termed the *formal operations* stage of cognitive development may still respond differently than adults to depression and its treatment, and because children and youth who are at Piaget's *concrete operations* stage will certainly respond differently than adults, the implementation of the intervention must be done in a manner that is developmentally appropriate.
- There is an active awareness (and, if necessary, treatment) of the emotional and behavioral disorders that are most likely to co-occur with depression in young persons, such as ADHD, conduct problems, or other internalizing disorders.

The following four sections of this chapter provide an overview of the basic steps of cognitive therapy for depressed adolescents and older children, and the specific techniques that can be used within each step. Some of the techniques used in these treatment steps are discussed directly, as they were introduced by the developers of this approach, and in some cases, I have introduced techniques and modifications that I believe will simplify the steps and make them more appropriate for younger or less sophisticated youth, and for school settings. It is important to recognize that these specific steps, and the treatment techniques involved with each, should not be viewed as something that the practitioner should feel compelled to use in a rigid or lockstep manner. These general steps, and the specific techniques within them, are flexible, general, and easy to modify; you can or pick and choose among them and make them appropriate for specific individuals or groups. If you are interested in a highly detailed treatment manual for depressed students that is based on Beck's cognitive therapy approach, I enthusiastically encourage you to get the excellent treatment manual developed by Wilkes and colleagues (1994).

There are four major steps in cognitive therapy. Before moving into the specific processes of each, it is useful to see how they fit together. Each step makes better sense within the context of the others.

*Step 1, Developing Awareness of Emotional Variability*, is aimed at helping students develop a greater conscious awareness of their own emotional states and how they are likely vary over time and across situations. This is a psychoeducational process whereby the individual or group members are taught to become aware of their own emotional variability. That variability can then be connected to specific cognitions and behavior. This chapter includes several possible techniques or exercises aimed at helping to promote emotional awareness.

*Step 2, Detecting Automatic Thoughts and Identifying Beliefs*, is aimed at helping students to identify their own individual patterns of thinking and the belief systems that underlie their thought processes and influence their emotions. This step is not aimed only at negative and destructive cognitive patterns; it focuses on creating a specific awareness of one's patterns of cognitions in general. Several techniques and exercises, such as the Cognitive Replay Technique and the use of Thought Charts, are included as potential resources in Step 2 to help achieve the desired goal.

*Step 3, Evaluating Automatic Thoughts and Beliefs*, moves from self-detection of cognitions into evaluation whether one's adopted "automatic" thoughts and belief systems are realistic or helpful. In many cases with depressed youth, they are not. Techniques such as the Three-Question strategy are used in this step to help students evaluate whether their automatic thoughts and beliefs are adaptive or maladapative.

Finally, *Step 4, Changing Negative Automatic Thoughts and Maladaptive Beliefs*, focuses on the process of actively attempting to change maladaptive thoughts and beliefs that have been identified through the previous steps. Note that the goal of this step, and the treatment as a whole, is *not only* to eliminate maladaptive thoughts and beliefs but also to *replace them*. Note, too, that some negative beliefs may be both realistic and adaptive, and so should not be changed. This chapter includes several therapeutic techniques that actively challenge students to change their patterns of thinking and adopt more realistic and constructive cognitions. For example, cognitive rehearsal, reframing, and relabeling may be used to challenge actively and change one's maladaptive cognitive patterns. In summary, these four steps each have specific aims and goals, yet they are flexible; the transition from one step to another can be made seamless.

## STEP 1: DEVELOPING AWARENESS OF EMOTIONAL VARIABILITY

This first step may be thought of as the first of a series of lessons on depression and social learning, in which the practitioner acts as a teacher and the depressed youngsters take the role of students. The general goal is to help them begin to understand how their thoughts, feelings, and behavior are interrelated. The specific goal of this step is to increase awareness of emotions and emotional variability. The variability of emotional states is then linked to variability in thoughts and behavior.

Treatment techniques for this step might include a homework assignment to keep a Daily and Weekly Mood Log (see Worksheet 5.1), and to keep a log of activities (see Chapter 6). It might also be useful to introduce the journal-writing technique covered in Chapter 6.

A couple of techniques that are often emphasized in this first stage of cognitive therapy with young persons may be particularly useful in aiding the process of helping older students become aware of their emotional states and mood variability.

### The Emotional Thermometer

**Purpose:** To help students understand that their emotions are expressed in degrees of intensity and are not just present or absent.

**Developmental level:** All ages, but keep emotional gradations simple for younger students.

The *emotional thermometer* is an exercise in illustrating emotional variability. The idea behind this technique is to convey the understanding that emotions are more than just present or absent, they are experienced in degrees of intensity, just like the temperature that is measured with a thermometer. Usually, the practitioner or group leader will draw a representation of a thermometer on the chalkboard or posterboard. The depiction of a thermometer must include graded variations or levels. For younger children, it would be most appropriate to keep the gradations simple, such as *low*, *medium*, and *high*. For more mature students, it would be more useful to label the thermometer gradations in smaller increments (say, 5 or 10 degrees). The emotional thermometer exercise is conducted by asking the participating children or adolescents to identify certain situations they might have experienced that involve particular emotions (such as angry, sad, fearful, etc.) and then select the appropriate level or gradation of emotional intensity for that situation.

## The Emotional Pie

**Purpose:** To identify the overall composition of mood states, or which moods/emotions are experienced more frequently than others.

**Developmental level:** Older children and adolescents.

**Supporting material:** Worksheet 5.2, "Emotional Pie."

Like the emotional thermometer, the *emotional pie* is a pictorial exercise that requires participants to evaluate their mood state in a more complex manner than simply identifying the presence or absence of particular emotions. This exercise works like a pie chart graph; the child or youth is asked to determine for a specific period of time (such as a specific day or an entire week) how his or her mood states were divided, like pieces of pie of varying sizes. This exercise will likely be somewhat difficult for younger or less intellectually sophisticated youth because it requires a fair amount of symbolic and spatial reasoning ability. However, it can be very helpful in the process of learning to identify emotional variability. The emotional pie exercise can also be helpful in setting goals for targeting certain emotions that children desire to increase or decrease as a proportion of the overall circle. Worksheet 5.2 includes a template that can be used with the emotional pie technique. An example of a completed worksheet is found in Figure 5.1.

## STEP 2: DETECTING AUTOMATIC THOUGHTS AND IDENTIFYING BELIEFS

After your students have developed a better understanding of their emotional variability through the exercises and lessons in Step 1, they are then ready to learn how to begin detecting their "automatic thoughts" and underlying beliefs associated with these thoughts. According to the theory that drives cognitive therapy, many of our thoughts or cognitions occur automatically in response to particular situations or stimuli. As a result, we tend to develop patterns of thinking without having made a conscious decision to adopt a particular strategy. Persons who are depressed often have developed patterns of negative automatic thoughts in response to many situations. In most cases, these negative automatic thoughts are maladaptive because they further fuel the depression, and because they are often distorted and unrealistic.

Related to automatic thoughts are underlying assumptions or beliefs that lead to them. Automatic thoughts are considered to be more specific responses to particular events or experiences, whereas beliefs are broader. They comprise a "schema," or pattern, through which we interpret various situations. For example, "I can't do this—I'm going to mess up," is a thought related to a specific situation, whereas the general underlying belief that shapes the thought might be "I am inferior; I am not a capable person." The negative thought and the depressed mood are connected.

The goal in cognitive therapy is to change maladaptive thinking patterns. This is done by first detecting the automatic thoughts and underlying beliefs. In the treatment manual

# Emotional Pie

Name *Devon*　　　　　　　　Time Period *this week*

This activity will help you describe how your feelings were divided up during a particular time, like a day or a week. Our feelings can be thought of kind of like a pie that is cut into slices of different sizes: Sometimes one feeling is bigger than another, in how much room it takes in our life. For the time period that you picked, divide the circle on this sheet into different sized "slices" to show how much room different feelings took in your life during that time. Pick at least two feelings, and label the slices of the pie using the first letter of that word. You might want to select the feelings from this list:

N = normal mood, okay　　H = happy　　　　　S = sad
T = tense　　　　　　　　A = angry or mad　　W = worried

Write down the names of the feelings, and the letters for them, that you are including in your chart:

B = bored　　　　　　A = angry　　　　F = frustrated

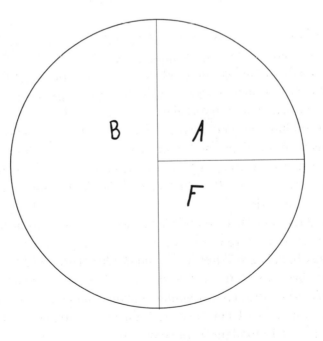

---

**FIGURE 5.1.** A sample completed worksheet using the Emotional Pie technique.

devised by Wilkes et al. (1994), detecting automatic thoughts comprises Step 2, and identifying beliefs comprises a separate step, Step 3. However, in practice, it is difficult to separate these steps, and as the authors acknowledge, detecting automatic thoughts and underlying beliefs is usually done in unison. Therefore, I have combined these two steps into one for this chapter. Several activities and techniques may be helpful in the process of detecting automatic thoughts and beliefs. Some of the more widely used techniques are described in the remainder of this section.

## Thought Charts

**Purpose:** To identify automatic thoughts starting from the situations and feelings that elicit those thoughts.

**Developmental level:** Older children and adolescents.

**Supporting materials:** Worksheet 5.3, "Thought Chart."

A thought chart is a simple technique that helps to summarize associated situations, feelings, and automatic thoughts. The practitioner/group leader can assist individuals or groups in doing this activity through the use of chalkboards, white boards, or poster charts. For example, the practitioner might summarize what he or she has observed about the automatic thought patterns of an individual. "Jamie, I've noticed that when you are given negative feedback, you often seem to automatically think that you are not capable of doing things right." Then, the individual child or youth might be encouraged to try the exercise on his or her own with feedback from the practitioner/group leader. With some simple instructions, individual children or youth can do this technique independently with a blank sheet of paper or by using a form such as the one found in Worksheet 5.3. Of course, although independent work for this technique is possible, it is best for the practitioner/group leader to help the individual child or youth process the activity so that it reflects reality and so that it becomes linked to the broader treatment goals.

## The Cognitive Replay Technique

**Purpose:** To identify automatic thoughts.

**Developmental level:** All ages, but younger and less sophisticated children will need more structure and feedback from the practitioner.

Some students, perhaps many, will not feel comfortable recording their thoughts or might simply write down what they think the practitioner/group leader wants them to write. In other cases, they might simply be too noncompliant or inattentive to the assignment to record their thoughts. An alternative technique for identifying automatic thoughts is one that is done in the "here and now" of the treatment session or group. In this technique, which is called *cognitive replay*, the practitioner guides the client through the process of discussing and thinking about a particular problem situation, with the goal of identifying negative automatic thought processes that may be a typical reaction to the situation. To make this technique effective, it is best to start by identifying a situation that specifically triggers depressed thinking or mood and have the children or adolescents relive it in their minds. As they think about particular experiences or situations, the practitioner can then guide them to identify the types of automatic thoughts they are experiencing. A natural extension of this process is to move from the detection of negative automatic thoughts to the beliefs that underlie them.

## Thought Forecasting

**Purpose:** To identify automatic thoughts.

**Developmental level:** Older children and adolescents; younger children may find this exercise too abstract and may not be able to generate realistic future situations.

This technique is similar to the cognitive replay technique except that the focus is on future rather than past situations. For children or adolescents who are resistant to reliving past situations or discussing current problems, the forecasting technique may prove to be a useful alternative way to detect automatic thoughts. An imaginary but realistic situation is created, and the children or adolescents "forecast" what might happen and how they might be thinking, through the imaginary process of walking through the steps of the situation. Again, it is a natural extension of this technique to move from thoughts to underlying beliefs. For example, a socially withdrawn and isolated youngster whose automatic negative thoughts interfere with his or her attempts to engage with peers might be asked to set up an imaginary situation that could realistically happen, in which he or she attempt to initiate interaction with peers. It is important for the practitioner to probe for how the youngster is feeling and thinking during the process, so that the forecasting technique does not stay confined to actions and behaviors.

## Hypothesizing/Guessing

**Purpose:** To detect automatic thoughts and beliefs.

**Developmental level:** All ages.

An additional technique that might be useful in detecting automatic thoughts and beliefs involves the practitioner/group leader offering a hypothesis (or making an educated guess) at what the child or adolescent might be feeling or thinking in a particular situation, or the underlying belief associated with these thoughts or feelings. This technique is essentially similar to *basic and advanced empathy techniques* that are used in counseling. Being effective at offering hypotheses requires the practitioner already to have formed a strong relationship with the student and be familiar enough with him or her to be able to predict with a good degree of accuracy what the student might be thinking, feeling, or believing in a given situation. If the practitioner is correct in his or her or hypothesis, the student might endorse the guess and also add other details or thoughts. If, on the other hand, the practitioner is incorrect in his or her hypothesis, the student might correct or deny it. When used with defensive or uncooperative youngsters, this technique can be difficult. For example, a disengaged adolescent might agree with the practitioner's hypothesis just to go along with it and avoid more work, even if the guess is incorrect. On the other hand, a highly resistant or defensive youth might actively combat or disagree with assertions made by the practitioner, even if these assertions are correct. Again, for all of these reasons, it is essential first to develop a strong relationship with the child to use this technique effectively.

## The Down Arrow Technique

**Purpose:** To identify underlying beliefs associated with negative thoughts.

**Developmental level:** Cognitively mature older children and adolescents.

This technique is an adaptation of the "vertical-arrow" techniques developed by Burns (1980) for treatment of adults with depression. Unlike most of the other techniques listed in this section, which are useful for detecting both thoughts and identifying beliefs, the down-arrow technique is specifically aimed at identifying beliefs. The name, the "down-arrow technique," is symbolic; its essential feature is that through a series of successive questions, the practitioner helps the client get to the key underlying beliefs associated with negative automatic thoughts and depressed mood. In essence, the practitioner will continually ask "So what?" "Why?" and "What does that mean?" to help guide the client beyond the basic or surface meaning of events and thoughts to the core belief he or she has adopted that may fuel depressive thinking and mood. For example, an adolescent who is experiencing depression might be continually troubled by thoughts such as "This isn't good enough," "I've got to do more," "I've got to do better," or "I've got to get a higher grade." Through a series of questions, the practitioner might be able to help this young person identify the core belief "I have to be perfect or else I am no good" that leads to such thinking processes. This technique is potentially very powerful, but it is not appropriate for some depressed youths. Those children or adolescents who are functioning at a more concrete level will probably have a difficult time with the down-arrow technique and may be easily frustrated by the continual probing questions that require them to go deeper than they are capable. The down-arrow technique is best used with cognitively mature youths who have developed a reasonable amount of insight and self-awareness. This technique also should not be used until a strong therapeutic relationship has been developed.

## STEP 3: EVALUATING AUTOMATIC THOUGHTS AND BELIEFS

After automatic thoughts have been detected and corresponding underlying beliefs have been identified, the next step in cognitive therapy is to evaluate these thoughts and beliefs. The purpose of evaluation is to determine whether thoughts and beliefs are realistic or unrealistic, adaptive or maladaptive. A realistic thought or belief is one that is supported by the evidence, whereas an unrealistic thought or belief persists despite all the evidence to the contrary. *An adaptive thought or belief is one that appropriately helps to solve whatever problem is the focus of concern.* A maladaptive thought or belief, on the other hand, typically gets in the way of solving the problem.

It is important for practitioners to realize that, in many cases, negative thoughts may be realistic, and negative beliefs may be adaptive. *The goal of treatment should not be simply to eliminate negative thoughts or beliefs. Rather, the intervention should help to change negative thoughts and beliefs that are unrealistic and maladaptive, and to replace these with thoughts and beliefs that are more realistic and adaptive.* This idea is an important distinction for beginning practitioners, who may try to challenge any negative thought or belief, regardless of how realistic or adaptive. For example, a boy whose alcoholic mother frequently becomes verbally and emotionally abusive toward him would be justified in thinking "My mom is being mean to me," or in believing "My mom has lots of problems and it is hard to depend on her." Because this thought–belief combination is supported by the evidence, and because it might help to propel the youngster to try and solve the problems that are within his control, there is no reason to challenge or combat them. Several useful techniques for evaluating automatic thoughts and underlying beliefs are described in this section.

## Identifying Cognitive Distortions or Thinking Errors

**Purpose:** Identification of basic errors in thinking, or distorted cognitions.

**Developmental level:** Older children and adolescents who are cognitively mature.

**Supporting material:** Worksheet 5.4, "Identifying Thinking Errors."

Persons who are depressed, regardless of their age or developmental level, tend to adopt erroneous ways of processing information that are commonly referred to as cognitive distortions or thinking errors. Such distorted, erroneous patterns of thinking about the world tend to fuel depression. Therefore, an important step in cognitive treatment is for the practitioner/group leader to assist clients in identifying whatever patterns of cognitive distortion or thinking errors are present. In outlining his cognitive theory of depression, Beck identified six basic errors in processing information that tend to fuel depression:

- *Arbitrary inferences.* Drawing a conclusion that is not supported by or is contrary to the available evidence.
- *Selective abstraction.* Focusing only on a detail taken out of context and ignoring the overall features of the entire situation.
- *Overgeneralization.* Drawing a general conclusion based on only a single event.
- *Magnification and minimization.* Magnifying small or negative events and minimizing positive or larger events.
- *Personalization.* Inappropriately relating external events to oneself when there is no basis for doing so.

- *Absolute, dichotomous thinking.* Thinking in very restrictive terms such as "good or bad," "all or none," "black or white," "yours or mine," and so forth.

In cognitive treatment, the practitioner teaches clients about these thinking errors and helps them to identify such distortions in their own thinking. Unfortunately, most children and many adolescents will probably find these six patterns difficult to comprehend because they are abstract and couched in fairly sophisticated language. Therefore, it is essential to teach younger persons about common thinking errors by using language and labels that are appropriate to their developmental level. The following include some examples of cognitive distortions (adapted from Wilkes et al., 1994; Burns, 1980) that are labeled and described in a more simple and straightforward manner that would be appropriate for most adolescents and many older children:

- *Binocular vision.* Looking at things in a way that makes them seem bigger or smaller than they really are. In *Binocular magnification*, a problem is viewed in a way that makes it look much bigger than it is. In *Binocular minimization*, a positive situation is viewed in a way that makes it seem to be much smaller than it really is.
- *Black-and-white thinking.* The tendency to look at things only in extreme or opposite ways. For example, thinking of things as being either *good or bad, never or always, all or none.*
- *Dark glasses.* Thinking only about the negative aspects of things; focusing only on the bad or undesirable aspects of any situation.
- *Fortune-telling.* Making predictions about what will happen in the future, without enough evidence. Like Eeyore, the dysthymic donkey in the *Winnie the Pooh* books, depressed persons have often developed a tendency to make negative predictions about future events, without regard to the evidence.
- *Making it personal.* Taking personal responsibility or blaming oneself for things that happen outside of one's control or are not one's responsibility.
- *Overgeneralizing.* As in the previous six patterns from Beck, drawing a general conclusion (e.g., believing that "life is unfair") based only on a single event (something happened that was unfair).
- *Labeling.* Putting simple (and usually negative) labels on things that are actually more complicated than the label suggests.
- *Discounting the positive.* Ignoring positive events or thoughts by discounting or disqualifying them: for example, refusing to accept a compliment, or twisting a positive situation into something that is negative.
- *"Beating up" yourself or others.* Insisting or demanding that things "should" or "must" be done a certain way. These unreasonable standards can be applied to oneself or to others and tend to set a person up to feel either inappropriately guilty or angry.

Most adolescents who participate in counseling find the identification of cognitive distortions to be a very interesting technique. Simply having them read through a list of thinking errors in session can be a very good use of time. I have actually had adolescents go through this exercise with me ask for a handout or list that they can take with them. Worksheet 5.4 provides a practical list of thinking errors in language to which most adolescents and many children will be able to relate.

## Examining the Evidence: Three Questions

**Purpose:** To evaluate whether automatic thoughts and underlying beliefs are realistic.

**Developmental level:** All ages, but younger children will require simplified questions and examples.

**Supporting material:** Worksheet 5.5, "Are Things Really That Bad?: Three Questions."

Another commonly used technique in the process of evaluating automatic thoughts and underlying beliefs involves holding them up to the standard of evidence. In other words, to determine whether an automatic thought is realistic, or an underlying belief is maladaptive, that thought or belief is scrutinized carefully based on available realistic evidence. This technique is easily done in session and is also easy to teach to students using a series of three questions than can be memorized:

• *What's the evidence?* By asking this question, the practitioner (and, ultimately, the child or adolescent who learns to implement the process) is directly challenging evidence that is interpreted in a way that supports a hopeless view of the world and the future. For example, a practitioner who notes that 15-year-old Keeshan has adopted the belief "Everyone hates me," might ask "What's the evidence that everyone hates you?" as a step in challenging and modifying that belief. In some cases, the evidence may be there to support an automatic thought or underlying belief, whereas in other instances, the evidence will be too thin to support it.

• *Is there any alternative evidence?* The second question in this process is designed to determine whether evidence exists that contradicts the distorted belief or thought. For example, if 11-year-old Catherine is asked to come up with some alternative evidence to the notion "I am never going to have any friends," she will be directed to identify times in her life when she actually has had friends. If the belief or thought that is supporting the depression is truly a distorted one, then there should be plenty of alternative evidence. However, because the young person is in the habit of viewing things negatively and in a distorted manner, the practitioner will likely need to help him or her along initially in identifying some alternatives.

• *What if?* The third question in the process, "What if?," is aimed is showing that the actual outcome of a feared event may not be as bad as the child or adolescent predicts. Again, if the young person's thinking is truly distorted and unrealistically negative, it should be relatively easy to show him or her that the worst case scenario in the *awful situation* he or she fears will not really be all that bad. For example, if 16-year-old Sandra believes "My life will be over if I don't make the varsity basketball team," the practitioner will help actively challenge this assumption. The practitioner's aim will be to help Sandra adopt the believe that even though not making the basketball team is something that could happen and would be unpleasant, her life will actually go on. "Okay, so you might not make the basketball team, but you won't know until you try. And even if you don't make the team, you'll be in good company. Only 12 girls out of about 700 at this high school are going to make the girls varsity basketball team, and my guess is that the other 688 will survive just fine."

The "three questions" approach is simple and straightforward enough that it can be easily memorized or illustrated in a visual aid format to serve as a prompt, or practiced within a group training session. Worksheet 5.5 may be useful in this regard.

## Evaluating Positives and Negatives

**Purpose:** Evaluation of whether automatic thoughts and underlying beliefs are realistic.

**Developmental level:** Older children and adolescents.

**Supporting material:** Worksheet 5.6, "Evaluating Positives and Negatives."

An additional straightforward and useful technique for evaluating automatic thoughts and underlying beliefs is conducting a pro and con evaluation, sometimes called a "cost–benefit" analysis. This technique simply involves helping the child or adolescent evaluate his or her cognitions by developing a list of advantages and disadvantages of particular situations. Once a complete and realistic list has been developed (with assistance from the practitioner/group leader), a more realistic evaluation can occur. This technique is particularly useful when one has adopted a very biased view and focuses almost entirely on the negative aspects of a situation. A simple tool that can be helpful in evaluating the positive and negative aspects of any given situation is Worksheet 5.6. An example of a completed positive–negative worksheet is found in Figure 5.2. A couple of cautions should be considered prior to conducting this technique. First, realize that a youngster who has developed a highly distorted and negative worldview will likely be resistant to identifying any positives for some situations, even when the positives seem obvious to the practitioner. For this reason, it is important for the practitioner/group leader to brainstorm collaboratively with the client as the pros and cons are listed. Second, the practitioner should avoid focusing only on the positive aspects of a situation. Realize that from the child's or adolescent's point of view, there may be many negatives to some situations. Simply discounting them will not necessarily help the youngster to do the same and may in fact provoke confrontation or disengagement from the intervention process. Rather, it is better to acknowledge that most situations have both positive and negative features, while helping the child or adolescent realize that the negatives do not always overwhelmingly win.

Remember that the overall goal in Step 3 of cognitive therapy is to teach the children or adolescents to detect their own negative automatic thoughts and thinking errors. The practitioner/group leader first must introduce these concepts, using the techniques that have been described in this section (or similar techniques) and then help the children or youth involved identify unrealistic negative thoughts and maladaptive beliefs. The participants need to practice monitoring their own thought processes and belief systems on a

## Evaluating Positives and Negatives

| Situation | List the positive things ("pros") about this situation. | List the negative things ("cons") about this situation. |
|---|---|---|
| A friend is constantly calling and wanting to do stuff, but it's getting annoying | She's a good friend, honest, loyal | She's getting on my nerves |
| I'm working a lot of hours at work— a lot more than I really want | I'm earning more money | It's making me tired and I don't have time for other things |
| I snuck out late at night and got caught | Nothing bad happened while I was out— I'm safe | I was grounded and my parents lost trust in me |

FIGURE 5.2. A sample completed worksheet for Evaluating Positives and Negatives.

continual basis. For youngsters who are not intellectually advanced, this particular stage may be difficult, because these thinking errors and maladaptive beliefs can be complex and rather abstract. It will help if the practitioner/group leader provides examples that are developmentally appropriate and simplifies the language that is used to describe these situations. The techniques described in this section are general enough that they should be useful for most adolescents and older children (i.e., ages 9–12) who are intellectually mature.

## STEP 4: CHANGING NEGATIVE AUTOMATIC THOUGHTS AND MALADAPTIVE BELIEFS

In cognitive therapy, it is not enough simply to identify and refute negative automatic thoughts that fuel depression: They must be replaced with cognitions (thoughts and beliefs) that are more realistic and adaptive. Because the processes that lead to negative automatic thoughts have likely become well ingrained in a depressed youngster's daily repertoire, changing his or her maladaptive thoughts and beliefs may not be an easy task. Fortunately, some excellent and straightforward cognitive techniques have been developed to assist in the process. The final step in the main phase of cognitive therapy is changing negative automatic thoughts and modifying maladaptive beliefs. Once Step 3 has been undertaken, and it has been determined that such negative and maladaptive thoughts and beliefs exist, the goal of therapy is to encourage change: Eliminate or reduce unrealistic negative thoughts and modify maladaptive underlying beliefs.

This section details a few therapeutic techniques that have been shown to be useful in the process of altering maladaptive thoughts and beliefs. These techniques can be introduced in separate sessions, but in some cases, using a combination of techniques within one session is useful. The intervention techniques selected for inclusion in this section are general and potentially useful across various age and developmental levels. For detailed descriptions of more specific intervention techniques, you are encouraged to refer to the excellent intervention manuals by Burns (1980), Clarke et al. (1990), and Wilkes et al. (1994).

## Daily Record of Thoughts

**Purpose:** To substitute appropriate and realistic thoughts for automatic negative and distorted thoughts.

**Developmental level:** Older children and adolescents.

**Supporting materials:** Worksheet 5.7, "My Daily Record to Spot Thinking Errors."

One of the techniques developed by Beck and his associates (1979) for modifying negative automatic thoughts involves keeping a "daily record of dysfunctional thoughts" that is divided into six columns: *situation, emotion, automatic thought, thinking error, rational response*, and *outcome*. Essentially, the person describes the situation in which a negative emotion occurred, records the automatic negative thought, identifies the type of thinking error it involved, comes up with a more rational response, and then records the outcome (how he or she feels) after substituting a rational response for the dysfunctional one. The system developed by Beck and associates may be too complex for most young persons, so I have developed a simplified daily log of negative automatic thoughts that may be more understandable for adolescents and easier to use. This log is found in Worksheet 5.7.

## Triple-Column Technique

**Purpose:** Identification of automatic negative thoughts and thinking errors, and substituting them with more realistic and adaptive cognitions.

**Developmental level:** Older children and adolescents.

**Supporting material:** Worksheet 5.8, "Changing Negative Automatic Thoughts."

Another tactic for substituting more realistic thoughts for dysfunctional ones is the "triple-column technique" originally developed by Burns (1980) for use with adults, which has been modified by many practitioners and writers for use with children and adolescents. This triple-column technique is similar to the six-column daily record of dysfunctional thoughts (see Worksheet 5.7) but does not include such a high level of detail. A dysfunctional thought log based on this premise and simplified for children and adolescents is found in Worksheet 5.8. A sample completed triple-column worksheet is found in Figure 5.3. The basis of this exercise is fairly simple: The maladaptive thought is identified, the type of thinking error that it reflects is selected, and then the maladaptive thought is replaced with a thought that is more realistic. To introduce this therapeutic exercise to students, it will be helpful first to provide some specific and realistic examples, perhaps using the worksheet on an overhead projector or chalkboard.

## Reframing and Relabeling

**Purpose:** To substitute adaptive beliefs or thoughts for dysfunctional ones.

**Developmental level:** Older children and adolescents.

The process of *reframing and relabeling* can be useful in helping to substitute a realistic adaptive belief or thought for a dysfunctional one. This process is very straightforward. The practitioner/group leader simply works with the children or adolescents to help them come up with a new label for a problem situation that they currently think is a terrible, catastrophic thing. Sometimes, simply putting a new label on a problem will make it seem more possible to cope, and the problem situation will not seem so awful. For example, helping adolescents to relabel as "a learning experience" or as "practice" their "failure" when they tried something that did not work as they wanted might help to make the circumstance seem less catastrophic. No special tools are needed for this technique; the prac-

## Changing Negative Automatic Thoughts

**Directions:** Use this worksheet to practice identifying your negative automatic thoughts and thinking errors. Identify some more realistic ways of thinking about these problems.

| What was my negative automatic thought? | What thinking error did I make? | What is a more realistic way of thinking about it? |
|---|---|---|
| Everything at home is bad | Dark Glasses | Some things at home seem bad right now, but there are some good things, too |
| I'm not going to find a summer job | Fortune Telling | I don't have a summer job lined up yet, but I still have several weeks to find one |
| It's awful that I fight so much with my dad | Binocular Vision | Most of the time I don't fight with my dad—just sometimes |

FIGURE 5.3. A sample completed worksheet for Changing Negative Automatic Thoughts, using the "triple-column" technique.

titioner/group leader simply assists children or youth in putting a new label on a situation that, although difficult or negative, is not as terrible or catastrophic as they initially thought. For younger and less intellectually sophisticated youth, this exercise will probably require a fair amount of modeling and participation by the practitioner/group leader, as well as the use of simple labels.

## Cognitive Rehearsal

**Purpose:** To rehearse appropriate and adaptive thoughts and beliefs.

**Developmental level:** All ages; younger children will require more concrete examples.

**Supporting material:** Table 5.1, "Suggested Techniques for Making Role-Play and Cognitive Rehearsal More Effective."

A widely used technique for practicing new thought processes within treatment sessions, cognitive rehearsal has been used in the intervention process for various problems such as social skills deficits, impulsivity, schoolwork difficulties, and anger management concerns. It is a natural technique for use in modifying the maladaptive thought and belief processes that may occur with depression. This very straightforward technique can easily be used with virtually all students, so long as the examples are tailored appropriately to their developmental level.

There are two usual ways of enacting cognitive rehearsal. The first involves an actual role play, in which the youth "thinks aloud" (rehearses) as he or she begins to engage in a particular problem situation. For example, an adolescent girl with an identified pattern of maladaptive thoughts and beliefs that occur in conjunction with arguments she has with her boyfriend might verbally rehearse some more realistic thought–belief patterns when role-playing a disagreement, with the practitioner playing the role of the boyfriend. With this type of cognitive rehearsal exercise, it is often useful for the practitioner/group leader to reverse roles with the youth (i.e., to play the part of the youth), to model for them some realistic and adaptive thought/belief processes. The second way of conducting cognitive rehearsal simply involves having the practitioner/group leader talk the child or adolescent through the steps within a particular sequence. For example, in the case of a 10-year-old

## TABLE 5.1. Suggested Techniques for Making Role-Play Exercises and Cognitive Rehearsal More Effective

- Make the role-play situation as much like the real situation as possible.
- Practitioner/group leader should correctly model the skill first.
- Have the child or youth practice the skill.
- Provide corrective feedback.
- Reinforce appropriate responses.
- Give a homework assignment that involves the parents.

boy experiencing severely negative and distorted automatic thoughts in conjunction with arguments between his parents, the practitioner might carefully guide the boy through a series of steps to practice engaging in more realistic and adaptive thoughts in response to the arguing.

Both methods of enacting cognitive rehearsal can be effective, but their success is often contingent on some of the basic strategies of generalization used in social skills training (e.g., Merrell & Gimpel, 1998): (1) make the rehearsal or role-play situation as much like the actual situation as possible, (2) have the practitioner/group leader model the skill first, (3) have the child or youth practice the skill, (4) provide corrective feedback on the child's enactment in the role play, (5) reinforce appropriate responses, and (6) give a homework assignment that involves the parents. Table 5.1 provides an outline for these strategies.

## Increasing Positive Self-Statements

**Purpose:** To practice making positive self-statements or affirmations that are realistic and personal.

**Developmental level:** All ages; younger children will require more support and structure.

**Supporting material:** Worksheet 5.9, "Increasing Positive Self-Statements."

A final useful technique for changing maladaptive negative thoughts and beliefs is to have the child or adolescent practice making positive self-statements. Such positive statements are considered to be affirmations that the youngster can rehearse in problem situations. Using the positive self-statement technique is more complex than simply saying "I'm good enough, I'm smart enough, and doggone it, people like me!" To be effective as a therapeutic technique for changing maladaptive thought and belief patterns, positive self-statements must be both *realistic* and *personal*. Simply having children or adolescents parrot some positive statements that are the oppositive of their negative thoughts is unlikely to have much of an impact. Rather, to be effective, such affirmations must be positive self-statements that the youngster has "bought into," and that seem realistic. This should not be a kind of rote recital exercise.

To develop and rehearse a list of realistic and appropriate positive self-statements, it is often useful for the practitioner/group leader to "brainstorm" with the youth to come up with a list of possible positive statements for various situations, to evaluate the list, and, ultimately to select the statements that make the most sense and seem most acceptable to them. If the young person is in the habit of thinking only in a negative way about certain situations, the practitioner/group leader may need to be very active in the brainstorming process. In some situations, it is actually useful for child or adolescent clients to finish this exercise by making their own chart of possible positive self-statements for various situations. They can take such a chart with them, post it on their bedroom wall, and so on, as a cue for later use. Worksheet 5.9 provides a worksheet that might be useful in developing a final list of positive self-statements for various situations.

## CONCLUDING COMMENTS

This chapter includes a practical description of cognitive therapy for depression, based on the work of Beck and Burns, later adapted by Wilkes and colleagues. Many of these techniques may seem too simple to be therapeutic, but in fact, when used as part of a comprehensive treatment package, they can be quite powerful. Although this chapter provides all the basics that you need actually to plan a cognitive therapy intervention with individuals or groups, it is important to recognize that this brief chapter on the topic is not all inclusive. Within each of the four steps, I have not included several commonly used treatment techniques because they are more complex or abstract, and probably only useful with more intellectually advanced adolescents. Also, please realize that the four steps outlined here comprise the "middle phase" of cognitive therapy (where the major intervention work occurs) as conceptualized by Beck and his colleagues. The initial phase of therapy involves the process of building rapport and developing a therapeutic alliance with the client, whereas the ending phase involves the complex issues of dealing with treatment-resistant clients or planning for termination. If you are interested in a more comprehensive outline of the entire process of Beck's cognitive therapy model, I encourage you to refer to the sources I have cited in this chapter.

# 6

# Changing Thoughts and Beliefs

*Rational-Emotive Therapy, Attribution
Retraining, Learned Optimism, and
Journal-Writing Strategies for Depression*

## INTRODUCTION AND OVERVIEW

There are several possible variations on what might be considered "cognitive therapy."
The focus of Chapter 5 was primarily a very specific approach, namely, the cognitive therapy originally developed for adults by Aaron Beck and later modified for use with adolescents and older children by Beck and his colleagues. Despite the prominence and importance of this particular type of intervention, it would be a mistake to think that it is "the
only game in town." Several other cognitive-based interventions have been developed for
use with depressed youth. This chapter describes and details three of the most widely used
additional cognitive intervention approaches: (1) Albert Ellis's *rational-emotive therapy*,
(2) *self-monitoring or self-control training*, and (3) the *attribution retraining* method, developed by Martin Seligman and his colleagues, which has more recently incorporated cognitive techniques for dealing with adversity and has come to be known as *learned optimism
training*. In addition, the use of *journal writing* as a cognitive form of intervention for
depression is illustrated. These additional interventions for depression are perhaps the
most popular and best validated of the cognitive methods besides cognitive therapy, but
they certainly do not represent everything that is currently being used. Cognitive and cognitive-behavioral treatment methods have become immensely popular since about the
1980s and are increasingly being used with children and adolescents. It seems that new
variations of cognitive interventions appear every year or so, but they all share a common
heritage with the techniques outlined in this chapter and in Chapter 5: Depression may be
treated effectively by systematically examining faulty or maladaptive thought–belief sys-

102

tems and learning to modify these cognitive processes in a more realistic and productive direction.

As you review the cognitive intervention strategies detailed in this chapter and Chapter 5, remember that your selection of a specific technique or collection of techniques for use in particular situations and with particular students should not be an "either–or" decision. In other words, selecting an appropriate cognitive intervention strategy should not be viewed as coming down to a decision regarding whether you use either cognitive therapy or rational-emotive therapy, or whether you include either attribution retraining or learned optimism training in your intervention plan. Remember that these techniques have many similarities and are based on a similar notion. Also consider that these cognitive strategies are often complementary. It is certainly possible, and often desirable, to use a one strategy to support another. In the end, your decision regarding which cognitive techniques to include in your overall treatment plan should be based on your own judgment regarding how much time is available, which technique(s) you think might be most appropriate for the particular student(s) with whom you are working, and which techniques you personally find more comfortable. Under a variety of circumstances, these cognitive intervention techniques are all good strategies for helping students overcome depression.

## DISPUTING IRRATIONAL THOUGHTS: THE RET APPROACH

**Purpose:** To teach students to dispute irrational maladaptive thoughts and replace them with more realistic and productive thoughts.

**Developmental level:** Older children and adolescents.

**Supporting material:** Worksheet 6.1, "Changing Irrational and Negative Thinking the RET Way."

One of the most enduring cognitive-based interventions is rational-emotive therapy (RET), originally developed by Albert Ellis (1962) several decades ago. In recent years, RET has also been referred to as rational-emotive behavior therapy (REBT). It is based on the assumption that many emotional problems such as depression and anxiety are caused by irrational thinking and mistaken assumptions, which in turn lead to low self-esteem, unnecessary guilt and shame, psychological stress, and maladaptive problem solving. In the RET approach, the solution to these problems is to adopt more positive and adaptive ways of thinking about one's life and problems. RET was not designed exclusively for treating depression, but it is certainly an appropriate tool for treating depression.

Like most therapeutic techniques originally developed and refined for use with adults, RET, has also been modified for use with older children and adolescents. During the 1960s and 1970s, when the RET approach was originally developed and refined, Ellis and his colleagues identified various well-known lists of "common irrational beliefs" that are considered to be central to the development of emotional problems. Practitioners who have modified the RET approach for use with children and adolescents have identified common irrational thoughts or beliefs that are more specific to this younger age group than to adults. Some of these common irrational thoughts or beliefs of children and adolescents include the following:

- "Nobody loves me."
- "Everything bad is my fault."
- "What's the use of trying?"
- "I'm no good."
- "I always say dumb things."
- "I'll never make any good friends."
- "I'm stupid."
- "There is something wrong with me."
- "Something bad is going to happen."
- "I can't try this because I'll be really embarrassed."
- "I'll never feel good again."
- "I am worthless."
- "There's no point in getting up in the morning."

The RET approach proposes that irrational thinking follows an "A-B-C" model of development. "A" stands for an *activating event*. "B" stands for a *belief* (irrational) that follows the activating event. And "C" stands for the *consequence* of the irrational negative thinking. For example, say that a high school student who has formerly received average grades in math classes does very poorly on a couple of math assignments, only getting 20% of the problems correct. These poor math performances would be considered the activating event. This girl then adopts the irrational–negative belief "I will never be able to do well in math because I am stupid." As a consequence of the activating event and the irrational belief, she feels worthless, quits trying to be successful in math, and gives up some of her goals in life that would have required her to take more math classes (such as going to college). She then feels depressed, worthless, and aimless.

In the RET approach, the irrational–negative thoughts are first identified, then actively disputed, and finally replaced with positive and more realistic patterns of thinking. In the process of intervention, the practitioner will need initially to help the student *identify*, *dispute*, and *counter* irrational thinking, because this way of being has become automatic, and he or she is probably not even aware of how pervasive it has become. Through active participation, modeling, and practice, the practitioner guides the student in this strategy and reinforces him or her for using it. As can be seen in Worksheet 6.1, this relatively straightforward process can be made into a poster or handout to be posted in a classroom or home as a prompt in how the process of RET works.

One of the essential elements for getting students actually to use RET or other cognitive change strategies is to *be honest and make things realistic to them* rather than simply trying to get them to recite positive statements like a mantra, which may not be realistic. Kids can easily see through phony attempts to put a positive spin on a tough situation, and many of them face myriad situations that can easily lead them to adopt negative or irrational thinking patterns. Realistically, many of the difficult situations (activating events) they face may actually be out of their control to a great extent. Therefore, use examples of disputing and countering that are positive but also realistic. Let us go back to our example of the high school student who developed irrational negative thinking after she did very poorly on two assignments. It would not be genuine to suggest that she replace the belief "I will never be able to do well in math because I am stupid" with a positive but equally irrational belief "I will probably ace the next math exam because I really am good at it." More realistic and appropriate would be to replace the negative belief with something like "Just because I did poorly on two exams doesn't mean that I can't do math; if I work hard at it, I can do better." Going back to our previous examples of common irrational–negative beliefs that students might adopt, the following are some examples of how to counter them with positive thoughts that are also realistic:

- "Nobody loves me." (*"Not everyone loves me, but I know that my mom and sister love me."*)
- "Everything bad is my fault." (*"Sometimes bad things just happen; it's not always my fault."*)
- "What's the use of trying?" (*"There's no harm in trying; if I don't succeed, I will still be okay."*)
- "I'm no good." (*"I'm not good at everything I do, but I am a good person."*)
- "I always say dumb things." (*"Sometimes I say really funny or smart things, too."*)
- "I'll never make any good friends." (*"I've had friends before, and if I keep trying, I'll end up making another friend."*)
- "I'm stupid." (*"I may not be brilliant, but I am not stupid; there are lots of things I can do better than lots of other people."*)
- "There is something wrong with me." (*"Everyone has things about themselves that they don't like, but there are also a lot of things that are right with me."*)
- "Something bad is going to happen." (*"Bad things happen, but not all the time; maybe something good will happen this time."*)
- "I can't try this because I'll be really embarrassed." (*"If I try this thing and it doesn't work, I will survive—I've been through worse things than this before!"*)
- "I'll never feel good again." (*"I've felt good before, and even though I've been feeling depressed, I can feel good again."*)
- "I am worthless." (*"Nobody is worthless."*)
- "There's no point in getting up in the morning." (*"Every day is a new day; maybe things will be better today."*)

RET was one of the first cognitive therapies developed, and its charismatic founder, Albert Ellis, was very effective in promoting its use. Therefore, it is widely known and is covered in most graduate training programs in the mental health fields. However, it is important to recognize that the empirical evidence for using RET is not overwhelming (Matson, 1989), and that there is even less evidence for using it as a treatment for helping depressed youth. But because RET includes strategies that are similar to tactics that have been empirically validated in other cognitive treatment methods, and because so many practitioners (including me) have found it to be effective for working with cognitively advanced children and adolescents, it is certainly worth consideration as a cognitive intervention tool.

## SELF-MONITORING AND SELF-CONTROL TRAINING

**Purpose:** To train students to monitor adequately their thoughts, activities, and feelings, and to attend to the results of these circumstances in a realistic and effective manner.

**Developmental level:** Older children and adolescents.

**Supporting material:** Worksheet 6.2, "Basic Steps to Self-Control and Self-Monitoring Interventions for Depression."

As is pointed out in Chapter 2, one of the most influential cognitive theories of depression proposes that this disorder develops as a result of deficits or failures of individuals to monitor adequately their thoughts, activities, and feelings, and to attend to the results of these circumstances in a realistic and appropriate manner. This notion, which was developed by Rehm (1977, 1990), is know as the *self-control model* of depression. Several proven cognitive and cognitive-behavioral treatment techniques have been developed by Rehm and others (e.g., Reynolds & Coates, 1986; Stark, 1990) based on the self-control model. The most common terms used to describe these intervention techniques are *self-control therapy, self-control training, self-instruction training*, and *self-monitoring training*. Although there are some differences in the specific ways that these treatment techniques are designed and implemented, most of them include several essential components. Participants are systematically taught the following:

- To monitor their self-statements and their activities.
- To increase their involvement in positive activities and the cognitions or self-statements that are associated with improved mood.
- To pay attention to the delayed consequences of their general behavior, as opposed to just the immediate consequences.
- To pay attention to the positive and delayed consequences that follow specific behaviors that are difficult to perform.
- To set standards for themselves that are realistic and attainable.
- To break down their individual goals into attainable, smaller goals.
- To make appropriate attributions for their successes and failures.
- To increase contingent self-reinforcement, while at the same time decreasing self-punishment.

In addition to the specific activities that comprise this general method of intervention, similarities among like methods include following a set of steps, procedures, or instructions that will lead to more positive cognitive and affective outcomes, and diminish the maladaptive thinking and behavior patterns that are so often associated with depression. Although these types of cognitive interventions are clearly useful for treating depression, particularly with adolescents and cognitively advanced children, they are not limited to depression. In fact, various modifications of self-instruction training, self-control training, or self-monitoring training have proven to be useful for working with children and youth with ADHD, learning problems, and conduct problems (Kaslow et al., 1998). Worksheet 6.2 provides the simplified, basic steps of the processes that are generally involved in self-control types of treatments. These simplified steps may be useful as both an aid for practitioners and as handouts for students participating in the intervention.

Self-monitoring and self-control therapy are best implemented in two ways: (1) In the "here and now" of the individual or group sessions, the practitioner points things out to the students and helps them develop and implement the appropriate strategies; and (2) in a structured psychoeducational or teaching process in classes, groups, or individually. For either the "in-session" or psychoeducational/teaching approach, Worksheet 6.2 may be very helpful; it may be enlarged and posted in a very conspicuous place for students to refer to, or it may be duplicated and given to students to use for reference as each point is being reviewed. In implementing this intervention, it is especially helpful to provide students with homework assignments to implement specific points that were practiced in session and to make sure that students know that they will report back during the next session. Having the student(s) keep a journal or record of their attempts to implement the specific points of intervention may also be useful.

## ATTRIBUTION RETRAINING AND LEARNING TO BE OPTIMISTIC

In Chapter 2, the concept of *learned helplessness* is briefly discussed as a cause and correlate of depression. This concept has become one of the more enduring notions of human motivation in psychology and education during the past two decades. Martin Seligman, a renowned psychologist most closely associated with articulating the construct of learned helplessness, has developed two closely related intervention models for treating depression that are linked to the idea of combating learned helplessness and the pessimistic view of the world that seems to go along with it. These two methods, attribution retraining and learned optimism, are illustrated in this section.

### Attribution Retraining

**Purpose:** To reduce cognitions that may lead to depression, by using a combination of environmental enrichment, personal control training, resignation training, and attribution retraining.

**Developmental level:** All ages.

Seligman's original method (1981) for combating depression associated with learned helplessness is a cognitive-behavioral technique that has come to be known as *attribution retraining*. Although retraining attributions is an important aspect of this method, it is only one of four treatment techniques originally proposed and shown to be effective as part of a comprehensive treatment program for combating depression. These four techniques, summarized in Table 6.1, include the following:

## Environmental Enrichment

Because learned helplessness may develop more easily in an environment where aversive outcomes are likely and desired outcomes are inconsistent or unlikely, environmental enrichment is aimed at manipulating specific environments (such as a classroom or home) so that aversive outcomes are less likely, and desired or positive outcomes are more likely. For example, in a home environment, the practitioner might work with the family of a depressed child to increase the number of positive statements and decrease the number of negative statements the parents make about the child, and to increase the availability of predictable reinforcing events in the home environment. Thus, this aspect of treatment is more behavioral than cognitive, because it primarily involves basic behavioral principles to make reinforcement more available and predictable, and to reduce aversive events (see the sections on reinforcement in Chapters 7 and 8).

## Personal Control Training

Because individuals who have developed learned helplessness typically have adopted beliefs that they have little or no control over what happens in their lives, they often behave in a manner that is consistent with such beliefs. Of course, such beliefs and patterns of behavior almost invariably fuel symptoms of depression and serve as a formidable barrier for overcoming it. *Personal control training* is a largely cognitive technique that assists in empowering individuals with realistic beliefs regarding their efficacy or control over important outcomes in life. Obviously, there are many situations over which we have little or no control. For example, a boy whose mother is an alcoholic may not be able to control his mother's drinking problem. Personal control training, however, is aimed at increasing perceptions regarding situations in which there is a realistic probability of having control over events and outcomes. The child in this situation, even though he may have little or no control over his mother's drinking problem, might be taught to focus on specific areas related to this problem that he can realistically learn to control: for example, his own behavior in relation to his mother's behavior or his belief that he is not destined to become an alcoholic himself. In essence, personal control training is a strategy for changing expectations from uncontrollability to controllability.

## Resignation Training

The title of this technique may be somewhat misleading. Far from being a technique that encourages "resigning oneself" to being depressed or adopting a negative view of things, resignation training is simply a strategy for making highly desirable (but perhaps somewhat unrealistic) outcomes less preferred. Resignation training is therefore a technique that can be used to "insulate" children and youth from being devastated by disappointments in life. For example, take the case of a 12-year-old girl whose parents have recently separated after years of marital conflict. It is understandable that this event should be troubling and upsetting to the girl. We would naturally expect such an outcome. But if this girl sets her sights on her parents reuniting as the *only* possible outcome that she can live with, then she may be setting herself up for a *huge* disappointment if they do not reunite. In resignation training, the goal would be for this girl to practice viewing the situation in a different manner than she currently views it. Rather than having reunification of her parents be the only outcome that she can live with, the practitioner would encourage her also to view other possibilities as being okay and not invest herself totally in only one desired possibility over which she has no control. Rather, the counselor might encourage her to practice thinking "It would be great if my mom and dad got back together, but even if they don't I still have two parents who love me."

## Attribution Retraining

The fourth technique in attribution retraining is the actual process of retraining individuals to attribute failures to more *external, unstable,* and *specific* factors, and to attribute successes to more *internal, stable,* and *global* factors. The rationale driving this technique is derived from years of research by Seligman and colleagues, who consistently found that depressed individuals often have a maladaptive attributional style. This maladaptive style of making attributions usually involves attributing successes to external, unstable, and specific factors, such as "I was lucky," or "The test was easy," and attributing failures to internal, stable, and global factors, such as "I'm stupid," or "Nothing ever works out for me." Therefore, the challenge in attribution retraining is to help the youngster learn to make attributions for things in a manner that is less likely to fuel depression. This process, like many cognitive techniques, involves instruction by the practitioner and having the depressed youngster practice the technique. For example, take the case of a 16-year-old boy whose depression has worsened since he was fired from his part-time job. He currently attributes being fired to internal stable factors: "I can never get anything right." Without trying to place blame externally in an unrealistic manner, the practitioner might work with this young man to try thinking of some other possible reasons for being fired, such as "Business was poor, so they needed to let someone go," or "The boss was having a really bad day, and he made too big a deal out of the mistake I made." Of course, you must be careful with this technique to avoid teaching young persons to blame every difficulty in life on some external power, even if they have some culpability in the matter. For example, if a student who consistently did poorly in a class because he or she did not turn in the assignments took this method to the extreme, he or she might avoid personal responsibility for the matter by adopting the belief "I am not doing well in this class because the teacher has it in for me." Such a belief system certainly reattributes failure to external factors, but in a very unrealistic and maladaptive way that is likely to create additional problems for the young person. Conversely, what if the young man in our example recently brought his grade in Algebra II up from a D to a B and attributes this success to "I just made lucky guesses on the last three tests?" In this case, the counselor would point out the likely hard work that went into the grade change and have the boy practice thinking about this success in a more internal manner, such as "I was able to bring my grade up by working harder and taking this class seriously."

## Learned Optimism Training

**Purpose:** To retrain pessimistic patterns of thinking into more optimistic and productive patterns.

**Developmental level:** Older children and adolescents.

**Supporting material:** Worksheet 6.3, "The Learned Optimism Worksheet: Your A-B-C-D-E Record."

During the 1990s, Seligman and his colleagues (Seligman, 1990, 1998; Seligman, Reivich, Jaycox, & Gillham, 1995) expanded on the notion of combating depression and learned helplessness by studying the characteristics of individuals who seemed to thrive and prosper despite adversity and difficult setbacks. The result of this endeavor was an articulation of the concepts of pessimism and optimism. Pessimism, or *the habit of perpetually viewing things from a negative perspective*, is closely linked to learned helplessness. Optimism, on the other hand, was identified as a trait that helps individuals to be resilient and successful, even when faced with adversity. Given that the trait of optimism appeared to be such a powerful mediating force in helping individuals to deal with adversity (and, ultimately, in preventing depression), the next logical question was "Can optimism be learned?" Seligman (1998) answered this question with a resounding *yes*:

> Pessimists can in fact learn to be optimists, and not through mindless devices like whistling a happy tune or mouthing platitudes . . . but by learning a new set of cognitive skills.

**TABLE 6.1. Four Techniques Used in Attribution Retraining**

| Technique | Description |
| --- | --- |
| Environmental enrichment | Manipulation of the environment to reduce the likelihood of aversive or punishing outcomes and to increase the likelihood of desired or reinforcing outcomes. |
| Personal control training | Changing one's expectations from uncontrollability to controllability; adopting the belief that one can control or impact realistic, selected aspects of their life. |
| Resignation training | Working to make highly preferred outcomes (especially those outcomes that are less realistic) less preferred; practicing acceptance of outcomes that are acceptable but not the most preferred. |
| Attribution retraining | Using cognitive strategies to change unrealistic attributions. Individuals should be retrained to attribute failures to more external, unstable, and specific factors, and to attribute successes to more internal, stable, and global factors. |

Far from being the creations of boosters or of the popular media, these skills were discovered in the laboratories and clinics of leading psychologists and psychiatrists, and then rigorously validated. (p. 5)

The specific techniques for learning to be optimistic, advocated by Seligman and colleagues in such popular books as *Learned Optimism* (Seligman, 1990, 1998), and *The Optimistic Child* (Seligman et al., 1995), are a kind of hybrid between the original attribution retraining methods they developed and the cognitive techniques used in rational-emotive therapy. Essentially, they are a process of identifying problem situations, irrational or helpless beliefs and their consequences, and actively disputing such beliefs.

### The A-B-C-D-E Process

The first step in learned optimism training is to teach the "ABC's" of the process to help identify the connection between problem situations, helpless or irrational beliefs, and their consequences. A modification of Albert Ellis's A-B-C (activating event–belief–consequence) model in RET, the first three steps in learned optimism training include the following:

- **A (adversity)**: A difficulty or problem situation that is encountered. *Example: A teacher yells at a student in front of the entire class.*
- **B (belief)**: The irrational or helpless belief that follows the problem situation. *Example: The student believes, "The teacher hates me and the whole class thinks I'm an idiot."*
- **C (consequence)**: The negative affect or further feelings of helplessness that follow the belief. *Example: The student feels depressed and helpless, and thinks, "I feel really sad. I wish I could disappear and never have to be in this class again."*

The first three steps in learned optimism training serve to teach the connection between negative thinking and negative affect. Once these steps are mastered, two additional steps are included, which comprise the positive treatment aspect of the intervention:

- **D (disputation)**: The individual actively disputes the irrational/helpless belief that followed the adversity, similar to the RET process of disputing and countering. The disputation should be aimed at replacing the maladaptive belief with an adaptive and realistic belief. *Example: "Okay, the teacher yelled at me, but that doesn't mean she hates me. She helped me with my project last week and told me I did a good job. She also seems to yell at about everyone in class once in awhile, so I guess that is just something she does when she's in a bad mood. The other kids in class probably don't think I'm an idiot because she yells at them, too, sometimes."*
- **E (energization)**: The modified and improved way that one feels after actively disputing the maladaptive belief that followed the adversity. *Example: "I'm still a little bit upset at getting yelled at in front of the whole class, but I don't think the whole class thinks I'm an idiot anymore, and I no longer wish that I could just disappear and never have to go back to this class."*

The steps in learned optimism training, which are very similar to those in RET, are easy to use in individual or group counseling, or in class- or schoolwide psychoeducational interventions or prevention programs. This technique is likely to be useful for elementary-school-age children as well as adolescents. In fact, Seligman (1998) has demonstrated through experimental studies that this treatment approach may be a powerful strategy for preventing depression in children and youth. Worksheet 6.3 can be used as a template or form for learned optimism training, using the A-B-C and A-B-C-D-E steps just detailed. A completed example of this worksheet is found in Figure 6.1.

## WRITING IT DOWN: JOURNAL WRITING AS AN INTERVENTION TOOL

**Purpose:** To keep track of thoughts, activities, and feelings in a structured way that allows for monitoring and reflection.

**Developmental level:** All ages, but journal activities will need to be simplified for younger children and for students with poor writing skills.

**Supporting materials:** Worksheet 6.4, "Weekly Journal Entry Form"; Worksheet 6.5, "Weekly Journal Entry Form with Mood Rating."

Having students keep a personal journal can be an effective intervention tool in treating depression, particularly when used in combination with cognitive approaches to treatment. Journal writing provides a structured way to keep track of thoughts, activities, and feelings. It also provides a time for personal reflection. When used as an integral and structured part of intervention, journal writing can help the student with depression and the intervention practitioner gauge progress toward treatment goals. Specifically, journal entries provide a permanent product by which to judge progress in reducing maladaptive negative and irrational cognitions and increasing the use of productive, realistic, and positive cognitions and self-statements.

Because journal-writing activities require insight, self-awareness, and the ability to self-evaluate, they are not be particularly suited for use with very young children or individuals who are at a very basic stage of cognitive development. Typically developing students at least 8 to 10 years of age are probably old enough to participate effectively in journal writing, as are older students who function cognitively at about that level. Younger, developmentally precocious children might also be able to participate in journal-writing activities without modifying the tasks involved. Children who have not mastered basic writing skills may still participate in journal writing but will require assistance from the practitioner or teacher, as well as a highly simplified way of keeping their journals.

There are many possible approaches to journal writing as part of a therapeutic intervention. There is a great deal of room for variation in how journals are used based on such factors as the cognitive and social developmental levels of the student, the setting in which

# The Learned Optimism Worksheet: Your A-B-C-D-E Record

Adversity (the problem):

*Fighting with my parents about curfew*

Belief (my belief after the problem happened):

*They don't want me to stay out and have fun*

Consequence (how I felt):

*Upset, frustrated*

Disputation (argue against the negative belief with a more realistic or helpful belief):

*They are worried about me and concerned about my safety*

Energization (the new way that I felt after I disputed the old belief):

*I still want to stay out later, but I'm glad to know my parents love me and are concerned about me*

---

FIGURE 6.1. A sample completed Learned Optimism Worksheet.

the intervention is being delivered, the specific intervention approach that is being used, and the general level of student cooperation. The following segments of this section provide some suggestions on the best uses of journal writing.

## How Often? Where?

Ideally, a student who participates in a cognitive or cognitive-behavioral intervention program for treatment of depression would be motivated to make journal entries on a frequent basis, maybe even daily. Although such a possibility is realistic for some highly motivated, self-aware students, it is not likely in most cases. Therefore, I recommend that journal writing for this purpose should typically be a once-a-week exercise in which students reflect on their thoughts, feelings, and activities for the past week. It is ideal to have a specific assignment for the day on which the journaling is done. For example, if students participated in individual or group counseling sessions on Mondays, then it would be ideal for them to set aside Sunday afternoon or evening to make journal entries for the past week, since they would need to bring their journal to session or group the next day. The parent, teacher, or practitioner might want to consider providing some kind of simple incentive as a reinforcer for compliance with the journal-writing assignment. Although this type of conscientious, dutiful, weekly implementation of journal writing will work for some students, the reality is that others, perhaps most others, will simply not have the motivation or organization to do it. Thus, there is an additional solution: Simply use the first 10 minutes of the weekly intervention session at school as a time for silent reflection on the previous week and structured journal writing regarding this time period. Although you need to be aware that the content of the journal entries might be influenced by the time and setting in which they are written, this method is acceptable and, in many cases, more realistic.

## Structure and Format for Journal Entries

Journal writing can be an open-ended exercise, with few or no rules or structure, or it can be highly structured. What is best in this regard depends on the purposes for which journaling is being used and, to some extent, on the motivation, developmental level, and compliance of the youngster. For use as a therapeutic technique in cognitive intervention for depression, it is essential that journal-writing activities focus on the *cognitions or thoughts* of the student and the ultimate connection of these cognitions to the student's affect and behavior. Therefore, it is my recommendation in most cases that journal writing used as part of a cognitive or cognitive-behavioral treatment program should be structured, so that students who make the journal entries understand that there is a particular task that should be done as part of the journal-writing process, namely, to write down how they are thinking and feeling. I also recommend the weekly journal-writing exercise as a time to do a structured mood rating for the previous week. Journal writing can be done in a specially purchased personal journal or in inexpensive spiral bound notebooks with lined paper. A more formal option is to use special journal entry forms that provide structure and organize the journal-writing task and save these forms in notebook binders or file folders. Worksheets 6.4 and 6.5 provide reproducible examples of two relatively simple, one-page journal entry forms, and Figure 6.2 provides a completed journal entry form. The form in Worksheet 6.4. is suitable for a younger or less sophisticated student (e.g., ages 8–12), whereas Worksheet 6.5 is for more mature or older students (age 13 or older), and also includes a weekly mood rating scale.

## Some Practical Considerations

Although journal writing in conjunction with cognitive treatment can be helpful, even if done separately from the intervention process and not monitored by the practitioner, it is best implemented in a planned, structured, and goal-oriented manner. To make the best use of journal writing, consider it a weekly (or even daily) assignment, provide instructions for how to do it, keep track of whether the writing assignments are completed, and, above all, use the journal-writing product as a way of evaluating progress and as a springboard for discussion with the student. Of course, allowing the teacher or practitioner access to the journal means that it is not going to be an entirely private journal, so there needs to be agreement to this effect before any assignment is made. Assuring confidentiality (within the usual limits) may help to some extent in this regard. You should also consider that an "open" journal in some cases might be a partially guarded journal, if students do not want to have certain feelings, thoughts, or activities monitored by their teacher or any other person. Therefore, use journal writing as an adjunct technique in treatment, and do not assume that every important detail will be revealed through this process.

## CONCLUDING COMMENTS

The cognitive intervention techniques illustrated in this chapter and in Chapter 5 have been a major development in treating depression and increasingly are being used with adolescents and children. Any one of the techniques outlined in these chapters has a high probability of being effective if implemented carefully, for the right concerns, and in a developmentally appropriate manner. Again, it is important to consider that none of these methods are the "best" or "right" techniques. Rather, the choice of technique, or combination of techniques, should be made individually, based on such factors as available time, developmental level of the student(s), and preferences of the practitioner. Remember that cognitive interventions require the ability to use personal reflection and insight, and also the ability to think in abstract or symbolic terms from time to time. With this consideration in mind, it is again worthwhile to note that cognitive intervention strategies will be of little use and limited effectiveness when used with developmentally immature students or individuals who have limited cognitive abilities. For such students, behavioral interventions are clearly the treatment of choice. A final consideration is that although cognitive interventions for depression may be quite effective when used alone, an increasing amount of empirical evidence indicates that the best treatments for depression, whether for youth or for adults, involve a combination of cognitive and behavioral techniques, such as the comprehensive cognitive-behavioral interventions detailed in Chapter 4.

# Weekly Journal Entry Form with Mood Rating

Name _Heidi_      Entry Date _____      Week _October 3-10_

Describe some of your *thoughts* about yourself, your world, and the future during this past week.

*I've been doing okay, but I've been kinda sad and irritable. I didn't get as much accomplished as I should have. I'm getting behind on schoolwork.*

Describe how you often *felt* during this past week. For example, did you feel happy, upset, angry, bored, depressed, excited, or other ways at times this week?

*depressed, irritable, lethargic*

Describe some of the activities that you did this past week. Also describe some of the thoughts and feelings you had during these activities.

*I've been going to school—it's all right, but can be pretty boring. I went to a party, but didn't like being around so many people, so I left. Went to the lake with some close friends—that was pretty fun.*

Write down anything else that you think is important about this past week.

*I haven't been feeling as social or energetic lately.*

**Rate your *usual mood* for the past week (circle one):**

| 1 | (2) | 3 | 4 | 5 |
|---|---|---|---|---|
| very sad or depressed | somewhat sad or depressed | okay, about average normal mood | pretty good happy | great, terrific! very happy |

---

FIGURE 6.2. A sample completed Weekly Journal Entry Form with Mood Rating.

# 7

# Behavior Change, Emotional Education, Interpersonal Problem Solving, and Conflict Resolution Strategies for Depression

## INTRODUCTION AND OVERVIEW

In terms of interventions for students with depression, this book clearly focuses on techniques that are usually lumped into the "cognitive" or "cognitive-behavioral" categories. This focus is not accidental. The emphasis on intervention techniques in these two areas is specifically targeted in this book for two reasons:

1. Cognitive and cognitive-behavioral interventions for depression are supported by more empirical evidence than any other psychosocial intervention techniques
2. Cognitive and cognitive-behavioral interventions are naturally suited for use with students in school settings, which is the focus of this book.

Despite the clear focus on these two general areas, it would be a mistake to think that they are the only promising approaches. On the contrary, several other promising intervention strategies for depression have emerged from other traditions. Although there is not as much evidence to support these other intervention strategies as being as effective as cognitive and cognitive-behavioral approaches for treating depression, the strategies included in this chapter do enjoy some empirical support and are very promising as tools for helping students overcome depression and other internalizing disorders. These techniques are not comprehensive intervention programs such as those presented in Chapter 4 but are often included in such programs and are useful for specific purposes and in conjunction with other intervention tools. This chapter includes descriptions of four of the most promising and widely-supported additional interventions for depression: behavior change techniques, emotional or affective education, interpersonal problem-solving and conflict resolution training, and social skills training (covered in more detail in Chapter 9).

## BEHAVIORAL INTERVENTIONS FOR DEPRESSION

Behavioral intervention strategies are unique because they are *externally rather than internally focused*. Rather than aiming at inner characteristics such as unresolved conflicts, guilt, or negative cognitive processes, behavioral strategies focus on *discrete behaviors* (those with a clear beginning and end) that are externally observable. Behavioral strategies tend to be highly structured and generally place less responsibility on the student or target child for implementing the intervention. Most behavioral tactics require that a teacher or parent be responsible for helping to implement and monitor the intervention. A variety of procedures may be used in behavioral intervention approaches, including the use of social and tangible reinforcers, shaping, chaining, fading, and modeling.

With the exception of modeling, which is historically linked to social learning theory, most techniques used in behavioral interventions are based on operant conditioning or learning theory. Although the empirical basis for behavioral treatments for child and adolescent depression is small in terms of specific studies based exclusively on behavioral interventions, a huge body of research supports the use of these strategies for other types of problems such as anxiety, phobias, and various externalizing behavior problems. Behavioral techniques do appear to have a strong potential for applications in treating child and adolescent depression and, as demonstrated in Chapter 4, are often a key component of comprehensive cognitive-behavioral interventions.

This section presents two types of basic behavioral interventions for treating depression in children and youth. First, activity scheduling tactics are discussed, and second, operant conditioning techniques are overviewed. This section cannot possibly do justice to the vast body of knowledge related to behavioral techniques. Readers who are interested in gaining a sound initial understanding of behavioral principles in assessment and intervention are referred to the following excellent basic texts on this topic: *Applied Behavior Analysis for Teachers* (5th ed.; Alberto & Troutman, 1999); and *Behavior Analysis for Lasting Change* (2nd ed.; Sulzer-Azaroff & Mayer, 1991).

## Specific Uses and Advantages

Because behavioral interventions are highly structured, place little responsibility for treatment on the student, and rely very little on the cognitive abilities of students, they are among the only psychological interventions for depression that are especially useful with very young students, as well as students with significant limitations in their cognitive abilities. Cognitive interventions and insight-oriented strategies typically require that the client function at what Piaget referred to as the "concrete operations" or "formal operations" stages of cognitive development. In practice, such strategies might have some uses for typically developing students at least 8 to 12 years of age but might be best used with typically developing students who are 13 or older. Behavioral strategies have no such underlying requirements for cognitive maturity. In contrast, they can be used with students of all ages and ability levels.

Another unique advantage of behavioral intervention strategies for depression is that they are perhaps the only tactics by which treatment effects might potentially be realized through indirect intervention or through the process of *consultation*. Practitioners who may not be in a position to provide a direct intervention to students with depression may still be able to effect positive changes through consulting with a teacher or parent and using them as the intervention agent that actually implements the treatment. Implementing behavioral interventions through the use of a "third party" in the consultation process may also help students who are resistant to becoming involved in group or individual counseling programs. This type of indirect intervention may also be useful in cases where comprehensive mental health services are not easily available.

## Activity Scheduling

**Purpose:** To increase the amount of time that is spent in purposeful, positive, and potentially reinforcing activities.

**Developmental level:** All ages.

**Supporting material:** Worksheet 7.1, "Weekly Planning Form for Scheduling Positive Activities"; Worksheet 7.2, "Baseline Record for Positive Activities."

Activity scheduling involves thoughtfully and systematically planning the student's daily schedule. Based on the premise that depression may be the result of insufficient "response-contingent reinforcement" (i.e., reinforcement that occurs following specific types of responses), activity scheduling seeks to increase the amount of time students spend in activities that are purposeful and potentially reinforcing. At the same time, activity scheduling seeks to reduce the amount of time students spend in isolation, without purpose, or in situations where they are likely to "ruminate" about their depressed state. In essence, activity scheduling is an attempt to break students' cycle of depression by adding response-contingent reinforcement to their daily lives, particularly reinforcing activities with other persons.

The theory behind activity scheduling is that as engagement in positive activities increases, depressed mood states should decrease. In practice, activity scheduling usually involves the practitioner and the depressed student. However, other variations as to who is involved in the scheduling are possible. In an indirect intervention, a consultant might educate the student's parent(s) regarding the purposes and processes of activity scheduling and then turn over the responsibility for actual creation and implementation of the daily schedule to the parent(s). Additionally, when depressed students are very young or have very limited cognitive ability, they may be able to provide limited input into the scheduling process, thus leaving the task primarily to the practitioner. However, it is almost always best to include the student actively in the process of designing and implementing the activity schedule. The more input and involvement students have, the more likely they will cooperate in taking part in these activities and find the activities enjoyable.

It is almost always desirable, and even necessary, to involve parents in the process of activity scheduling, because it is often the parents who end up monitoring students' adherence to the schedule and providing the means (such as transportation, resources, or materials) to make the activities happen. An additional benefit of parental involvement in activity scheduling is that successful maintenance and generalization of treatment effects will be more likely if someone in the student's immediate environment is involved in the means and ways of keeping the intervention going.

Activity scheduling should start out simple and gradually increase the amount and complexity of tasks or events. It is unlikely that seriously depressed students in a cycle of engaging in very few purposeful or pleasurable activities will immediately be able to change course. It is more likely that as a few reinforcing activities are added to their daily and weekly life, students will become increasingly invigorated by the process, as well as increasingly amenable to the addition of more activities.

External reinforcement and careful external monitoring of the activity schedule may be necessary at first. Although the types of activities scheduled should have a high likelihood of being reinforcing in and of themselves, it is best to not leave reinforcement to chance in such cases, if the cycle is to be broken quickly and the activity scheduling continued. In my own clinical work, and in the work of graduate student practitioners I have supervised, I have found that it is always necessary at first for the practitioner to monitor closely the activity schedule and provide a high rate of social reinforcement (such as praise, encouragement, and other positive statements) anytime that students engage in the scheduled activities or even approximate such engagement. In some cases, it may even be necessary initially to use material reinforcers to accomplish engagement and participation in the scheduled activities. If you are philosophically opposed to such tactics and view them as "bribery," get over it! The reality is that serious depression (as well as seriously depressed youngsters) can be quite stubborn and may require every tool that is at your disposal. It is not uncommon for seriously depressed children and adolescents to be resistant to engagement in any potentially positive activity that parents, teachers, and practitioners might attempt to help them plan. Such cases require more than just good intentions. Items such as tokens, movie tickets, small prizes, or even cash may prove to be valuable tools, at least initially, in getting students engaged in the activity schedule. I know of a psychologist in private practice who has successfully used a small pool of money (provided up front by the parents) as an external incentive for the youngster to engage in the scheduled activities. It works something like this: "If you meet your goals for positive activities this week, I'll give you $10 so you can plan for some things next week that might require money." An additional benefit of initially using external reinforcement for engagement in scheduled activities is that the reinforcers can be carefully selected, so that future social engagement and response-contingent reinforcement are more likely. For example, an external reward of two movie tickets for meeting a week's goals might result in a student going to the movies with a friend.

To gauge the effectiveness of activity scheduling interventions, as well as to help students understand the connection between what they do and how they feel, this type of intervention is perhaps best implemented in conjunction with monitoring mood levels. Worksheet 7.1, a weekly planning form for scheduling positive activities, provides a structure for activity planning that will help to determine the type of activity, the persons involved, and the materials or resources needed to complete the activity. This particular form would likely be completed by the student and practitioner, but could also be completed by the parent and student, if the intervention were being done indirectly. A sample completed activity scheduling planning form is presented in Figure 7.1. Worksheet 7.2, used to collect baseline data on the number of specific positive activities in which students participate, would likely be completed individually by the student as a homework assignment and then reviewed weekly or biweekly.

## Operant Conditioning Techniques

**Purpose:** To reduce symptoms of depression by increasing behavioral responses that are incompatible with feeling depressed.

**Developmental level:** All ages.

Operant conditioning techniques such as reinforcement of desired behavior and extinction of undesired behavior are widely used in treating externalizing conduct problems but are seldom mentioned as an important component of treating depression. Although operant conditioning techniques may seldom be the *central* component of interventions for depression, they certainly have many applications, especially with younger children. Used as part of a comprehensive treatment program, operant conditioning techniques potentially help to reduce behaviors that maintain depression and to increase behaviors that help in overcoming depression.

### Reinforcement

By far, the preferred operant conditioning technique for treating depression (and just about any other behavioral or emotional problem) is *reinforcement*. By definition, of course, reinforcement is strengthening behavior, or making the behavior more likely to occur in the future, by presenting a positive consequence (or reinforcer) immediately following the behavior. *Positive reinforcement* is probably most useful for treating depression. *Negative reinforcement* also strengthens behavior, but through a different process—by terminating an aversive or annoying stimulus following the occurrence of a desired behavior. For example, successfully nagging a depressed child to leave him or her room and engage in some positive outside activity is negative reinforcement. The child, tired of the annoying nagging, finds it reinforcing to get out of the house, if for nothing else than to terminate the nagging. This discussion on reinforcement is limited to positive applications of reinforcement, which are theoretically more congruent with treatment of depression.

Reinforcers may be *social*, such as praise or recognition. They may also be *tangible*,

## Weekly Planning Form for Scheduling Positive Activities

| | Monday | Tuesday | Wednesday | Thursday | Friday | Saturday | Sunday |
|---|---|---|---|---|---|---|---|
| Date | June 1 | 2 | 3 | 4 | 5 | 6 | 7 |
| Goals for positive activities | go to a movie | ride bikes | swimming | play baseball | run a lemonade stand | play basketball | roller skate |
| Persons who will be involved | Oliver | Abby | Skippy | Nelson Bill | Dillon | David | Fred Jill Carl Lenny |
| Materials or resources needed | money | bikes | money swimming equipment | baseball equipment | lemonade stuff | basketball | skates |

FIGURE 7.1. A sample completed Weekly Planning Form for Scheduling Positive Activities.

such as a token, a desired object, or access to a desired activity or food. A common mistake made by parents or teachers responsible for actually delivering the reinforcer is to assume that something they deem to be a reinforcer should actually be reinforcing to the child, and then thinking that "reinforcement doesn't work" when it fails to increase the target behavior. What children may find reinforcing is not necessarily the same as what adults believe may be reinforcing to them. So it is often useful for the practitioner to solicit input from students to find out what might be most reinforcing to them, and to encourage parents or teachers to have a variety of reinforcers available. *Immediate delivery of the reinforcer following the desired behavior is essential.* It is also often necessary to start a reinforcement program by delivering the positive consequences most times, or every time the desired behaviors occur and then gradually thin the reinforcement schedule.

Perhaps the most useful way to develop a positive reinforcement system for treating depression would be the use of *differential reinforcement*, which involves targeting behaviors that are incompatible or incongruent with depressive symptoms. There are two basic methods of differential delivery of positive reinforcement. *Differential reinforcement of other behavior* (DRO) is a schedule whereby any class of behavior other than the targeted problems may be reinforced. The idea is to decrease the overt manifestation of depressive symptoms by increasing "other" behaviors, or those behaviors that are inconsistent with the syndrome of depression. The second and probably the best method of differential positive reinforcement for treating depression is *differential reinforcement of alternative behavior* (DRA), in which a specific class or limited number of classes of behavior that are incompatible or inconsistent with depression are specifically targeted and reinforced. Although both types of differential reinforcement may be effective in reducing the occurrence of problem symptoms, DRA is preferable to DRO in this case, because it targets desired behavior more specifically and may thus be more useful in increasing the types of responses that may be more critical in overcoming depression. In essence, DRA may be useful in teaching a new repertoire of desired skills.

## Child Behaviors to Target for Positive Reinforcement

Although the specific behaviors targeted for reinforcement in treating depression are varied and should be based on the unique symptom manifestation and behavioral repertoire of the student who receives the intervention, the following list may provide some guidance regarding what types of "nondepressed" behaviors might be targeted in a differential positive reinforcement intervention:

- Smiling
- Making eye contact with other persons
- Delivering a positive social greeting
- Interacting with peers in a positive manner
- Appropriate speech volume, tone, or clarity
- Peer-directed talk
- Volunteering to participate in activities or to assume responsibility for tasks
- Actually participating in various positive activities

- Making positive self-statements
- Making positive statements regarding other persons or events
- Engaging in physical exercise

You may have noticed that some of these examples of targets for positive reinforcement are similar to those found in social skills training. Realistically, in many of these instances, a training component of demonstration, modeling, practice, feedback, and reinforcement may be most effective in reinforcing behaviors that are inconsistent with depression. Therefore, whether the intervention is considered to be social skills training would depend on the specific behaviors that are targeted. Although social skills training should also usually include a cognitive treatment component, it can certainly be considered a specific example of positive reinforcement. Social skills training as an intervention for internalizing problems is covered separately in this chapter and in more detail in Chapter 9.

## Extinction and Punishment

In addition to reinforcement, other operant conditioning approaches used successfully in treating behavioral and emotional problems of children and youth include punishment (presenting an aversive consequence following an undesired behavior, in order to reduce its occurrence) and systematically withholding reinforcement. Planned ignoring of a targeted problem behavior (i.e., *extinction*) and the use of "time-out" techniques are both examples of eliminating access to reinforcement. Although variations of these other operant conditioning techniques have proven to be successful short-term interventions for externalizing conduct problems, particularly when used in conjunction with reinforcement techniques, they are not recommended with any enthusiasm for use in treating depression. There is virtually no literature to support the use of punishment, time-outs, or extinction in treating depression, and in many respects, such techniques are counterintuitive; they simply do not seem appropriate. Three of the most common problems experienced by depressed persons of all ages are *excessive self-punishment, insufficient response-contingent reinforcement*, and *social isolation*. It seems likely that using punishment or time-outs to treat overt symptoms of depression (such as making negative self-statements or withdrawing from the company of other children) would only increase problems in these three areas. Treating social isolation by further isolating a child makes no sense. Neither does punishing a child who is already punishing him- or herself excessively. Furthermore, the use of punishment may lead to avoidance and aggressive behaviors, neither of which help the child to overcome serious depression. Therefore, applications of operant conditioning for treatment of children and youth with depression should be focused primarily on positive reinforcement, particularly the DRA approach.

## EMOTIONAL EDUCATION

Emotional education (also referred to as *affective education*) is a psychoeducational intervention technique that is often used as one component of comprehensive treatment programs for depression. For example, cognitive therapy (Chapter 5) and combined cognitive-behavioral programs for treating depression (Chapter 4) increase students' understanding and awareness of their emotions as an important step in the overall intervention process. Emotional education is also often included as one component of more generic interventions, such as social skills training. Even when emotional education is used as a stand-alone prevention or intervention technique, it seems to have solid potential for producing beneficial effects in the behavioral, social, and emotional functioning of children and youth (e.g., Eisenberg, Wentzel, & Harris, 1998). In fact, empirical studies increasingly provide evidence that emotional education techniques can promote positive changes in both emotion and behavior (e.g., Greenburg, Kusche, Cook, & Quamma, 1995).

As an intervention for treating moderate to severe depression, emotional education is best used as only one part of a comprehensive treatment package. However, for less severe cases of depression, and for situations when prevention is the goal with children and youth who are "at-risk" for developmental social–emotional problems, emotional education techniques may be an excellent choice. They may be used with individual students but are clearly very well suited for use with groups, such as pull-out interventions groups of targeted students or entire classrooms.

There is a tremendously wide variety of emotional education techniques available, many of which have been designed specifically for use with children and youth in school settings. For example, a handbook for educators on promoting social and emotional learning (Elias et al., 1997) lists 24 model programs in the United States as examples of effective emotional education programs and references a large number of specific published curricula. Although differences exist among the many specific techniques and programs available for emotional education, there are probably more similarities. The main objective of almost all emotional education techniques and curricula is to increase students' understanding of emotions in general and their own emotional functioning in particular. Like most cognitive and cognitive-behavioral interventions that utilize an affective educational component, many emotional educational techniques are also aimed at helping students to understand the connection between their emotions, behavior, thoughts, and external events. This section provides descriptions of several of the most popular emotional education techniques used in a variety of programs. Because most of these techniques are concrete and relatively structured, they are easy to use with groups or classes of students, and several reproducible handouts are linked to this section.

## Identifying Comfortable and Uncomfortable Feelings

**Purpose:** To increase awareness of one's emotions in general and to evaluate "feeling words" based on whether they are linked to feelings of comfort or discomfort.

**Developmental level:** All ages.

**Supporting material:** Worksheet 7.3, "Feelings Identification."

One of the most basic techniques in a variety of emotional education programs is identification and evaluation of comfortable and uncomfortable feelings. This technique is useful for increasing awareness of emotions in general, and for evaluating "feeling words" based on the criterion of whether they are positive or negative, comfortable or uncomfortable. Although there are several ways to conduct this identification exercise, perhaps the most common way is simply to present students with a list of feeling words or emotion labels that are appropriate for their developmental level and then ask them to divide the list into words that express comfortable feelings and words that express uncomfortable feelings. This technique can be done individually or in a group or class format. For some students, it will first be necessary to define what is meant by comfortable and uncomfortable. A simple way to teach this concept is to state (and maybe post) the following definition, adapted from Berry (1987):

> *Comfortable feelings make people feel good. They can help you have fun and enjoy life. Uncomfortable feelings make people feel bad. They can also help people grow and change for the better. Uncomfortable feelings can help people notice and appreciate their comfortable feelings.*

Notice how this definition teaches that both positive and negative emotions are important and useful. The goal of emotional education should not be to teach students to expect or value only positive feelings. Rather, it should first increase children's awareness of emotions and the purposes they serve. In cases where negative emotions are overpowering, interfering with children's ability to function, or the result of maladaptive cognitions, more advanced techniques can be used to reduce them. However, it is important to recognize that emotional education seeks to increase awareness and understanding of emotions of all kinds, whether comfortable or uncomfortable, positive or negative.

Worksheet 7.3 is a useful tool for structuring an emotional identification and evaluation exercise. This particular worksheet is divided into two levels: Feeling List 1 includes a list of feeling words that is most appropriate for younger students; Feeling List 2 includes a more complex list of feeling words and is therefore more appropriate for older and more mature students. When using this worksheet with individuals, small groups, or classes, practitioners should instruct students regarding which list to use. Students who complete this workshop are instructed to put a + (plus) next to words that describe comfortable feelings, and a − (minus) next to words that describe uncomfortable feelings. A key to making this technique or similar exercises effective is to process the activity with a discussion afterward, preferably in a group situation, so that students can discuss specific feeling words and learn from their peers regarding differences in how feelings are experienced. Follow-up discussions of the feeling words are especially important for students who do not have an adequate grasp of the various emotions involved; such discussions promote increased understanding and awareness. Another benefit of follow-up discussions for this exercise is to help clarify that emotions are complicated, and not all emotions can be easily described or labeled as comfortable or uncomfortable. For example, "surprised" can be both comfortable and uncomfortable, depending on the situation. Likewise, "love" is not only a comfortable emotion but also can create some discomfort.

One potential pitfall to consider in implementing this exercise is that some students may evaluate the comfortability or uncomfortability of certain feelings based on what they think is expected rather than how they actually feel. For example, students might expect that they should be comfortable with the feeling "love" and endorse it positively, because they have been told that it is a good thing, despite the fact that this emotion is complicated and can make them feel quite uncomfortable. To avoid this social desirability pitfall, emphasize that there are no right and wrong answers, and also be careful regarding your own reaction to the evaluations that students produce. For example, if students identify "hate" or "anger" as emotions that they are comfortable with, do not express disappointment or dismay. Rather, use the exercise as a tool to help students increase their emotional awareness, which should ultimately prove to have numerous benefits.

## Learning to Express Feelings: The Incomplete Sentence Technique

**Purpose:** To increase self-identification of one's patterns of emotionality.

**Developmental level:** All ages.

**Supporting material:** Worksheets 7.4 and 7.5, "About My Feelings."

A widely used strategy for teaching children and adolescents to identify their own particular patterns of emotionality is the incomplete sentence technique. This technique is usually implemented by providing a stimulus, usually in the form of a worksheet (see Worksheets 7.4. and 7.5), where the task is to go over several sentence starter stems that involve various emotions and to complete the "blank" space by writing a situation in which that particular emotion was present. The rationale or basis for such incomplete sentence techniques is that they provide a structure for an emotional situation that is linked to an ambiguous ending. Students are required to analyze situations from their own life to determine when they experienced particular emotions. The technique is aimed at increasing awareness of actual situations in which students experienced particular positive and negative emotions. For example, the sentence stem "I became angry when . . . " requires students to identify particular instances when they experienced anger. Ideally, this technique should be used as a springboard to discussing (preferably in a group or class) situations in which particular emotions are likely. As a result, students who participate in the activity will not only increase awareness of their own emotional states but also learn about differences and similarities among their peers regarding how emotional situations are experienced. Worksheet 7.4 provides a sentence completion worksheet that is suitable for younger and less sophisticated children, whereas Worksheet 7.5 provides sentence stems that are more appropriate for older and more sophisticated youth.

One potential pitfall with these incomplete sentence techniques is that some students, particularly those who are disengaged from the process or are oppositional, may not take the exercise seriously, providing silly answers or "going through the motions." Other than working to develop good rapport with students before this exercise is implemented, there is no simple solution to this problem. However, appropriate modeling and feedback from the practitioner may go a long way toward reducing the chances of such problems occurring in the first place. Another potential pitfall with this and similar exercises is the tendency of some students (particularly younger and less intellectually mature students) to be exceptionally brief and concrete in the responses they provide. One way to help students process these exercises using higher level thinking strategies is to model the exercise carefully for them beforehand and provide specific, positive feedback for their efforts to expand and elaborate.

## Identifying and Expressing Feelings: "How Do You Feel?"

**Purpose:** To increase one's emotional vocabulary and enhance awareness of emotional states that accompany specific events or circumstances.

**Developmental level:** All ages.

**Supporting material:** Worksheets 7.6 and 7.7, "How Do You Feel?"

A variation on the sentence completion technique in which the sentence stems are much more ambiguous and students are asked to select from a menu specific listed emotions to complete each sentence, this technique essentially requires students to select the feelings they will describe rather than having each sentence structured for them in advance. For example, when the sentence stem "I feel _____ when _____" is used, students are required to select a particular emotional or feeling word from a list to place in the first blank and then to fill in the second blank in their own words. Although this technique requires more effort on the part of students, it has the advantage of exposing them to a wider variety of feeling words as they select from among several possibilities. The central goal of this variation on sentence completion is still the same as that for more structured sentence completion methods: to help children and adolescents become more aware of their emotions and the situations that trigger these emotions. Again, you should use this technique with groups of students when possible, so that individuals can learn about differences and similarities of emotionality among their peers. Worksheets 7.6 and 7.7 provide practical worksheets for conducting this technique, with the former designed for younger and less sophisticated children and the latter for adolescents and more sophisticated youth. A sample completed worksheet of this type is found in Figure 7.2.

## The Reacting to Emotional Situations Technique

**Purpose:** To practice or rehearse reactions to common emotionally charged situations.

**Developmental level:** Older children and adolescents.

**Supporting material:** Worksheet 7.8, "Reacting to Emotional Situations."

A widely used technique in emotional education programs is to have students practice reacting to common, emotionally charged situations. Such in-session practice not only provides students an opportunity to practice engaging in potentially difficult interactions within a safe setting but also provides the practitioner a good opportunity to observe and subsequently supply feedback to students. There are a variety of ways to conduct such an exercise. The practitioner can simply describe some common situations, one at a time, to the students involved and ask them to identify what emotion, or emotions, would most likely be present for them in such a situation. More structured ways of conducting this

# How Do You Feel?

**Directions:** From the list of feelings at the bottom of this sheet, choose words to write in after the "I feel" part of each sentence, and then use your own words to describe when you feel that way.

I feel _excited_      when _I start school._

I feel _happy_      when _I finish a grade._

I feel _bored_      when _There is nothing to do._

I feel _lonely_      when _I'm up at night._

I feel _angry_      when _My brother hit me._

I feel _safe_      when _My mom & dad are around._

I feel _worried_      when _I'm sick._

I feel _scared_      when _I hear a noise._

## List of Feelings

| | | | |
|---|---|---|---|
| happy | bored | joyful | thrilled |
| lonely | angry | thankful | safe |
| excited | proud | stupid | worried |
| scared | tense | hyper | upset |

**FIGURE 7.2.** A sample completed "How Do You Feel?" worksheet for identifying feelings that correspond to situations.

exercise are also possible. For example, Worksheet 7.8 provides a list of common emotionally charged situations for students of all ages, both at home and at school. Student are asked to read each situation, write down the label for a feeling they think they might have in such a situation, and think about "why" they might feel that way. As with the other emotional education exercises presented in this chapter, it is very useful to process this technique with a group discussion at the end. What might be particularly helpful about such a processing discussion is for students to learn that certain common situations might produce different levels of the same emotion in different persons, or even different emotions. Learning about individual differences in how various situations affect people may be a very useful process in both expanding student's range of emotional understanding and learning to have empathy for other people. A sample completed "Reacting to Emotional Situations" worksheet is found in Figure 7.3. One potential pitfall of this exercise is that some students (particularly younger or disengaged students) may provide superficial, "pat" responses to the stimuli situations, without really thinking at a more critical level about how they might feel. There are a couple of ways to improve the outcomes for this exercise. First, once the students provide the response, help them to evaluate their responses and reinforce their efforts to think critically and become engaged in the activity. Second, the use of rehearsal or role-play activities may help to create an environment in which the emotional situations seem to be more realistic and less abstract.

## Expressing Feelings: A Self-Rating Inventory for Communicating Feelings

**Purpose:** Self-appraisal of one's confidence and ability at communicating feelings.

**Developmental level:** Older children and adolescents.

**Supporting material:** Worksheet 7.9, "Expressing Feelings Inventory."

Developing an increased awareness and understanding of emotions is no guarantee that any particular child or adolescent will be able to translate him or her increased awareness into better communication of feelings. Therefore, after various emotional education exercises have been completed, it is often useful to end the emotional education training by having students complete an inventory of how well or how easily they are able to express various common emotions. Such an activity may be useful for setting goals for future work or change and helps to instill the idea that becoming more aware of one's feelings is only one step toward effectively communicating those feelings.

The self-rating inventory found in Worksheet 7.9 may be a useful tool for helping students appraise their competence in expressing or communicating various emotions, and for helping them to set goals for future social and emotional growth. The particular emotions included in this inventory are general ones that should be familiar to children and youth of a variety of ages (mid-elementary age to high school age) who have completed some emotional education activities individually or in groups. If students indicate on this inventory that they have a great deal of difficulty expressing particular emotions, then that area might be considered for goal setting or future education or intervention activities. I

# Reacting to Emotional Situations

**Directions:** For each situation listed on this worksheet, describe the feeling you would probably have if it happened to you. Also, think about "why" you think you might feel that way.

| Situation | Feeling |
|---|---|
| You are invited by three different students to sit with them in the cafeteria. | Popular |
| One of your friends doesn't want to spend time with you anymore. | Angry |
| You can't think of anything to do. | Bored |
| You get picked last to play on a team. | Left out |
| You are home alone at night. | lonely |
| You get picked first to play on a team. | happy |
| You don't want your mom or dad to see your report card, because of some poor grades you received. | stupid |
| You teacher says, "Great job. You got 100% right!" | confident |
| Your teacher says, "Your work is too sloppy. Do it over again." | frustrated |
| A student says, "I don't understand how to do this. Will you help me?" | Important/ smart |
| Your parents are having an argument. | I'm not sure. |
| There isn't enough money to get something you want. | poor |
| Your mom or dad says, "You're too young. Wait until you're older." | I don't know. |
| You are getting ready to go on a trip for which you have been waiting a long time. | excited |
| A family member is very ill. | disgusted |

FIGURE 7.3. A sample completed worksheet for Reacting to Emotional Situations.

recommend that if this, or similar, self-report inventories are used at the conclusion of an emotional education intervention, the practitioner should meet individually with each student to help him or her evaluate the inventory, set goals for the future, and discuss any concerns. It is important to realize that there are no right or wrong answers on such an inventory—it is simply a tool for helping students to understand the progress they have made, and want to continue making toward being able to effectively understand and express their emotions.

## INTERPERSONAL PROBLEM SOLVING AND CONFLICT RESOLUTION TRAINING

**Purpose:** To increase skills in solving interpersonal problems and conflict.

**Developmental level:** All ages, but younger children will require higher levels of structure and support.

**Supporting material:** Worksheet 7.10, "Five Steps for Solving Conflicts."

## Why Teach Conflict Resolution?

By definition, conflict occurs when two or more persons have mutually incompatible goals. In other words, one persons wants one thing, and the other wants something incompatible with that thing. Interpersonal conflicts are a part of everyday living and not necessarily something pathological. However, the development of maladaptive problem solving and conflict resolution skills can certainly promote behavioral and emotional problems. For example, children who grow up in families where interpersonal conflicts are dealt with by using high levels of *power assertion* or *avoidance* usually do not have good conflict resolution and problem-solving skills. The use of *coercive tactics* ("pain control") to achieve goals is particularly damaging to the development of appropriate negotiation and conflict resolution skills. In schools, intense conflict that is not appropriately resolved is one of the most common causes of students' aggressive and antisocial behavior, and it may also increase school dropout, substance abuse, and depression. Therefore, an additional intervention strategy that may be helpful in working with depressed students in school settings is problem solving and conflict resolution training. These two tactics are discussed together as one idea because they have so much in common, both theoretically and practically.

Although enhancing students' abilities to solve problems and resolve interpersonal conflicts may be beneficial in many respects, it may be particularly important in combating depression. Researchers and practitioners alike have noted that poor problem-solving skills and difficulties in resolving interpersonal conflicts may not only increase the risk of developing depression but may also worsen and lengthen depressive symptoms. Therefore, providing structured training to students in how to solve their interpersonal problems and conflicts more effectively is a natural strategy for prevention and treatment. In fact, some of the best-known programs for treating depressed adolescents include problem solving and conflict resolution training as a major component. For example, interpersonal psychotherapy for depressed adolescents (IPT-A), discussed in this chapter, is based to a great extent on the notion that depression usually occurs within the context of relationship difficulties, and also includes as a major focus of treatment improving conflicts in interpersonal relationships. Several comprehensive, combined cognitive-behavioral treatment programs for depression (see Chapter 4) include both problem solving and conflict resolution as a major focus of treatment. In fact, the *Coping with Adolescent Depression Course* (Clark et al., 1990) devotes 4 of its 16 treatment sessions to teaching negotiation and problem solving for interpersonal conflicts—more sessions than are devoted to any other intervention topic. Clearly, instruction and practice in interpersonal problem solving and conflict resolution is an area that should be included in most comprehensive interventions for depressed children and youth, and that may be potent a prevention strategy in its own right.

## Step 1: Learning about Maladaptive Styles of Problem Solving

The first step in interpersonal problem solving and conflict resolution training should be a psychoeducational process wherein conflict is defined, and both positive and negative examples of dealing with conflict are provided. A useful guide for teaching students about maladaptive styles of dealing with conflict is found in Table 7.1, which provides an overview of four common ways of dealing with interpersonal problems or conflict: *avoidance, dominance, pliancy,* and *trivialization.* None of these ways is particularly helpful, and all tend to worsen problems. However, because they are so common, even insidious, it may be helpful to review them with students. Most students will find this exercise to be interesting and directly applicable, because almost everyone resorts to one or more of these maladaptive styles at times, and it is useful and revealing to find our which one(s) we tend to use. Younger students (younger than age 12) and those with cognitive impairments may find this exercise too abstract and challenging, so practitioners should modify or eliminate this step as needed. One simple suggestion for modifying this exercise for younger students is to avoid the use of the more technical and advanced terms (such is "pliancy" and "trivialization") and instead focus on concrete examples of ineffective ways of dealing with problems.

### Avoidance

Avoidance is characterized by being very uncomfortable with conflict or acting in a "passive–aggressive" style. Avoidant persons will change the subject or stay away from the problem situation. They may also vent their frustration in other unhelpful ways, such as becoming anxious or depressed, using chemical substances, and so forth. *The solution to this style is to be more assertive and direct in dealing with problems.*

### Dominance

Dominance as a style of dealing with conflict is characterized by the need to "be right" and to feel in control. Dominant persons will not let other people respond during a disagree-

**TABLE 7.1. Four Maladaptive Styles of Dealing with Conflict**

| Style | Description | Solution |
|---|---|---|
| Avoidance | May be very incomfortable with conflict, or act in a "passive–aggressive" manner. Changes the subject, stays away from the problem situation, and vents frustration in other ways. | Learn to deal with conflict directly. |
| Dominance | Has a need to feel in control and to "be right." Will not let others respond in a conflict situation. May resort to intimidation or threats to silence the other person. | Learn to slow down, to listen to the point of view of others and not have to "be right." |
| Pliancy | May feel responsible or take responsibility for the problem, even when it is not their fault. May be overly shy and self-critical. | Learn to be more assertive and direct. |
| Trivialization | Laughs or shrugs off problems. Does not take problems seriously. Minimizes things and says, "It's not a big deal." | Learn to respect the other person and take the problem seriously. |

ment. They tend to cut the other person off and try to dominate the argument. In some cases, dominant individuals may also resort to threats, intimidation, or coercion to stay in control. *The solution to this style is to learn to listen to the point of view of others and to slow down in the argument.* Additionally, it is helpful to learn that it is not necessary always to be in control or have to be right.

## Pliancy

Pliancy as a style of dealing with conflict is characterized by feeling responsible for the problem or taking responsibility for it. Pliant persons often feel shy and self-critical. The problem with this style is that it places the responsibility for solving the problem on one person, when, in fact, it takes two persons to create a conflict. Pliancy may also lead to feelings of guilt, shame, and increased self-doubt, which are all associated with depression. *The solution for overcoming pliancy in conflict resolution is to learn to be more assertive and direct.*

## Trivialization

Trivialization of conflict is characterized by laughing or shrugging off a problem. Persons with this style do not take the problem seriously. They minimize things and think "It's no big deal." The problem with this style is that it does not lead to resolution of the problem or conflict—the other person may become angry and the conflict may likely continue. *The solution for this style is to learn to respect the other person and to take the problem seriously.*

## Step 2: Training in Conflict Resolution

Training in conflict resolution can be conducted in a variety of ways, ranging from simple problem-solving steps to complex, schoolwide interventions involving formally trained peer mediators. Any of these possible ways of training students to solve interpersonal problems or resolve conflicts may be helpful. My recommendation for including conflict resolution training as one component of a comprehensive strategy aimed at preventing or treating depression is to make the training module moderate in simplicity and detail. For example, one whole session or class period could be devoted to this aspect of training, with follow-up reviews as needed. It is particularly important to model and role-play examples of realistic conflict resolution to make this technique effective. Specifically, I recommend a five-step training technique that is similar to countless conflict resolution strategies used with children and youth in school settings. These five steps include the following:

1. *Define the problem.* Many students who have poor problem-solving skills have a tendency to get into conflict situations, even extreme conflict situations, without really understanding what the problem is. In many cases, the "problem" may be a result of misunderstanding another person, being overly defensive, or attributing hostile intentions to someone when such is not the case. To ensure that students enter into conflict resolution attempts with a clear definition of the problem, I suggest that the following procedures, adapted from Clark et al. (1990), should be considered:

- *Begin with a positive statement.* For example, a statement such as "I know we are having a fight, but I would like to get things straightened out, and I think we can" will help to set a productive tone for actually solving the problem.
- *Be specific.* In other words, describe specifically what you consider the problem to be, or your concerns.
- *Describe what the other person has done or said.* Make the description very specific—something that anyone present could easily observe. For example, saying something like "She was being mean" is not as descriptive as saying "She took my lunch card and called me bad names."
- *No name-calling!* This will only add to the problem by increasing the intensity of emotional reactions on both sides.
- *Say how you feel.* Simply stating what the other person has done or said that you are unhappy with is sometimes not enough. It is best also to describe how you feel about the situation. For example, saying "When she took my lunch card and called me names, I felt really hurt and upset" brings the situation to a more personal level.
- *Admit your part.* In almost all cases, it takes two people to start a conflict, meaning there is at least some culpability on both sides. By admitting that you have some part in the conflict may defuse an angry response from the other side.
- *Don't accuse.* Again, be descriptive in describing what concerns you. It is better to say "She took my lunch card" than "She is a thief," which will only add fuel to the conflict.
- *Keep it short and simple.* Be brief and do not let the description of the problem drag on. Get things out on the table, so that you can solve the problem.

By going through this simple problem definition process, working with the core issues will be easier and it is more likely that the conflict will be resolved amicably.

2. *Generate solutions.* The next phase of conflict resolution involves generating or "brainstorming" as many possible solutions to the problem as is possible. If the problem involves two or more conflicting problems, which is typical, all parties should be involved in the brainstorming process, so that they will all have a say in what solutions are considered. The essential characteristic of brainstorming is to come up with as many potential solutions as possible without judging, evaluating, or criticizing.

3. *Evaluate the solutions.* After several possible solutions have been generated through brainstorming, they must be evaluated to determine their worth in actually solving the problem. Some of the things to consider in evaluating various solutions are as follows:

- How realistic is the solution?
- Why would this solution work or not work?
- Would this solution help all the persons involved in the conflict to achieve their goals?
- Is this solution fair to all persons involved?

4. *Choose a solution.* This step can be one of the most difficult parts of conflict resolution. The solution that is chosen must be agreed on by all persons involved and should best meet the needs of all parties. The goal of problem solving and conflict resolution training as one component of an intervention for depression should be aimed at helping students develop the skills needed, so it is important that students practice this step (and all steps involved) using realistic situations, and without too much control from the group leader or teacher, who likely will not be around when a real conflict has to be solved. If a solution cannot be agreed on by all parties involved in the conflict, then it is worth going back to Step 3 and trying to brainstorm more possible solutions.

5. *Make and seal an agreement.* After a solution has been chosen, each person in the conflict should state specifically that he or she agrees on the solution and will accept it. Shaking hands on the deal is often a good way to formalize or seal it. It is also useful in some situations actually to write out a formal contract, signed by each person, that specifies what the solution will be, and what each person will do to achieve that solution.

These five steps to resolving interpersonal conflicts are simple, but they will work, and if learned well, they generalize into skills that can be used in various situations that children and adolescents may encounter. Worksheet 7.10 provides a handout or poster than can be given to students to be used as a prompt or guide in learning and practicing the steps of problem solving. This worksheet can also be used by practitioners in teaching or training situations, particularly if made into an overhead transparency or enlarged into a poster. In summary, interpersonal problem solving and conflict resolution training can be a very helpful technique not only in preventing and treating depression but also in aiding with other social–emotional problems.

## SOCIAL SKILLS TRAINING

**Purpose:** To increase skills for interacting appropriately and effectively with other people.

**Developmental level:** All ages.

For many years, researchers and clinicians alike have known that there is a connection between depression and social skills problems. This connection seems to exists for children, adolescents, and adults. In general, it can be said that individuals who experience depression are more likely to evidence problems or deficits in social skills than individuals who are not depressed. And likewise, individuals who have significant deficits in social skills are more likely to report being depressed than individuals who have adequate social skills. The relationship between social skills and depression is complex; depression may in some cases be a cause of social problems, whereas in other cases, it may be a result of social problems (Merrell & Gimpel, 1998).

Regardless of the exact nature of the connection between social skills and depression, social skills training has often been recommended as an intervention for children and adolescents who are experiencing depression, and there is actually a reasonable amount of evidence indicating that this form of intervention may be effective in reducing depression. In some cases, social skills training for students who are depressed has been shown to be as effective as other interventions; in other cases, it has been shown to be a useful part of a comprehensive intervention package. The effectiveness of social skills training as an intervention for depression is probably due to two factors: First, social skills training is almost always conducted within social groups of peers, and therefore provides a rich source of additional social reinforcement during the training sessions, regardless of whether students actually have social skills deficits; second, for students who have significant social skills deficits, the behavioral and cognitive changes that may occur through the social skills training can provide them with the tools to be more effective in obtaining higher rates of social reinforcement outside of the training sessions.

The process of social skills training as an intervention for students with internalizing problems is covered in more complete detail in Chapter 9, where information, procedures, and recommendations provide a strong general framework for social skills training with students, regardless of whether their primary problems involve depression or anxiety. However, there are certain considerations in social skills training that may be particularly important in treating depression as opposed to anxiety. The following four suggestions, adapted from recent work in this area (Merrell & Gimpel, 1998) may be particularly useful in using social skills training as an intervention for students with depression.

- *Incorporate social skills training with other treatment approaches for depression,* such as cognitive restructuring, emotional education, activity scheduling, self-monitoring, and so forth. Because the particular mechanisms that make social skills training effective for treating depression are not well understood, it makes sense to use social skills training as part of a comprehensive intervention package for treating depression in most cases.

- *Include students who exhibit similar types of social deficits or problems within an intervention group.* Not all depressed students have the same types of social problems. It makes sense to try and focus the social skills training on the specific types of skills that are most needed by students in the group.
- *Teach skills that will increase the chance that students will interact with others.* Because one of the main premises for the effectiveness of social skills training in treating depression is that it increases social reinforcement, maximize the potential for such reinforcement actually occurring.
- *Recognize that boys and girls may respond somewhat differently to social skills training and have different social difficulties related to their depression.* Although depressed students of either gender may benefit from social skills training, and should both be included in training groups in most situations, routine social skills training will probably not be sufficient to address the range of concerns.

In summary, social skills training may be an excellent intervention tool for treating depression. Refer to the more expanded coverage of social skills training in Chapter 9 for the particulars regarding when and how to implement this intervention technique.

## CONCLUDING COMMENTS

The strategies described in this chapter can serve several purposes. Behavioral intervention strategies, emotional education techniques, interpersonal problem solving training, and social skills training can all be used as class- or schoolwide prevention techniques, or as part of a personal health or emotional growth curriculum. These four techniques can also be very useful components of an overall, comprehensive treatment strategy for helping depressed children and youth. Although cognitive and cognitive-behavioral intervention strategies are the focus of much of this book and clearly have the most empirical support at the present time, consider that there are other promising strategies from which to develop intervention plans for students who are struggling with depression. In the end, the specific needs and characteristics of the student(s) who are the focus of concern should guide the selection of an appropriate intervention approach.

# 8

# Behavioral Treatments for Anxiety
## *Systematic Desensitization*

## INTRODUCTION AND OVERVIEW

Unlike behavioral interventions for depression, which are generally used in specific circumstances or as one part of a comprehensive cognitive-behavioral treatment program, behavioral interventions have long been a mainstay treatment for anxiety symptoms such as fears, phobias, and general anxious arousal. The tradition of using operant and classical conditioning methods in treating anxiety symptoms dates as far back as the early 1900s, and includes applications for children and adolescents as well as adults. In fact, one of the most famous research studies in the early days of psychology, that of "little Albert," involved the application of classical conditioning techniques by John B. Watson to demonstrate how anxiety and fear responses could be acquired (and, ultimately, treated) in children. Although cognitive and pharmacological interventions for anxiety disorders of children and adolescents now offer additional treatment choices, behavioral treatments are still invaluable and widely used tools.

Within this chapter, the most widely used behavioral interventions for anxiety are presented, with specific emphasis on how they might be applied with children and adolescents in school settings. The first is systematic desensitization, a complex but very practical intervention strategy that has been used for several decades. Systematic desensitization makes use of relaxation training, development of an anxiety hierarchy, and graded exposure. Following the discussion of systematic desensitization, some other basic behavioral intervention techniques, such as modeling and variations of reinforcement, are presented. The interventions presented in this chapter may actually involve more than just behavioral principles in the strictest sense. For example, it is difficult to analyze the three phases of systematic desensitization without realizing that cognitive as well as behavioral techniques are being utilized, and the same might be said for social learning–based modeling interventions. Nevertheless, these interventions have developed within the behavioral tradition. The more recently developed cognitive and cognitive-behavioral treatment techniques for anxiety clearly spring from a separate theoretical perspective. These cognitive-oriented interventions are presented in Chapter 9.

## OVERVIEW OF SYSTEMATIC DESENSITIZATION

One of the oldest and most time-honored treatments for anxiety, fear, and phobic responses is *systematic desensitization*, a behavioral intervention based in great measure on the principles of classical conditioning. Originally developed in the 1950s by Joseph Wolpe, systematic desensitization has historically been the most widely used treatment for reducing children's fears and phobias.

The basic assumption behind systematic desensitization is that a fear response can be reduced or inhibited through substituting an activity that is incompatible or antagonistic to it. Wolpe referred to this process as *reciprocal inhibition*. Typically, the activity or response that is used as a substitute for the anxiety or fear response is relaxation and calmness. In other words, the relaxation and calmness responses are practiced in the gradually increasing presence of the feared stimuli, and eventually, this process weakens the connection between these stimuli and the anxiety responses that they may provoke. The process of systematic desensitization is usually done gradually, and the exposure to the feared stimuli typically begins imaginally in school settings, with the child imagining the feared stimuli. In cases of school phobia, *in vivo*, or real-life, desensitization may be appropriate.

As a very simplified example of how systematic desensitization might be implemented, consider a situation in which a child has developed an extreme fear or anxiety response to almost any class of bugs. First, the fear is identified, and the practitioner teaches the child some very specific and simple methods of relaxation. The child practices these relaxation methods until they are mastered and can be effectively implemented with little prompting. Second, the practitioner helps the child develop an anxiety hierarchy of the feared stimuli (bugs). This involves identifying various feared bugs that are then ordered in terms of the amount of fear they produce, from least to most. Third, the practitioner works to help "expose" the child to the feared bug situations, starting with the least feared. As the child practices the relaxation responses, the situations gradually increase in severity. This third step in the process usually takes several sessions. As the intervention progresses, the child should eventually be able to approach bugs without having the extreme fear responses, because he or she has learned to be in the presence of the feared bug stimuli while maintaining a state of relaxation and calmness. Essentially, the child has practiced responses that are incompatible with anxiety and fear he or she experienced while in the presence of stimuli that formerly produced those anxiety responses. Each of the three major steps in systematic desensitization (relaxation training, development of an anxiety hierarchy, and systematic desensitization to the feared stimuli) is discussed in more detail in the remainder of this section.

Although systematic desensitization has generally been conducted and researched in clinical or medical settings rather than school settings, it is a widely studied intervention that does seem to have potential utility in school settings, particularly when group-based relaxation training, development of anxiety hierarchies, and imaginal forms of exposure are used. Of course, for effective use in school settings, the targeted anxiety or fear-producing situations should be directly related to school situations. Table 8.1 provides a brief outline of the basic steps in systematic desensitization.

To help understand each phase of this intervention and how they fit together, it is useful to consider the typical time requirements needed. Unlike some types of intervention, the number of minutes for each session in these three phases does not need to be extensive. In many cases, 15- or 20-minute sessions are sufficient, particularly after rapport has been obtained, and after the student has some basic proficiency in using relaxation. However, even though the sessions can be relatively brief, it will likely take several sessions on

### TABLE 8.1. Basic Steps in Systematic Desensitization

**1. Relaxation training**
- May occur in groups or individually.
- Practitioner teaches relaxation techniques such as progressive muscle relaxation (Table 8.2) and quick relaxation (Table 8.3), following scripted directions.
- Use relaxation imagery instead of or along with active relaxation techniques if necessary.
- Students practice relaxation techniques for three to four sessions, until they are fully proficient and can become fully relaxed on command.

**2. Development of the anxiety hierarchy**
- May occur in groups or individually.
- Students make a list (with input from parent and teachers, as appropriate), of Specific situations within their targeted area of fear that produce anxiety, fear, or discomfort.
- Student is provided with ten 3″ × 5″ index cards.
- Student writes down situations on cards.
- Student rates how much fear or anxiety each situation produces, using a scale of 10 to 100 in multiples of 10 (Worksheet 8.1).
- Cards are ordered from least- to most-feared situation.
- Intermediary situations are added if there are gaps.

**3. Desensitization proper**
- May occur in groups or individually, but individual sessions are preferred.
- Desensitization sessions occur in a quiet, comfortable environment with few distractions.
- Student spends 5 minutes relaxing and signals to practitioner when full relaxation is reached.
- Practitioner presents student with three to four situations, one at a time, from anxiety hierarchy cards, beginning with the least-feared situation; student attempts to imagine vividly those situations while in a state of relaxation; each situation is practiced three to four times, with a maximum exposure of 10 seconds per situation.
- If tension or anxiety is experienced while the situations are imagined, students signal to practitioner, who gives them a "zero-state" situation to imagine and prompts them in the relaxation technique.
- If failure occurs (anxiety is prompted), return to a lower situation in the hierarchy.
- Sessions should be brief (15–25 minutes) and preferably occur more than once per week.
- Practitioner gradually introduces higher levels from the hierarchy in successive sessions, until students can imagine the highest level while maintaining a full state of relaxation.

a continual basis (once or twice a week) for effective treatment. Consider the following range of numbers of sessions for each phase as a general guide:

- Three to five sessions of relaxation training
- Two to three sessions of building an anxiety hierarchy
- Three to six sessions of systematic desensitization proper

Also, remember that these ranges are only general guidelines, and individuals will vary in terms of how much time and how many sessions are needed. However, if you consider using systematic desensitization, realize that it may take at least eight sessions of 15–20 minutes each, and that it will likely take more than eight sessions, perhaps as many as 14–15 sessions. So, realize that you are making a commitment with this intervention.

## Step 1: Relaxation Training

**Purpose:** Relaxation training is essential in systematic desensitization for anxiety to teach students to become completely relaxed and in preparation for practicing relaxation when exposed to anxiety-provoking stimuli; it is also used in treatment of depression.

**Developmental level:** All ages, but particularly students in grade 3 and higher.

**Supporting material:** Table 8.2, "Progressive Muscle Relaxation Script"; Table 8.3, "Instructions for Abbreviated Relaxation Technique."

Relaxation training is an important first step in the process of conducting systematic desensitization. If the child or adolescent does not learn to prompt a state of relaxation and calmness, then the desensitization phase of the process will probably be ineffective, because the fear-producing stimuli will not be paired with a state that is incompatible with anxiety. Therefore, the initial phase of the process should begin with a few sessions aimed at helping students become comfortable with the intervention setting and teaching them how to enter into a deep state of relaxation. Morris and Kratochwill (1998) have stated that it usually takes three or more sessions of relaxation training for a child to learn relaxation techniques effectively, to the point that they can practice them independently and be prepared for the other phases in the desensitization process.

There are many ways to conduct relaxation training with students, and it is important for practitioners to select a method of training that is best suited for the specific students involved in the intervention, and for the particular circumstances under which the intervention is being delivered. Perhaps the oldest of the many psychological methods for teaching relaxation is the *Jacobson relaxation technique*, which was initially promoted by Edmund Jacobson in the 1930s, and detailed in his book *Progressive Relaxation* (1938). The Jacobson technique is considered to be an *active* muscle relaxation method because it involves very specific physical tensing and relaxing of the major muscle groups in a progressive manner, in which the student learns the difference between states of tension and relaxation, and by alternately tensing and relaxing the major muscle groups, brings on a very deep state of relaxation.

## Progressive Muscle Relaxation

There have been a great many variations on the Jacobson technique over the years, but all of them have some common elements. Some variations of the Jacobson technique are highly detailed and use language that may be too sophisticated or abstract for many children to understand. Table 8.2 provides a basic script for progressive muscle relaxation, based on the principles of the Jacobson technique but simplified, in language appropriate for older children and adolescents. Depending on the particular circumstances and the students being trained, it might take 10–20 minutes on average to go through a progressive muscle relaxation exercise. When using this script, and all other scripts for relaxation techniques, practitioners should strive to speak in a *very clear, relaxed, calm voice*, using a somewhat slower pace of speaking than would be appropriate for normal conversation. Additionally, between each set of instructions or steps in the script, pause long enough that students will not feel rushed. The voice of the practitioner who reads the script for relaxation exercises needs not only to be part of the therapeutic technique but also to facilitate relaxation.

It also might be helpful to make a voice audiotape of yourself or a colleague reading the script. The script can be recorded under controlled conditions, where the focus is specifically on reading the script with the right pacing and the most relaxation-producing tone of voice possible. An advantage of recording relaxation scripts on audiotape is that the practitioner can focus on the progress of the students during the exercise rather than on reading the script. Additionally, copies of the tape can be given to the students for practice at home.

When conducting relaxation training with students, there are some practical issues. First, consider the physical space in which you conduct the relaxation training. It should be comfortable, somewhat private, and not too bright. School desks and chairs are usually a very poor setup for promoting total relaxation. If there is a carpeted room available, consider using it and having the student(s) sit or lie on the floor. Another alternative is to use padded mats from the physical education room, cushions, or beanbag chairs, if available. Some students will initially be uncomfortable or self-conscious doing a relaxation training exercise, particularly if they are the only student with whom you are working. The self-consciousness should decrease over time, but you can initially reduce it by spending some time doing something fun or relaxing before the relaxation training begins. Other students may laugh or become disruptive during relaxation training in groups. If this is a problem situation for you, talk to those students beforehand and explain how important it is to not disrupt the exercise. You might also consider having students sit so that they are not facing each other or in too close proximity to each other.

## Abbreviated Relaxation Technique

The progressive muscle relaxation script found in Table 8.2 should be very helpful for relaxation training in most circumstances with children and adolescents, but there are times when other types of relaxation exercises may be needed. For example, there are times when a brief relaxation exercise might be helpful but there is not enough time to go

**TABLE 8.2. Progressive Muscle Relaxation Script**

1. **First, your hands and arms.** Make a tight fist with your hands (*pause*). Now tense your arms. Hold them very tight (*pause*). Notice how strained the muscles in your hand and arms feel (*pause*). Now slowly open up your hands and relax your arm muscles (*pause*). Notice how comfortable and relaxed your hands and arms feel.

2. **Now, your shoulders, neck, and back.** Pull up your shoulders toward your neck as high as you can (*pause*). Make your shoulder, neck, and back muscles go as tight as you can (*pause*). Hold those muscles very tight (*pause*). Now slowly let out a deep breath and let your shoulders drop down, and let the muscles in your shoulder, neck, and back relax all the way (*pause*). Notice how those muscles are relaxed and comfortable.

3. **Now, your face and head.** Lift your eyebrows (*pause*). Squint your eyes as tightly as you can (*pause*). Clench your teeth (*pause*). Wrinkle your forehead (*pause*). Do you feel the tension? Hold it there (*pause*). Now breathe out very slowly and feel the difference as you relax all of the muscles in your face and head (*pause*). Notice how relaxed those muscles are now.

4. **Next, your mouth and jaw.** Breathe in and make a tight forced smile with your mouth (*pause*). Pull your lips hard against your teeth (*pause*). Your lips and cheeks and jaw should feel very tight. Hold it (*pause*). Now slowly let your breath out and relax the muscles on each side of your mouth (*pause*). Say to yourself, "Relax and let go" (*pause*). Notice how relaxed your mouth and jaw are now.

5. **Now, your chest and stomach.** Take a deep breath and hold it. Pull your stomach muscles up tight (*pause*). Tighten your chest and main body as much as you can (*pause*). Hold it. Keep it tight, tight, tight. Hold it some more. Now relax (*pause*). Breathe out, and let yourself breathe normally (*pause*). Relax all of those muscles (*pause*). Notice your deep, relaxed breathing and how smooth and calm it feels.

6. **Next, your legs and feet.** Lift your legs and bend your toes toward your knees (*pause*). Tighten your calves as much as you can (*pause*). Now press your toes against the floor. Tighten your feet. Turn them up and toward your head (*pause*). Hold your legs and feet as tight as you can (*pause*). Now relax. Let all of the tension in your body go out through the tips of your toes (*pause*). Every bit of tension and energy is leaving your body through your toes (*pause*). Breathe out a deep, slow breath. You are totally relaxed now. Imagine the sun shining on your totally relaxed body (*pause*). You are totally relaxed and don't have any worries.

7. **Close your eyes.** Breathe in and out slowly in very deep, relaxing breaths (*pause*). Focus on each muscle group in your body, one at a time (*pause*). They should all be calm and relaxed. With each breath out, focus on a different muscle group, and notice how relaxed you are. First your hands and arms (*pause*). Then your shoulders, neck, and back (*pause*). Now your face and head (*pause*). Now focus on your mouth and jaw (*pause*). Notice how relaxed, calm, and warm everything feels. Now focus on your chest and stomach muscles (*pause*). Now your legs and feet.

8. **Slowly open your eyes** (*pause*). Move your arms and legs, wiggle your fingers and toes. Slowly bring your body back to normal (*pause*). You are now totally relaxed, calm, and alert. You have no worries (*pause*). Doesn't it feel great?

through an entire progressive relaxation script, or the physical circumstances are not right for it. In such cases, consider a simple and abbreviated relaxation exercise. Table 8.3 presents the instructions for this type of abbreviated relaxation technique. Some students might find that their thoughts become easily distracted as they try to focus on relaxation. You may solve this problem by having them practice redirecting their attention and focusing on breathing and repeating a particular word or phrase, such as "I am calm and relaxed," or something else that works for them. An additional consideration for some children in practicing active–progressive muscle relaxation is that their muscles may spasm or cramp, or they may otherwise be bothered by the physical sensations of the exercise, or be unable to do it for some other reason. In such situations, it may be better to practice mental imagery or visualization exercises associated with relaxation (passive relaxation) rather than progressive muscle relaxation. Such alternative exercises may be done quite simply by having the students shut their eyes and think about being very relaxed and calm in a favorite, comfortable place. A few creative phrases from the practitioner can help greatly to facilitate this type of mental imagery.

Relaxation training is an essential aspect of systematic desensitization for reducing fear and anxiety responses. However, it is also a very useful technique even when used apart from systematic desensitization and as part of an intervention for depression and other internalizing problems. In fact, the comprehensive cognitive-behavioral interventions for depression that are detailed in Chapter 4 tend to include relaxation training as an important treatment component. There is even some evidence that relaxation training, even when it is used without the benefit of other treatment components, may be effective in reducing symptoms of depression. Therefore, consider relaxation training as more than just one phase of systematic desensitization. The instructions and scripts introduced in this chapter for teaching relaxation have very broad potential use as an intervention for depression, anxiety, and related problems.

## TABLE 8.3. Instructions for Abbreviated Relaxation Technique

1. Find a quiet comfortable place.
2. Get into a relaxed and comfortable position.
3. Sit quietly.
4. Close your eyes.
5. Focus on your breathing; draw in deep, full breaths, let them out slowly, and feel yourself relax as you breathe out. Let your worries go.
6. Tense and tighten your muscles, group by group. Then let them relax. Notice how calm they feel as you let them relax.
7. Let your whole body relax, and continue to breathe in and out in deep, slow breaths.
8. Think about being in a favorite place, and being very relaxed and calm.
9. Do these steps for a few minutes, then sit quietly for a few minutes more.

## Step 2: Development of an Anxiety Hierarchy

**Purpose:** To help students grade anxiety-producing stimuli from least to most feared, in preparation for graded exposure to these stimuli during Step 3.

**Developmental level:** All ages, but particularly students in grade 3 and higher.

**Supporting material:** Worksheet 8.1, "Listing and Rating Your Fears."

As the relaxation training progresses, the practitioner will need to begin to develop a hierarchy of anxiety-producing situations for the particular student(s) with whom he or she is working. There is a large amount of variation among individuals regarding how much fear or anxiety particular situations might produce, even when the situations all involve the same type of feared stimuli. For example, one adolescent who has an extreme fear of being alone at home might find it most frightening to be home alone when it is dark outside, whereas, for another youth, the fear of this situation may be worse if he or she enters an empty house after his or her parents have left the house for awhile, regardless of whether it is light or dark outside. In addition to the variation among individuals regarding fear-producing situations, most persons who have extreme fear responses tend to have different degrees of fear to variations of the same stimuli. For example, a child who has an extreme fear of eating food from the school cafeteria because of a worry about contamination from germs might be more afraid of eating warm food than cold foods, or loose foods than solid foods.

Because of these variations in fear responses among and within individuals, it is possible to develop a hierarchy of anxiety-producing situations. This is a very important step in systematic desensitization. After an anxiety hierarchy is developed, it will play a crucial role in sequencing exposure to fear-producing situations or objects during the final phase of intervention. It is recommended that the practitioner plan an anxiety hierarchy with the student (and where appropriate, with the student's parents and teachers) for each fear-producing situation that has been identified as a significant problem. The hierarchy is a list of all related, fear-producing situations or objects, ordered from least to most anxiety-producing. Morris and Kratochwill (1998) have recommended targeting only those fears that the child and the practitioner agree are in need of change. The practitioner, or a parent or teacher, should not impose a particular treatment on the child if he or she does not agree that it is a problem and needs to be changed. Otherwise, the treatment will likely be ineffective. So what if the student disagrees with a particular target for desensitization training? The best course of action is to work toward finding some common ground with the student, even if there is some disagreement regarding whether the target is the most important issue to address. If this course of action is taken, and is effective, then the student will likely have more confidence in allowing the use of systematic desensitization for other concerns as well. However, it must be understood that systematic desensitization requires the full cooperation of the student/client to be effective, and unless good rapport and cooperation can be obtained, it may be best to select other, less direct methods of treatment (such as modeling and reinforcement).

Typically, the actual way that the anxiety hierarchy is developed is first to give the student ten 3" × 5" index cards. Then, with input from parents and teachers, when appropriate, ask the student to write down brief descriptions of particular situations that produce problem levels of fear or anxiety. Each of the situations on the 10 cards is then given a rating (up to 100, in multiples of 10) of how much fear or anxiety it produces, with 100 being the highest level of anxiety and 10 indicating very little anxiety. During this task, it is often helpful for the practitioner to provide the student with some behavioral anchors for particular ratings, so that the multiples of 10 have some tangible meaning. For example, you could give students a sheet of paper with all the values between 10 and 100 listed, and some specific descriptions of what particular gradations in the hierarchy might indicate, or go through this type of exercise on the chalkboard. Worksheet 8.1 provides an example of such a behaviorally anchored rating system that could be used by students. Of course, in some situations it may be best to work with students in developing their set of values or anchors for the rating values that are specific to their particular concern.

After students have completed the 10 cards and assigned ratings, the practitioner should go over them with students to clarify any of the situations or ratings that are confusing or seem incongruent with what students have said previously about their fears. Next, the practitioner should discuss the cards with students and add additional items, if needed, so that each of the 10 values from 10 to 100 is represented in the hierarchy. For example, a student might develop a list of 10 fear-producing situations and rate them all with an 80, 90, or 100. If such is the case, then there will not be enough low-fear situations in the hierarchy. If the student cannot immediately think of appropriate situations to fill the gap, the practitioner should work with him or her by suggesting possibilities, asking questions about past fearful experiences, or having the student imagine various situations until sufficient examples have been identified. Situations will also need to be added to the hierarchy if large gaps occur in the values assigned to the 10 situations, for example, if a student has used only values of 20, 60, and 100. For effective implementation of the desensitization phase, it is important to have a complete range of fear-producing situations.

Morris and Kratochwill (1998), noted experts in implementing systematic desensitization with children and adolescents, have indicated that once the hierarchy is completed and all of the values in the range of ratings are represented, there will typically be 20 to 25 items. However, in particular circumstances, there may be more or fewer items. The most important issue in this regard is that the student's most problematic fear-producing situations are included and that enough intermediary situations are added, so that the complete range of fear-producing values from 10 to 100 is represented as closely as possible. Additionally, the practitioner should determine with students some *zero-level* situations (Morris & Kratochwill, 1983) that they consider to be very relaxing and can easily imagine. These zero-level situations will eventually be used in the desensitization phase for the purpose of shifting to and from fear-producing situations and situations that are more compatible with relaxation and calmness. It generally takes two or three sessions with a student to develop fully and refine the complete anxiety hierarchy prior to the desensitization phase (Morris & Kratochwill, 1998).

Although systematic desensitization is based on the behavioral notion of classical conditioning, there are certainly some cognitive components to this intervention, and nowhere is the cognitive aspect more apparent than in the second phase of intervention, when the anxiety hierarchy is constructed. The tasks involved in construction of the anxiety hierarchy require the student to think both abstractly and symbolically, and to have a fair amount of insight regarding his or her fears. Although most youth in grade 3 or higher should be able to develop an anxiety hierarchy successfully with some guidance, there will be some situations in which a student's level of cognitive sophistication is simply too low for this intervention. In such a case, as is true in cognitive therapy for depression, the cognitive-based intervention should not be pushed and more concrete and externally controlled types of intervention choices should be selected.

## Step 3: Desensitization (Graded Exposure)

**Purpose:** To eliminate unwanted anxiety responses by helping students experience relaxation in the presence of anxiety-provoking stimuli, imagined or real.

**Developmental level:** All ages, but particularly students in grades 3 and higher.

The final phase in desensitization is a process of systematic exposure to the feared stimuli. By the time the desensitization phase begins, the child or adolescent should have had a sufficient amount of practice and feedback in relaxation training that he or she can relax effectively and completely when asked to do so. At this point, the anxiety hierarchy (or more than one hierarchy, if necessary) should also have been developed and put into its proper order. If more than one anxiety hierarchy has been developed, the practitioner should first work on the hierarchy that is most distressing to the student. There are two types of exposure. The most common in school settings is *imaginal desensitization* of the feared situations in the anxiety hierarchy. This method of conducting systematic desensitization is almost always the preferred way to work with an anxious student in a school setting because of the low risk of an extreme anxiety reaction. The second variation on exposure, *in vivo desensitization*, involving exposure to the actual feared situation or object, has been used frequently in the clinical world. With a few exceptions, however, it is not recommended for school situations. A brief discussion is included later.

### Imaginal Desensitization

The initial desensitization session should begin by having students spend about 5 minutes relaxing in a comfortable position. They are instructed to signal by raising their right index finger when a state of deep relaxation has been reached. Once the signal is given, the practitioner should ask students to imagine the situations from the anxiety hierarchy, beginning with the least feared situation. Students are instructed to imagine the scene vividly, as if they were actually there. When the fear-producing situations in the hierarchy are presented imaginally, it helps if students close their eyes, so that they can imagine the situations and relax without distraction. If students begin to feel even a small amount of anxiety or tension as they imagine the fear-producing situations, they should signal by raising their right index finger. If the signal is given, the practitioner presents them with a "zero-level" scene to imagine (one that produces no fear or anxiety) and guides them through the steps until a state of relaxation has once again been reached and students signals to this effect.

When students have again achieved relaxation, the practitioner instructs them to imagine the scene once again. Students should again signal if they begin to feel anxiety. If the student signals, then the zero-level scene should be evoked until relaxation is again achieved. The cycle continues until the student can imagine the initial scene without fear or anxiety. When he or she has done this three consecutive times, the practitioner asks him or her to imagine the next-level scene in the anxiety hierarchy, and the cycle repeats until that new scene can be imagined without anxiety.

Morris and Kratochwill (1998) have suggested that each hierarchy scene should be presented in ascending order (from least feared to most feared), "three or four times, with an exposure time of 5 seconds for the first presentation and with a gradual increase up to 10 seconds for subsequent presentations" (p. 100). They have also suggested that only three or four scenes from the hierarchy should be presented each session, and that sessions typically last 15–20 minutes. Remember that the student should be instructed to relax for a few seconds between each scene in the hierarchy. The session should end with a short period of relaxation.

Following the initial desensitization session, the same general format is used for subsequent sessions. The practitioner should help the student gradually move up the anxiety hierarchy of feared scenes at the rate of three or four per session, gradually increasing the time exposure of each scene up to 10 seconds. *Each scene should be presented until the student has had three consecutive successes, or exposures, without an anxiety response.* If there are two consecutive failures (i.e., if feelings of fear or anxiety accompany the scenes), the practitioner should "back up" to the scene that was most recently imagined without fear. The process is repeated for several sessions, and it is helpful to conduct the sessions at the rate of more than one per week, to reduce the amount of relearning that will need to occur each time.

Eventually, the student should be able to imagine the most feared situation in the hierarchy concurrently with a full state of relaxation. Theoretically, as students pair being relaxed with imagining the feared situations in the hierarchy, they become increasingly "desensitized" to these situations. With successful implementation of the intervention, students should eventually learn to be exposed to the situation that previously produced fear, without having a major fear or anxiety reaction.

## In Vivo *Desensitization*

With *in vivo* desensitization, the same processes that have already been discussed are used for relaxation training and construction of the anxiety hierarchy, but the student is gradually exposed to the actual fear-producing stimuli rather than only imagining them. Consider the case of an 11-year-old girl with an extreme fear of walking alone in the halls at school. With imaginal presentation of the anxiety hierarchy, while in a relaxed state, she would vividly imagine being alone in the halls. But with *in vivo* presentation of the hierarchy, she would gradually be required to walk alone in the halls as she focuses on her relaxation techniques. It is also possible to combine imaginal and *in vivo* desensitization, gradually moving from the former to the latter. Although the *in vivo* method may potentially be effective in many cases, school-based practitioners should be very cautious about using it and should generally use imaginal procedures. The reason for this recommendation is simple. School environments are generally not highly controlled or predictable and, in fact, may involve a fair amount of unpredictability. The risk of failure and even a severe reaction from the student (such as a full-blown panic attack), is great enough and poses enough liability that school-based practitioners, in my opinion, should stick with imaginal rather than *in vivo* procedures in the vast majority of situations. There are some exceptions to this recommendation, of course. The most important exception is treatment of school phobia, or school refusal behavior that involves extreme anxiety reactions. In such cases, it is almost always important actually to expose the student to the anxiety-provoking situation of being at school, preferably as soon as possible. Removal from the anxiety-provoking school setting too easily may serve inadvertently to worsen the problem, through the very powerful escape conditioning it might provide. Table 8.4 provides some additional suggestions for treatment of anxious school-avoidant students.

How many sessions are needed in the desensitization phase of treatment? As many as needed to achieve relaxation when the feared stimuli are presented. The actual number of sessions will vary depending on many circumstances and conditions, but consider that it will probably take at least three sessions and perhaps as many as six. Remember that these sessions should not be very long—perhaps 15–20 minutes each will do. If there is no progress after three or four sessions, consider evaluating how well the anxiety hierarchy has been constructed and the relaxation training learned. These first two phases are both

### TABLE 8.4. Tips for Working with Anxious Students with "School Phobia"

- Do not assume that all school refusal behavior is the result of an anxiety problem or "school phobia." In some cases, refusal to attend school may be the natural avoidance reaction to being in an aversive environment. If the school environment is indeed aversive, work on making the environment more positive rather than simply getting students to fit in to the environment.

- Realize that significant fear or anxiety reactions to attending school are not uncommon with young children, particularly those in kindergarten and first grade. For these young students normal school anxiety problems usually diminish quickly when there is a firm expectation of school attendance, coupled with a nurturing environment at school.

- For students who are in a pattern of staying at home because of school-related anxiety, work with the parents to make school attendance a clear and firm expectation and to remove any unusual reinforcers available in the home setting when school is missed.

- Combine anxiety-reduction procedures such as systematic desensitization and cognitive-behavioral techniques with positive reinforcement for school attendance.

- For anxious students who have ceased school attendance altogether, start with smaller goals for attendance, such as part-day attendance.

- For students who have more than one teacher during the school day, make sure that all of their teachers are following a consistent plan for dealing with anxiety behaviors that are related to school attendance.

- Educate parents and other school personnel regarding the causes of school refusal behavior and what intervention efforts are most effective.

- Maintain complete records of intervention efforts and school attendance, so that progress can be evaluated and the intervention modified if necessary.

essential building blocks for effective systematic desensitization. If continued efforts do not produce improvement, consider that the student may not be amenable to this type of treatment. Although systematic desensitization is perhaps the most widely documented psychological intervention for anxiety problems, it may not work in all situations and with all persons.

## OTHER BEHAVIORAL INTERVENTIONS

In addition to systematic desensitization, several other behavioral techniques are also commonly used as interventions for anxiety symptoms. Modeling and the use of positive reinforcement have both been shown to be effective interventions for anxiety and fear responses in specific situations. In addition, some variations on positive reinforcement, such as shaping and extinction, may also be useful. These basic behavioral interventions for anxiety problems are described in this section.

### Modeling

**Purpose:** To reduce anxiety and fear responses by having students observe another individual who deals appropriately with the anxiety-provoking stimuli.

**Developmental level:** All ages.

Based primarily on social learning theory as articulated by Bandura (1969, 1971, 1986), modeling is another important behavioral tool for treating the anxiety disorders, fears, and phobias of children and youth. The premise behind the use of modeling is that behavior change may result from observing the behavior of another person, and the consequences of that behavior. However, modeling is much more complex than simple imitation of behavior. Effective behavior change through modeling involves several distinct phases, as well as attentional, memory, motor, and motivational processes. An excellent discussion of the use of modeling in treating fears and phobias of children is found in Morris and Kratochwill (1998), whose review of the research in this area provides convincing evidence of the potential therapeutic uses of modeling.

Modeling may be *live* or *symbolic*. With live modeling, the observer watches the behavior of another student as it occurs in a naturalistic or analogue setting (i.e., the classroom, playground, cafeteria, or office). Live modeling involves actual demonstration of the target behavior by the model. For example, a student who experiences anxiety or fear in response to eating lunch with other students in the school cafeteria might observe another student performing that behavior in the cafeteria setting. Equally important as observing the live enactment of the target behavior is observing the consequences of that behavior, which should be positive, for the model. In other words, the student who experiences extreme fear toward eating lunch with other students in the school cafeteria should observe another student performing that behavior, which should then be followed by positive consequences, such as the student talking and laughing with other students as they eat lunch. This process is referred to as *vicarious reinforcement*; the student learns that positive consequences may likely follow the target behavior.

Symbolic modeling is similar to live modeling except that it involves presentation of the model enacting the target behavior through film, videotape, photograph, or some similar medium. For example, a student with an extreme fear of getting on and riding the school bus might watch a video of a model going through the complete sequence of behavior involved in getting on and riding a school bus. Again, it is important that the model's enactment of the target behavior be followed by an appropriate, positive consequence and a lack of negative consequences, so that the observer student will be more likely to experience vicarious reinforcement. One popular variation of symbolic modeling involves reading stories to students that involve other children successfully negotiating feared situations or events. Many school-based practitioners maintain a library of children's books that they can read to students to help them cope with feared situations, such as visiting a doctor or dentist, separating from parents, being home alone, dealing with the severe illness of a family member, moving, and so forth.

## Differential Positive Reinforcement

**Purpose:** To reduce symptoms of anxiety by increasing behavioral responses that are incompatible with those symptoms.

**Developmental level:** All ages.

Many variations of reinforcement have been used to treat children and youth who exhibit maladaptive anxiety responses. Positive reinforcement, the most widely used and effective reinforcement procedure, is an operant conditioning technique and may be used alone or in conjunction with other intervention procedures. The basic premises behind the use of positive reinforcement are detailed in Chapter 7, and need not be repeated in detail here. However, a brief review of some principles of reinforcement as they apply to treating anxiety symptoms may be helpful.

Generally speaking, the preferred use of positive reinforcement in treating anxiety symptoms is *differential reinforcement* of behaviors that are incompatible with the troublesome anxiety responses. As these nonanxious responses are reinforced and strengthened, students are less likely to exhibit the anxiety symptoms, because they have learned new behaviors that are incompatible with the anxiety responses. Differential reinforcement may involve *differential reinforcement of other behavior* (DRO; reinforcement of any behavior other than the targeted anxiety response), or *differential reinforcement of alternative behavior* (DRA; reinforcement of selected appropriate and adaptive behaviors that are incompatible with the targeted anxiety response). As is true in the case of using behavioral methods as a treatment for depression, the use of alternative differential reinforcement procedures is the preferred method because it targets selected responses or behaviors that are important in overcoming the anxiety, fear, or phobia. Differential reinforcement of alternative behaviors may be used for the following common, school-based, anxiety-producing situations:

- School attendance
- Public speaking
- Eating lunch in the school cafeteria
- Getting on and riding the school bus
- Entering or initiating conversations with other students
- Responding to a question by the teacher
- Talking to a member of the opposite sex
- Using the school restroom
- Asking other students to play during recess periods

These examples all reflect common anxiety-provoking situations, and the behaviors that constitute these responses are the alternative behaviors that will be reinforced. For example, a student may have a great deal of anxiety regarding initiating conversations with other students. The maladaptive behavior in which he or she engages as a way of preventing additional anxiety is to avoid any conversation with other students. Thus, the alternative behavior that is reinforced is what the student is not currently doing: entering into conversations with his or her peers. The specific alternative behavior or behaviors that are selected for reinforcement must be carefully identified through an analysis of the problem situations of particular students.

## Conducting a Reinforcer Preference Assessment

It is important to recall that there are many potential types of reinforcers, and if reinforcement is to be an effective intervention, then the right types of reinforcers must be selected. Reinforcers may be social, such as praise, or a pat on the back or attention from a teacher, counselor, and so forth. Reinforcers may also be of the tangible variety—some object that has some value to the student or some symbol of that value (i.e., a token that may redeemed in the future for a valued object). In school settings, there are a wide variety of potential activities available that may also provide a rich source of reinforcement for students. For example, extra time on the computer or at recess, being assigned as the teacher's helper, or being given the "privilege" of cleaning the chalkboard and erasers may all serve as powerful incentives for certain students. The number of potential reinforcers is limited only by the creativity of the practitioner and the preferences of the student. Thus, an important aspect of using reinforcement effectively is to conduct a brief "preference assessment" with students for whom interventions will be implemented. A simple way of conducting such an assessment is to present the target student with a long list of potential reinforcers and ask him or her to underline or circle the activities or things that he or she would most like to have. Another way to conduct a reinforcer preference assessment is to allow the student access to a variety of potentially reinforcing objects or activities for limited time periods and then observe and record their selections, which may be then be used as part of the reinforcement menu. Whether the reinforcer preference assessment is conducted systematically or informally, it is important to do it so that the potential reinforcers used have a greater likelihood of actually being reinforcing to the student. Otherwise, you are likely to hear complaints from parents and teachers to the effect that "Reinforcement doesn't work," because the specific items or activities used as reinforcers had little value to the student. Again, to restate the obvious, a consequence is only reinforcing if it increases behavior.

## Methods of Delivering Reinforcement

In a school setting, many potential persons might be in a position to reinforce selected alternate behaviors. Reinforcement may be delivered by teachers, administrators, or support service professionals who work with the student. It may occur through the use of a written contingency contract that specifies desired behavior and the positive consequences when that behavior has occurred according to some specified criterion. Reinforcement may also be designed and delivered by parents in the home setting as part of a consultation intervention in which a school-based practitioner helps the parents identify the specific alternative behaviors to reinforce and educates them regarding basic behavioral principles. Because school-based interventions may involve so many potential persons who monitor the student's behavior and deliver the actual reinforcers, special care must be taken to ensure consistency and communication across various classrooms and other school settings. In situations where a student exhibits extreme maladaptive fear and anxiety responses across various settings within the school, it is generally best to have the intervention managed by a single individual, such as a counselor, psychologist, or social worker, who will take on the responsibility of consulting with all other personnel who need to be involved, to make sure that the intervention is delivered in a consistent and effective manner.

## Variations on Reinforcement: Shaping and Extinction

Although positive reinforcement is the most widely used behavioral technique for treating anxiety problems, it is not the only technique, and several variations on positive reinforcement might be potentially useful in certain situations. Two of the most common variations of reinforcement that may be useful in treating anxiety problems in school settings are *shaping* and *extinction*.

In situations where students have great difficulty engaging in the desired anxiety-incompatible behavior all at once, *shaping* may be helpful. Shaping is a reinforcement procedure that involves teaching the student to engage in the desired behavior in a series of small steps rather than all at once and reinforcing each successive step in the behavior sequence. For example, it is appropriate to select "eating lunch with other students in the school cafeteria" as an alternative target behavior for a student who has a great fear of eating in the cafeteria. However, if the fear and consequent anxiety responses are intense, it may be more realistic to get the student to engage in this desired behavior in small steps. On the way to performing the ultimate desired behavior of eating lunch in the cafeteria with other students, a student might perform the smaller steps of entering the cafeteria during lunch, sitting down at a table by him- or herself, sitting with other students, and actually eating lunch with other students. Each step in the shaping process must be carefully planned and then reinforced immediately.

Another variation on reinforcement that may be useful in treating anxiety problems in school settings is *extinction*. By definition, extinction involves removing any reinforcing consequences that occur following problem behavior that is perhaps being inadvertently maintained through reinforcement. For example, consider again the situation of a student who has developed an extreme fear of eating lunch with other students in the school cafeteria. This student exhibits significant anxiety responses such as crying, screaming, shaking, and begging the teacher when it is time to go to the cafeteria. In response, the teacher comforts the student and allows him or her to eat lunch in the classroom with the teacher. Although such a compassionate response from the teacher is well-intentioned, it could ultimately serve to make the problem worse by reinforcing the problematic anxiety responses. In a situation such as this, extinction would involve *planned ignoring* of the anxiety responses to the greatest extent that is feasible. The teacher would simply ignore the problem behavior to the greatest extent possible, so that his or her own behavior does not reinforce the anxiety problem. Before using extinction as an intervention for anxiety problems, realize that the problem possibly will get worse initially, once extinction begins (the so-called "extinction burst" phenomenon), and that extinction is usually best used in conjunction with reinforcement for engaging in the desired behavior.

Of course, other variations of behavior principles are also possible in treating anxiety problems but may be of questionable use in school settings. For example, the use of punishment, or presentation of aversive consequences following the undesired behavior, may theoretically act to suppress or reduce that undesired behavior in the future. However, the use of aversives may also elicit avoidance and aggression, and poses many potential ethical and legal problems. As a general rule, it is best to avoid the use of punishment or aversive consequences in school settings to the greatest extent possible and to rely on positive means of intervention that may actually help to teach new behaviors rather simply suppress problem behaviors.

## CONCLUDING COMMENTS

Behavioral techniques have long been, and will continue to be, important and effective intervention tools for treating anxiety disorders of children and youth. Systematic desensitization, and other behavior-oriented interventions, such as modeling, reinforcement, shaping, and extinction, are in many ways naturally suited for treating anxiety-related problems. Although the large majority of reported applications of these behavioral interventions have occurred in clinic settings, they could be implemented in many ways in school settings as well. Some of these techniques, such as relaxation and modeling, can be done in groups, even in classes, using a psychoeducational approach, with plenty of opportunities for practice. These techniques are well suited to school settings. Other techniques, such as systematic desensitization, are more difficult to do in school settings because they require a commitment to several ongoing sessions and must generally be done on an individual basis rather than in groups. However, one consideration might make such work possible in the schools. Although several sessions are needed, the time for each session may not need to be extensive—15- to 20-minute sessions are often sufficient. Implementing reinforcement and variations such as shaping and extinction is more straightforward in a school setting, and a skilled practitioner consultant may be able to work with parents and teachers to deliver these techniques indirectly, thus potentially affecting many students positively. If you are a school-based practitioner who works with students who struggle with anxiety disorders and related problems, consider some of the following ways you might implement behavioral intervention tools: with individual students, in small groups, or in self-contained classrooms. Although these behavioral techniques have long been the mainstay treatments for anxiety problems of children and youth, this field is not static, and new, effective intervention approaches have been developed during the past several years. One of the most exciting developments in this regard is the use of behavioral intervention techniques as part of a comprehensive cognitive-behavioral treatment package for anxious children. Chapter 9 complements the present chapter by detailing the use of some of these more recent cognitive and cognitive-behavioral intervention techniques.

# 9

## Social Skills Training and Other Cognitive-Behavioral Treatments for Anxiety

### INTRODUCTION AND OVERVIEW

Behavioral interventions such as systematic desensitization, relaxation training, and variations on reinforcement procedures have long been the standard intervention methods for anxiety disorders and related problems of children and youth. However, since about the mid-1980s, cognitive intervention strategies have begun to make significant inroads in this area. The earlier attempts at cognitive interventions for anxiety problems consisted primarily of adaptations of the cognitive techniques that had become widely used for treating depression. During the 1990s, the first comprehensive cognitive-based interventions designed specifically for use in treating anxiety problems of young people became established. For the interventions in this area that have been adequately refined and evaluated, the term "cognitive" is best used with a hyphen and the word "behavioral" linked to it. Almost all of these interventions are cognitive-behavioral in nature, in the sense that they utilize important aspects of each theoretical approach. In this chapter, five such cognitive-behavioral interventions are described and illustrated: *self-control training,* self-instructional training, the *"Coping Cat" program* developed by Kendall and his associates, the *transfer of control approach* refined by Silverman and Kurtines, and *social skills training.* These five approaches to intervention for anxiety problems of young people are varied. Some are rather narrowly focused, whereas others should be considered comprehensive cognitive-behavioral approaches to treatment. These interventions represent a promising approach to delivering treatment to young people with anxiety disorders and related problems.

## SELF-CONTROL TRAINING FOR ANXIETY

**Purpose:** To train students to monitor their thoughts, activities, and feelings adequately and to attend to their consequences in a realistic and effective manner.

**Developmental level:** Older children and adolescents.

Self-monitoring as a treatment for depressive symptoms is discussed in detail in Chapter 6. Out of this same general area of theory and research, a method of intervention for anxiety symptoms has also evolved and is referred to as self-control training. The basic premise of self-control training as a treatment for anxiety is similar to that of self-monitoring or self-control methods of treating depression, namely, that emotional–behavioral problems such as depression and anxiety develop as a result of deficits or failures of individuals to adequately monitor their thoughts, activities, and feelings, and to attend to the consequences of their thoughts, feelings, and behaviors in a realistic and appropriate manner. Therefore, self-control training methods of intervention for anxiety problems seek to reduce anxiety symptoms through the general mechanism of teaching individuals to become the primary agent in regulating and directing their thoughts and behaviors in ways that lead to specific positive outcomes and consequences.

Self-control training as a treatment for anxiety is not so much a specific technique as a collection of techniques based upon common principles. Because self-control training methods are based on the premise that the individual must learn how to regulate his or her own behavior and thoughts in a productive manner, these methods place a good deal of responsibility on the individual client. The practitioner's role is that of a teacher and motivator who helps the student begin the process of change. Self-control training also requires a fair amount of intrapersonal insight as well as the ability to think somewhat abstractly. Therefore, the best candidates for treatment using self-control training methods are older children and adolescents (ages 10–11 and older) who have average or above intellectual ability and are likely to be willing to assume responsibility for an active role in the intervention process.

Although it is difficult to list a specific set of steps that might be used in self-control training for anxiety, because the treatment is based on a premise rather than a set of procedures, it is still possible to identify some specific elements that might be used in this treatment method. Typically, students who participate in self-control training for treatment of anxiety problems are systematically taught the following:

1. To monitor their self-statements associated with situations that produce anxiety, fears, or panic.
2. To increase their cognitions or self-statements associated with states of relaxation or calmness.
3. To understand the connection between the way they think about an anxiety-provoking situation and the way that they actually respond to that situation.
4. To set standards for themselves that are realistic and attainable.
5. To break down their individual goals into attainable subgoals or smaller goals.
6. To make appropriate attributions for their successes and failures.

There is some limited evidence supporting the use of self-control training as an intervention for students with anxiety problems (see Morris & Kratochwill, 1998). However, much of the available evidence in this area involves self-control training as part of an overall comprehensive treatment plan that might also include systematic desensitization or modeling. Because self-monitoring has not been fully developed at this point in time for the specific purpose of treating children and youth with anxiety disorders, relatively few supporting materials are available, and this method is probably best used by practitioners as an adjunct rather than as a primary intervention. However, it is a very promising treatment method for treating both depression and anxiety.

## SELF-INSTRUCTIONAL TRAINING FOR ANXIETY

**Purpose:** To learn to alter maladaptive thoughts and behavior appropriately through the use of carefully scripted self-talk

**Developmental level:** All ages, but scripts for younger children must be very simple.

Self-instructional training, a specific type of cognitive-behavioral treatment approach, was originally developed by Meichenbaum and his colleagues in the early 1970s for teaching reflective problem-solving skills to impulsive students. This approach was later modified for other uses (e.g., Meichenbaum, 1986), including treatment of anxious children. The basis of self-instructional training is that students can learn to alter their thoughts and behavior through the use of carefully scripted self-talk. Initially, students observe an adult (e.g., the teacher or practitioner) model the scripted self-talk strategies and ultimately are expected to use these strategies on their own, when faced with specific problems situations. For example, a student who exhibited extreme test-taking anxiety could go through the steps of self-instructional training using a scripted set of instructions designed to reduce anxiety regarding the test, and to facilitate effective performance (e.g., "Am I feeling anxious? Okay, I need to follow my plan. I need to do only one problem at a time, and then take a deep breath and relax when I am done with each problem. I can do this!").

Meichenbaum (1986) proposed that self-instructional training for children should include the following five steps:

1. An adult (the teacher or practitioner) performs some task while modeling the cognitive training procedure (reciting the scripted self-talk out loud).
2. The student performs the same task with external guidance and overt direction from the adult model.
3. The student performs the task while he or she provides self-guidance through overt recitation of the scripted self-talk.
4. The students whispers the instruction to him- or herself while proceeding through the task.
5. The student performs the task and at the same time uses inaudible, private self-talk to guide his or her performance.

The five steps of self-instructional training detailed in the previous paragraph are general and may be used in response to a variety of problems, not just anxiety. However, there is some evidence that this process can be modified specifically for use in successfully dealing with anxiety-provoking situations. Although self-instructional training has not been studied very extensively for use in treating anxiety problems with children and youth, it certainly has logical face value as a simple and potentially effective intervention, and it has been incorporated as one element of comprehensive cognitive-behavioral treatment packages, such as the one discussed in the next section.

## THE "COPING CAT" PROGRAM FOR ANXIOUS YOUTH: AN INNOVATIVE, COMPREHENSIVE TREATMENT APPROACH

**Purpose:** A comprehensive cognitive-behavioral program for group and individual treatment of anxiety.

**Developmental level:** Older children and adolescents.

One of the most innovative cognitive-behavioral approaches to treating anxious youth is the "Coping Cat" program, a set of manualized treatment packages developed by Phillip Kendall and his associates at the Child and Adolescent Anxiety Disorders Clinic at Temple University. The complete Coping Cat program includes a comprehensive package of treatment manuals: the *Coping Cat Workbook* (Kendall, 1992) for use by children and adolescents in treatment and three accompanying therapist manuals—one for individual child treatment (Kendall, Kane, Howard, & Siqueland, 1990), one for group treatment (Flannery-Schroeder & Kendall, 1996), and one for treatment of families of anxious children (Howard & Kendall, 1996). Table 9.1 provides the complete titles of these manuals, as well as relevant information for obtaining them.

This treatment program includes a systematic combination of plans for treatment sessions based on empirically supported premises of cognitive and behavioral change, and is designed for use with older children and adolescents. Although the lower end of the appropriate age range for this program is not rigid, it appears that a reasonable minimum level for effective participation would be typically developing children ages 9 or 10 (e.g., grade 3 or 4). The individual and family treatment components of the Coping Cat program include 16 sessions each, whereas the group component includes 18 sessions. The guidelines for treatment sessions are general and fairly flexible, but it should be assumed that each session would require at least 1 hour to complete.

Although this treatment program is flexible and is not "scripted," treatment generally follows two distinct phases, whether it is delivered to individuals, to groups, or to families. The first phase of treatment (approximately eight sessions) involves a psychoeducational process to teach children to identify the somatic, cognitive, and behavioral components of anxiety. The second phase of treatment involves application of the new skills in real life (*in vivo*) situations tailored to the specifics of the child's anxiety problems. A combination of

**TABLE 9.1. Treatment Manuals from the "Coping Cat" Program for Anxious Youth**

- *Coping Cat Workbook* (Kendall, 1992)
- *Cognitive-Behavioral Therapy for Anxious Children: Therapist Manual* (Kendall, Kane, Howard, & Siqueland, 1990)
- *Cognitive-Behavioral Therapy for Anxious Children: Therapist Manual for Group Treatment* (Flannery-Schroeder & Kendall, 1996)
- *Cognitive-Behavioral Family Therapy for Anxious Children: Therapist Manual* (Howard & Kendall, 1996)

<u>Available from:</u>
Workbook Publishing, Inc.
208 Llanfair Rd.
Ardmore, PA 19003
Phone: 610/896-9797
Fax: 610/896-1955

cognitive and behavioral techniques are used to accomplish the treatment goals. For example, self-monitoring, identification of distorted and unrealistic cognitions, evaluation of physiological symptoms, disputation of irrational cognitions, relaxation training, self-instruction, and self-reinforcement are all used to some extent. An example of this eclectic cognitive-behavioral mix of treatment treatment techniques is found in a four-step plan for coping and managing anxiety symptoms that is presented in the first (psychoeducational) phase of the Coping Cat program. The acronym FEAR is used to illustrate steps toward mastering unwanted anxiety symptoms:

- **F** (*Feeling frightened?*). Students ask themselves this question as they learn how to recognize their internal or physical signs of anxious arousal and learn and practice relaxation techniques.
- **E** (*Expecting bad things to happen?*). Students ask themselves about the potential "catastrophes" that they might be worrying about, and actively think of other possible outcomes. Students also learn to identify anxiety-related thoughts.
- **A** (*Actions and attitudes that help*). Students are taught a variety of cognitive and behavioral strategies that they can use to reduce and overcome anxious arousal.
- **R** (*Rate and reward*). After the first three steps are completed, students learn to rate the outcome of their attempts to manage anxiety and reward themselves for making progress.

Research on various applications of the Coping Cat program, as detailed by Kendall and Treadwell (1996), provides impressive evidence of the potential utility of this comprehensive cognitive-behavioral treatment approach. Although this program was initially developed and field-tested in clinical settings, it appears to have a great deal of promise for use in school settings as well. In fact, the structured psychoeducational nature of the program, coupled with the practical and realistic manner in which new skills are practiced, appear to make the Coping Cat program an excellent choice for treatment of anxious students in school settings.

## THE TRANSFER OF CONTROL APPROACH

**Purpose:** To reduce anxiety and phobia symptoms through gradually increasing exposure to the problem stimuli and gradually transferring control over the treatment techniques from practitioner to student.

**Developmental level:** Cognitively mature older children and adolescents.

An interesting model for treating internalizing disorders of youth that primarily involve anxiety and phobia symptoms, the *transfer of control* approach, developed by Silverman and Kurtines (1996a, 1996b) and their colleagues, is referred to by the authors as pragmatic, because it is not grounded in any one specific theory but borrows from several theoretical models and approaches that they have found to be effective in their research and clinical work with children. According to the authors (1996a), the transfer of control approach

> holds that effective long-term psychotherapeutic change in youth involves a gradual transfer of control, in which the sequence is generally from therapist to parent to youth. Within this approach, the therapist is viewed as an expert consultant who possesses the knowledge of the skills and methods necessary to produce therapeutic change. Furthermore, it is the therapist who initially controls the use of these skills and methods, but then transfers the use of these skills and methods to the parent, who subsequently transfers the use of these skills and methods to the youth. (pp. 65–66)

In other words, a key feature in the transfer of control approach is expert consultation and a gradual shifting of the control of the intervention from the practitioner to the parent to the youth. Although the transfer of control approach was developed, refined, and researched in clinical rather than school settings, its reliance on consultation and its emphasis on "what works" appears to make it very well suited for possible use by practitioners in school settings.

The most important specific intervention procedure in the transfer of control approach is *exposure*. Youth who participate in this program are informed at the onset of treatment that they will learn how to cope with their fears, anxiety, and phobic reactions through exposure to the stimuli that are associated with the uncomfortable reactions. In essence, youth who participate in transfer of control training are taught to "face their fears." However, exposure is done very gradually and in a carefully planned manner, and participants are initially informed of that fact to ease their concerns about facing uncomfortable situations. Consistent with the overall theme of the transfer of control approach, exposure to the anxiety- or fear-producing situations is initially directed by the practitioner, who eventually trains the parents to take on this role, when it is appropriate, and the target child or adolescent ultimately placed in charge of the exposure situations. Exposure, as well as the transition from practitioner to parent to youth, occurs gradually to assure step-by-step success in implementing the procedures. Exposure to the feared situations or objects is done both *in vivo* and imaginally, and in a carefully graduated manner consistent with the general notion of systematic desensitization.

In addition to the major emphasis on exposure as a treatment technique, the transfer of control approach includes several other therapeutic techniques that are designed to facilitate the effective occurrence of exposure. Parents are provided with basic training in behavioral techniques in the form of behavioral contingency management contracting. The goal of this strategy is that parents induce successful exposure of the youth to the anxiety/fear provoking stimuli through the use of carefully worded contracts that specify particular steps to be taken and rewards that will be provided for fulfilling the contract. This behavioral parent training component is not conducted haphazardly. Parents not only receive specific instruction, practice, and feedback but are a detailed set of instructions to take with them to use in the home setting.

The other primary therapeutic strategy that is used to facilitate exposure is self-control training of the youth. This strategy is aimed at helping the child or adolescent who is experiencing significant internalizing symptoms to use appropriate cognitive strategies to approach exposure to the feared objects and situations. The implementation of self-control training in this approach is very similar to many of the cognitive techniques for combating depression, which are detailed in Chapters 5 and 6. Silverman and Kurtines (1996a) suggest that self-control training in this approach should be done very systematically and in a highly structured manner. They have successfully used a set of cognitive rehearsal steps for this strategy called "STOP fear," in which the acronymn STOP refers to the following structured steps:

- **S** (recognize when I am *scared*, anxious, worried, nervous, or afraid)
- **T** (what are my *thoughts*? . . . what am I *thinking*?)
- **O** (what are *other* thoughts or things I can do?)
- **P** (*praise* myself for controlling my fear)

It is interesting that the major obstacle to the transfer of control approach reported by the authors is what they have referred to as the "protection trap." This label refers to the seemingly natural instincts of parents to protect their children in anxious or fearful situations. What may happen due to this phenomenon is that parents may be reluctant to enforce the conditions of the contingency contracts they make with their child, or to facilitate exposure to the feared stimuli. Of course, such actions are countertherapeutic. The best way to reduce the negative effects of the "protection trap" is careful training and monitoring of the parents as they help to implement their end of the intervention in the home setting.

Silverman and Kurtines's (1996a, 1996b) transfer of control approach to treatment is an innovative and practical strategy for helping children and adolescents who are experiencing significant internalizing distress in the form of anxiety, fear, nervousness, worry, phobias, and the like. Although the field-testing and research to date with this approach have focused on clinic-based populations of youth, it seems to have a great deal of promise for use in school settings, particularly when parental involvement is possible. The authors have described some variations on this basic approach to treatment, such as individual- and group-based applications of the strategy, but the essential characteristics remain the same. Reductions in significant internalizing symptoms are accomplished through a program of self-control training, contingency management, and exposure, which is initially orchestrated by the practitioner, then by the parents, and ultimately by the youth.

## SOCIAL SKILLS TRAINING

**Purpose:** To increase skills for interacting appropriately and effectively with other people.

**Developmental level:** All ages.

Social skills training has long been used as an intervention for socially withdrawn and anxious students. Most socially withdrawn youth tend to experience significant anxiety regarding their social experiences. They may feel a great deal of fear in tackling common school situations, such as answering a teacher's question in front of the whole class, speaking in public, asking questions of teachers or other students, or initiating conversations with their peers. In addition to exhibiting shyness and withdrawal, and not interacting with their peers, socially withdrawn or anxious students may often have poor social problem-solving skills and are less likely than most of their peers to engage in social problem solving after they have experienced a failure in trying to deal with a social situation. In other words, socially anxious students who withdraw from social situations at school because of their discomfort in these situations are less likely than most of their peers to possess the skills needed to negotiate these social situations effectively. They are likely to "give up" and withdraw from social situations rather than risking the discomfort and embarrassment that they perceive will occur if they fail in these situations. For socially anxious and withdrawn students, social skills training offers a practical intervention tool to increase their ability to deal with social situations. This intervention is best described as cognitive-behavioral in nature, because it includes components ranging from cognitive rehearsal and self-evaluation of performance to overt behavioral demonstration and modeling. Additionally, most social skills training programs include an affective component, making this intervention truly eclectic in nature.

## Skills Deficit or Performance Deficit?

Practitioners should not automatically assume that students who exhibit social problems necessarily have *deficits* in social skills. Although many students who fail to engage in appropriate social behaviors have not yet mastered the requisite behavioral skills to do so (evidence of a skills deficit), there is another type of student to consider. Some students actually may have learned the particular social skills but fail to use them. Such circumstances reflect *performance deficits* rather than *acquisition deficits*. The student has acquired the skill but fails to perform it when needed.

The prevailing explanation for performance deficits is the *competing emotions model* (Merrell & Gimpel, 1998), which model contends that students who have already acquired a social skill may fail to perform it because of *maladaptive emotional or cognitive states*. For example, a student who possesses the appropriate skills needed to invite another student to play at recess may fail to do so because he or she is overcome with anxiety about the outcome. Or the student may engage in negative self-talk (e.g., "I can't do this, she will think I am stupid" or "Nobody will want to play with me anyway") that further fuels maladaptive cognitions and inhibits performance of the social skills needed in a given situation.

A simple way to determine whether the social skills problem is an acquisition deficit or a performance deficit is to role-play common social situations with students individually and observe them carefully to make a determination. Can they perform key social skills in a contrived situation, where there is little stress and a high degree of control within the environment? If students appear to have true social skills acquisition deficits, then the best intervention is to identify the specific skills they lack and assist them in learning those skills through a structured social skills training program. In Chapter 3, Table 3.3 includes a list of general purpose behavior rating scales, many of which include social skills screening subscales and may be useful for planning social skills training interventions. If social skills problems are a major concern, the use of standardized behavior rating scales designed specifically to assess social skills is particularly recommended. Behavior rating scales such as the School Social Behavior Scales (Merrell, 1993), Home and Community Social Behavior Scales (Merrell & Caldarella, 2001) and Social Skills Rating System (Gresham & Elliott, 1990) are particularly recommended in this regard. If a student appears to have a performance deficit, then the best intervention is to work on the underlying affective or cognitive difficulties, using an appropriate cognitive restructuring or affective education program, such as any one of several that are discussed in this book.

## Basic Steps in Social Skills Training

Because social skills training has been such a popular method of intervention for so long, many models of social skills training have evolved and numerous packaged social skills training programs are available (for a comprehensive review of programs, see Merrell & Gimpel, 1998). Given the wide variety of models and training programs, it is understandable that there are some notable differences among social skills training methods. For example, some social skills training programs are highly behavioral in nature, whereas others place a large emphasis on cognition or self-instruction. But despite the differences among the most widely used social skills intervention programs, there are considerable similarities. More often than not, the similarities among the many social skills training programs stem from a combination of empirical support and what is "tried and true" in clinical practice.

In the book *Social Skills of Children and Adolescents* (Merrell & Gimpel, 1998), my colleague and I conducted a careful analysis of the most widely used models and programs for teaching social skills to children and youth, and identified the common core elements among them. The result of this analysis was a synthesized or integrative eight-step model of social skills training that should be considered cognitive-behavioral in nature. This integrated eight-step model provides a practical framework for developing and conducting social skills interventions across the age span and range of social skills acquisition problems. The eight steps described in the following bulleted sections are also summarized in Table 9.2.

- **Introduction and problem definition.** The group leader first presents relevant problem situations to the students and then assists them in defining the actual problem. Then, the group leader works with students to generate alternatives for solving the problem.
- **Identification of solutions.** After the problem has been defined and some appropriate alternative solutions have been noted, the group leader assists students in identifying the social skill components of the best solution. After an optimal best solution has been identified, the group leader provides specific instructions to students regarding how to engage in the desired social behavior.
- **Modeling.** Before the students actually practice the new social skill, the group leader should model it correctly for them. Because social skills training for our purposes is based on a cognitive-behavioral premise, the modeling should include two components: cognitive and verbal rehearsal, in which the group leader "thinks aloud" the steps in the process of enacting the skill and demonstrates actual behavioral enactment of the new social skill. By using these two components of modeling, students are able to observe not only the correct enactment of the new skill but also the correct self-instructional process that accompanies it.
- **Rehearsal and role playing.** After the group leader has modeled the desired social behavior both verbally and behaviorally, the students are guided through the steps of enacting the behavior. An important aspect of rehearsal and role playing is that students

---

**TABLE 9.2. Eight Essential Steps of Social Skills Training as a Cognitive-Behavioral Intervention**

1. Introduction and problem definition
2. Identification of solutions
3. Modeling
4. Rehearsal and role playing
5. Performance feedback
6. Removal of problem behaviors
7. Self-instruction and self-evaluation
8. Training for generalization and maintenance

are asked to perform the desired behavior through the use of role-play situations that are realistic and relevant to them.

• **Performance feedback.** After the students have engaged in rehearsal and role playing of the desired social behaviors, they must immediately be given feedback regarding their performance. Reinforcement (praise) should be provided if students correctly enacted the social behaviors, and corrective feedback and additional modeling should be provided if the students' role plays were incorrect. If corrective feedback is given, then it is important to give the students an additional opportunity for rehearsal and role playing, until the behavior is enacted correctly. Any feedback to students during this step, whether reinforcement or correction, should be highly descriptive of their behavior, so that they will know exactly what aspects of the skill enactment they performed correctly or incorrectly.

• **Removal of problem behaviors.** This step is not always needed, but when students in social skills training groups are engaged in off-task, noncompliant, antisocial, or other problem behaviors during the group sessions (which is typically more often than not), then removal of these problems is absolutely essential if the intervention is to have any meaningful impact. Most experienced social skills trainers find that the use of a positive reinforcement-based behavioral plan, perhaps using a token economy system, is an integral part of running a group. It is often helpful to spend part of the first training session developing a simple and very brief list of behavioral expectations and rules for the sessions, and then posting these rules where they are plainly visible in all subsequent sessions. Reinforcement, and corrective reduction procedures, if needed, should be used in a manner that stresses and teaches the rules.

• **Self-instruction and self-evaluation.** Students are asked to "think aloud" during training sessions, as modeled by the group leader. Self-statements that reflect distorted thinking or maladaptive thought–belief systems should be identified, using the same procedures already noted for cognitive treatment of depression and anxiety symptoms. As part of this step, training sessions should include a gradual shift from overt instruction and appraisal of performance by the group leader to self-instruction and appraisal. Ultimately, the students should develop the skills to guide themselves through problem situations and to provide themselves with appropriate feedback.

• **Training for generalization and maintenance.** It is important to emphasize the value of this final step for the ultimate success of the intervention. If effective training for generalization and maintenance of the newly learned social skills does not occur, then whatever gains are realized through the intervention will likely end at the doorway of the room where the training sessions are conducted. Throughout the intervention, the situations, behaviors, and role plays selected should be as realistic or close as possible to natural social situations that the students encounter at school, at home, and in their neighborhood. Appropriate homework assignments, with home–school communication, will help to achieve this end. Classroom teachers and parents should be enlisted to monitor homework, encourage practice of the social skills, and provide reinforcing and corrective feedback to the students. Although none of these training procedures guarantees that gains made from social skills training will generalize across settings or be maintained over time, it is very unlikely that such will be the case without them.

This particular model of social skills training is straightforward, easy to use in designing social skills training groups, and based on empirically supported principles from the research literature and the most widely used intervention manuals. Table 9.3 provides an example of a social skills training outline or script that might be used for a specific skill with socially anxious students—initiating a conversation with peers. If you are interested in a more thorough description of social skills training than is possible in this section, you are encouraged to check out any or all of the following social skills training guides: Elksnin and Elksnin's (1995) *Assessment and Instruction of Social Skills*, Merrell and Gimpel's (1998) *Social Skills of Children and Adolescents*, and Sheridan's (1995) *The Tough Kid Social Skills Book*. Other excellent manuals and texts in this area are also readily available and may be helpful in developing expertise on social skills interventions for students with social behavior problems.

## Training Suggestions for Socially Withdrawn and Anxious Students

The eight-part integrated model for effective instruction in social skills training just presented provides a solid basis for intervention with all students who experience social difficulties. However, students whose social problems are related to social anxiety or social withdrawal may benefit from some specific approaches, understanding, and emphasis within social skills training programs. The following six suggestions, adapted from my previous work in this area, may be particularly useful in planning and conducting social skills training interventions with students who are withdrawn and socially anxious:

• Before conducting social skills training, try to determine whether the social behavior problem is due to a *skills deficit* or a *performance deficit*. Social problems due to skills deficits require extensive training and practice of new social skills. Social problems due to performance deficits require efforts to practice the skills under varying conditions to remove competing emotional or cognitive conditions that interfere with the performance of appropriate social behaviors.

• Understand that social withdrawal may be a cause as well as a consequence of social difficulties. Different groups of students who experience social withdrawal may need different intervention approaches to social skills training based on this issue.

• Rather than implementing a generic social skills training curriculum, identify the specific social skills in which children are most deficit and focus training efforts on those skills.

• Realize that a student who does not interact with other students may not necessarily have deficits in actual social skills. Rather, the lack of interaction may be due to anxiety caused by negative cognitions. In such cases, an intervention aimed at modifying the negative cognitions will be more appropriate than social skills training.

• Make sure that students receive adequate opportunities to practice newly learned social skills in "real-life" settings, where they are more likely to experience difficulties with social withdrawal or social anxiety.

• If a student's social withdrawal is associated with a more severe anxiety disorder

**TABLE 9.3. A Sample Social Skills Training Script/Outline for Initiating a Conversation with Peers**

**Introduction and problem definition**

- Today we're going to practice the skills we need to start a conversation with another person.
- What is a conversation? (Generate discussion with group members.)
  *Possible answers: (1) talking with another person about something you are both interested in, (2) communicating with another person by speaking and listening.*
- Have you ever noticed someone trying to start a conversation the wrong way? What was that like? (Discuss ineffective ways to start conversations.)
- Why is it important to know how to start conversation in a way that works well? (Assist group members in developing some answers.)
  *Possible answers: (1) so you can make friends, (2) so you can learn about things from other people, (3) so you can tell other people something that is important to you.*

**Identification of solutions**

- This is how you start a conversation:
  Look for a good time to start (don't interrupt).
  Greet the other person (say "Hi").
  Look the other person in the eyes.
  Make sure the other person is listening to you (looking at you).
  Tell the other person what you want to say to him or her.
- Now, I need you to help me go over the steps that I just told you about. What are the things you need to do to start a conversation?
  *Assist group members in identifying the steps; make sure each one is reviewed.*

**Modeling**

- Watch how I begin a conversation with another person using the five steps we just went over.
  *With another adult or one of the student group members acting as the person you want to talk with, model the five steps, both physically and verbally (think aloud).*

**Rehearsal and role play**

- Now I want all of you to practice these skills. First, we need to review the five steps. (Briefly review each of the five steps from a chalkboard or poster.)
- Now you are going to try it.
  *Each student should take a turn at trying out the five steps for beginning a conversation, using other students in the group as the listener, and receiving prompts as needed.*
  *Help students choose realistic situations for the role plays; the coactors for role playing should be as similar as possible to the persons who would be encountered in the actual situation.*

**Provide performance feedback**

- (If the role play was correct and all steps were followed:) That was great!
  *Note the specific steps the student followed correctly.*
- (If the steps were not all followed correctly:) That was a nice try, but there are a few things we still need to work on.
  *Point out the steps that students followed correctly and incorrectly; model the steps needing correction and have the students enact the steps again until they get it right.*

(continued)

**TABLE 9.3.** *(continued)*

---

**Self-instruction and self-evaluation**

- Now, let's practice how to go over these steps by ourselves.
  *Model covert rehearsal for self-instruction and prompting; have students practice the same.*

- Now, let's figure out how we know when we have started a conversation the right way.
  *Provide training for self-evaluation—all the steps were followed, the conversation was successful, and a positive outcome occurred.*

**Training for generalization and maintenance**

- You have done a good job working on the skills for starting a conversation. Each of you should practice these skills over the next few days, and then let the group know how it went when we meet again. What are some situations where you could practice starting a conversation?
  *Help students generate some ideas for situations where they can practice the skill steps—get specific commitments from each student that they will practice and then report on their experience at the next meeting.*

---

(such as social phobia), consider combining social skills training with other interventions as part of a comprehensive treatment program.

In summary, although it may be used for treating students with a wide variety of behavioral, emotional, and social problems, social skills training is a particularly important intervention tool for use with students who exhibit significant problems with anxiety, fear, and social withdrawal. Social skills training may be the primary intervention of choice, or it may be used in conjunction with other interventions within a comprehensive treatment program.

## CONCLUDING COMMENTS

The five intervention approaches detailed in this chapter represent the most fully articulated and refined accomplishments in cognitive and cognitive-behavioral treatment of anxiety disorders of children and youth during the latter two decades of the 20th century. These five approaches have made some important inroads in effective interventions for young people with anxiety problems. Nevertheless, it is important to recognize that the development of the art and science of treatment in this area has just begun. Hopefully, the advances in cognitive applications in treating anxiety disorders of children and youth will continue and the next two decades will include important new developments in this area. Applications of this general approach within school settings are particularly needed and represent an area of tremendous potential importance.

# 10

# Finding More Help

*Referral Guidelines for Mental Health Counseling, Psychiatric Medications, and Alternative Treatments*

## INTRODUCTION AND OVERVIEW

The first nine chapters of this book provide a foundation for understanding depression, anxiety, and related internalizing problems of children and adolescents, a model for assessing these problems, and a comprehensive guide for delivering proven school-based psychoeducational and psychosocial interventions. Any school-based practitioner who learns these strategies and implements them effectively on a regular basis will undoubtedly prove to be a change agent that has positively affected the lives of many students and helped diminish a significant amount of distress. Despite the tremendous promise held by such school-based work, there are times when such work is simply not sufficient to help students who are suffering from *severe* emotional and behavioral problems. There are some obvious natural limits to what can be done in a school setting by a school psychologist, counselor, social worker, or consultant. Although individual and group counseling and psychoeducation to help students deal with social and emotional problems are usually considered to be an appropriate use of resources, few schools are equipped to provide the comprehensive health services that are needed to adequately help students whose problems have become both severe and chronic. Because of this limitation, there are times when it may be necessary to make referrals to professionals outside of the school system for help in dealing with such severe problems. Individual mental health counseling or psychotherapy and psychiatric medications are the most likely services for which outside referrals may need to be made.

This chapter begins with a discussion of the process of making referrals for outside mental health services and addresses several common questions relative to this process.

The bulk of this chapter deals specifically with issues regarding psychiatric medications. The section on medication begins with some basic issues and concerns. Common medications used for depression are discussed first, then common medications for anxiety. Finally, some promising alternative treatments for depression and anxiety are noted, along with cautions regarding the many nonmainstream interventions that offer little more than empty hope.

## MAKING REFERRALS FOR MENTAL HEALTH COUNSELING AND PSYCHIATRIC MEDICATIONS

The process of making referrals for students to receive mental health counseling services or psychiatric medications raises several important questions for school-based practitioners. This section addresses some of these common questions.

## When Should I Make a Referral?

A general recommendation for school-based practitioners who are working with students with depression, anxiety, and related problems is that, whenever possible, school-based psychosocial and psychoeducational interventions should be tried before making referrals for outside mental health counseling or psychiatric services. However, school-based interventions of the amount and quality needed to help students are not always possible. There may be issues such as lack of professional training or expertise, excessive caseloads, lack of administrative support, problems with confidentiality, or excessive severity of social–emotional problems that require additional outside help.

### Mental Health Counseling

Most school-based practitioners work in situations in which the counseling and psychoeducational intervention services they provide are developmental in nature, supportive of the overall goal of academic progress, and time-limited. In such situations, it may be necessary to make a referral for outside mental health counseling or psychotherapy. How does outside mental health counseling differ from the counseling a school-based practitioner might provide to individual students or groups of students within a school setting? Actually, there are more similarities than differences. The two main differences will likely be the training of the practitioner and the length of time available for sessions. Most individual therapy sessions in private practice or mental health sessions are approximately 1 hour long, but school practitioners may find their caseload and time demands too great to spend that much time working with an individual student on a regular basis. Independent mental health specialists, especially psychologists, psychiatrists, and social workers, are more likely than most school-based practitioners to have extensive training and experience in identifying and dealing with abnormal behavior. Thus, the right independent mental health specialist may be able to provide more intensive services to students than those typically available in schools. With these two primary differences noted, *consider making a referral for outside individual mental health counseling when two or more of the following circumstances are present*:

- The problem symptoms are severe.
- The problem symptoms are chronic or long-standing.
- The problems appear to interfere significantly with the student's personal and academic adjustment.
- There is significant concern that the student may harm him- or herself or somebody else.
- It is not possible to implement the needed intervention services within the school setting.
- School-based interventions have been implemented but have not resulted in adequate improvement in the problem symptoms.
- The student of concern is willing, motivated, and has sufficient maturity and verbal skills to participate in direct, intensive counseling.
- The student's parents are willing to seek such additional help.

## Psychiatric Medications

An additional form of outside professional help for behavioral, social, and emotional problems is prescription and management of psychiatric medications to help alleviate symptoms. The empirical evidence supporting the use of psychiatric medications for children and youth with internalizing problems is not necessarily any stronger than the evidence in favor of psychological interventions. Medication should not necessarily be viewed as the "best" or most powerful option. Yet there are definitely times when such help is of great potential benefit for the student and their family. *Consider making a referral for evaluation of psychiatric medication when two or more of the following circumstances are present*:

- The problem symptoms are severe.
- The problem symptoms are chronic or long-standing.
- The problems appear to interfere significantly with the student's personal and academic adjustment.
- There is significant concern that the student may harm him- or herself or somebody else.
- The student exhibits possible symptoms of psychotic behavior (such as auditory or visual hallucinations, abnormal or disconnected thought processes, or highly bizarre social–emotional behavior).
- School-based interventions have been implemented but have not resulted in adequate improvement in the problem symptoms.
- There is a strong family history of mental health problems.
- There are possible health or medical complications to the social–emotional problems.
- The student's parents are willing to seek such additional help.

*Services Are Not Mutually Exclusive*

As you can see in the two previous lists of reasons to make an outside referral, a substantial amount of overlap exists among the reasons for making referrals for mental health counseling services or psychiatric medications. It is important to remember that the two types of services are not necessarily mutually exclusive. In other words, it is not always a matter of deciding on one type of service versus the other type. Also, consider that there is not an exact science for deciding when to refer for additional services. When you are faced with situations in which you feel that a student may require more help than can be provided in the school setting, consider the concerns noted in the two lists, consult with a colleague, and make a referral decision based on what you believe is in the best interest of your student.

## Who Provides Services?

Counseling or psychotherapy services for children and adolescents may be provided outside of school settings by a wide array of professionals. The most likely professionals to provide such services include psychologists, social workers, psychiatrists, marriage and family therapists, and mental health counselors. Psychiatric medications may be prescribed only by licensed physicians and, in some cases, by nurse practitioners or physician's assistants.

## Medical Generalist or a Specialist?

When making referrals to medical professionals for help with psychiatric medications, one of the issues you will need to consider is whether the referral should be to a generalist or a specialist. Because many of the newer psychiatric medications are relatively safe in comparison with the previous generation of medications, most prescriptions are written by primary care physicians, such as family practice doctors, pediatricians, or internists. For medication evaluation in general or straightforward cases of depression or anxiety, there is no reason the referral could not be made to the student's primary care physician. In rural areas, specialists such as child psychiatrists may be very difficult to find, and such a referral may necessitate a long time on a waiting list and travel difficulties for the family. Therefore, *the primary care physician should always be involved to some extent.* However, referrals should be made to specialists (i.e., psychiatrists) whenever the symptoms are complex or involve an array of psychiatric or medical problems. For example, if a child who was being treated for ADHD through the use of a stimulant medication developed a serious and treatment-resistant internalizing disorder, referral to a psychiatrist might be needed. And without question, the presence of psychotic symptoms, such as delusions of thinking, detachment from reality, or visual or auditory hallucinations, should precipitate a referral to a psychiatrist rather than to a primary care physician. When in doubt, it is advisable to refer to the primary care provider, who can then refer to a medical colleague if needed, or at least to consult with him or her about the situation.

## How Do I Find a Good Referral Source?

If you are new to a community or to a particular professional position, you may not be aware of the best sources for mental health counseling or psychiatric medication referrals. *The best way to develop a list of potential referral sources is to ask trusted colleagues with whom you work.* They are likely to have developed relationships with practitioners who have provided good care to students referred by them. Such colleagues can often advise you regarding some of the particular matters of which you should be aware in making such referrals.

If you are working without the benefit of a large cadre of colleagues with whom to consult about medical referrals, consider making an appointment to visit with some medical and mental health practitioners who work with children and their families in your community. Introduce yourself as a professional who might be a potential source of referrals to their practice, and take the opportunity to find out their limitations and preferences for practice, as well as their general style of working with children and adolescents.

## What Can I Do to Facilitate the Referral?

If you are a school-based practitioner, there are most likely three things you can do to facilitate a referral for medication evaluation:

- If you are not experienced in making medication referrals, you should *consult with more experienced colleagues* regarding the particular case with which you are concerned. Such consultation can be helpful in determining whether a referral is warranted and perhaps identify potential referral sources.
- It will almost always be absolutely necessary to *meet with the parents of the student* with whom you are working to discuss your concerns and to determine whether they are willing to consider such a referral.
- A brief, *written referral letter or memo*, perhaps one to two pages in length, to the outside practitioner can be of great help in facilitating treatment. Such a letter should contain a concise description of your concerns and observations, as well as a brief history of the problem and a summary of any relevant assessment or treatment information that you may have. Because a physician may only see the child in his or her office for a few minutes, your letter can be a huge help in piecing together some of the relevant bits of information that may not be obvious during the office visit. Of course, it will be necessary to obtain the appropriate consent and permission from the parents to release information prior to sending such a referral letter.

## Whose Financial Responsibility Is It?

Several years ago, when students were referred by school personnel for outside mental health or medical services, there was seldom any question regarding whose financial responsibility it was to pay for these services. It was simply assumed that any costs incurred would be the family's financial responsibility. However, new education laws, court rulings, and changes in public expectations during the past two to three decades have made the situation more complex for educators and support service professionals. Beginning in 1977, with the initial enactment of the Education for All Handicapped Children Act (EHA, or Public Law 94-142), the scope of what is considered to be a "free and appropriate public education" for students with disabilities has broadened considerably. Although most rules and regulations for implementing this law initially made it fairly clear that medical treatment and mental health counseling for students with disabilities would not be considered the financial responsibility of the schools, later court decisions and modifications of the law through congressional reauthorization carved out some new territory. Although this particular issue changes constantly and is more complex than can be dealt with adequately here, there is an important main point: Increasingly, some parents may legitimately feel that their child with a disability (e.g., a serious emotional disturbance) may be entitled to have the school pay the cost of psychiatric or other mental health services when school personnel make the initial referral. This issue is particularly complex in some states that require a psychiatric evaluation (paid for by the school district) prior to a student being classified as emotionally disturbed for special education eligibility purposes. What about the cost of any medications that are recommended, and what about the cost of continuing treatment?

Although the Individuals with Disabilities Education Act and various higher court decisions have not *specifically indicated* that schools are required to pay the cost of psychiatric medications and outside mental health services for students with disabilities, many financially strapped school systems are understandably concerned about this possibility. As a result, it is not uncommon to find that school administrators at both the local and state level are implementing official or unofficial policies prohibiting school personnel from making referrals to families for mental health or medical services for their children such as psychotherapy, family counseling, and evaluation for psychiatric medications for depression, anxiety, ADHD, and so forth. The reasoning behind such policies is that if the referral is made by the school, then the parents of the student may contend that the school is responsible for paying for services, because the school has initiated the process. In my travels around the United States to conduct professional training workshops, I have been told by numerous school psychologists, counselors, and social workers in several states that they work in a type of climate in which they are discouraged, or even forbidden, from making referrals for outside services they believe might be beneficial. Such policies are understandably frustrating because in so many instances, professionals feel a conflict between what they think is best for a child, and how their administrator is encouraging or requiring them to behave.

There is no simple solution to this dilemma. The schools and the parents both have legitimate points of view that can be taken into consideration when conflicts occur over payment for psychiatric evaluations and medications. It is essential for school-based practitioners to work out situations such as this with their administrators, so that they can provide appropriate referral services without feeling that their jobs may be threatened. To avoid making a referral for additional services when it is clear that the student needs them is both unethical and *not* in the best interest of the student. If we believe the axiom that our first responsibility to our clients is to "do no harm," then it is essential that we must be able to discuss with families the services that may be needed to help their children who are in distress.

One possible way around this legalistic dilemma is to work out with your administrator a procedure for "suggesting" that parents consider particular services for their child as opposed to making a mandate or specific referral that may take on the appearance that the school requires such services. In other words, the way that the referral suggestion is made may be a key to whether it will be acceptable to budget- and lawsuit-conscious administrators, as well as to parents. For example, rather than stating, "We feel that you must take your daughter to see a doctor to get a prescription for an antidepressant medication," the issue could be stated in the following manner: "We are really concerned that your daughter's depression is getting worse even though we are working very hard to try and help. You may want to consider taking her to see her pediatrician to see if there are any medical reasons for the depression, or any medical treatments that might help." Such small tactics might help all interested parties to work together for the good of the child rather than to engage in conflict over financial interests. See Table 10.1 for recommendations on when to make outside referrals.

## USING MEDICATIONS TO TREAT CHILDREN'S SOCIAL–EMOTIONAL PROBLEMS: SOME BASIC ISSUES AND CONCERNS

Two or three decades ago, the use of psychoactive medications (prescription drugs designed to alter psychological functioning) to treat children's emotional and psychiatric disorders was a very controversial practice. The available medications during those years were generally not sufficiently tested for use with children and often posed significant health risks. Furthermore, specific cognitive-behavioral and related psychosocial treatments had not yet been refined for use with children. The most popular psychodynamic-based interventions emphasized dealing with unresolved conflicts and traumas from earlier developmental stages. In subsequent years, the development and field-testing of new medications, coupled with increasing dissatisfaction over the traditional psychosocial treatment choices, resulted in a more widespread use and acceptance of psychiatric medications for children and youth. Today, there are still some controversies regarding this practice but the professional community and lay public alike have generally accepted the use of psychiatric medications for young people. Additionally, the available treatment evidence, though more sparse for children than for adults, has provided reasonable evidence that many medications may be effective in treating the symptoms of internalizing and other disorders of childhood and adolescence. Despite these advances and the increased acceptance of using psychiatric medications with children and adolescents, there are still a number of important concerns to consider. This section briefly addresses some of the more common concerns and problems that school-based practitioners may have regarding psy-

**TABLE 10.1. Recommendations for When to Make Outside Referrals for Mental Health Counseling Services or Psychiatric Medications**

| Mental health counseling | Psychiatric medications |
|---|---|
| *Consider making a referral for outside individual mental health counseling or psychotherapy when two or more of the following circumstances are present:* | *Consider making a referral for evaluation of psychiatric medication needs when two or more of the following circumstances are present:* |
| • The problem symptoms are severe. | • The problem symptoms are severe. |
| • The problem symptoms are chronic or long-standing. | • The problem symptoms are chronic or long-standing. |
| • The problems appear to interfere significantly with the student's personal and academic adjustment. | • The problems appear to interfere significantly with the student's personal and academic adjustment. |
| • There is significant concern that the student may harm him- or herself or somebody else. | • There is significant concern that the student may harm him- or herself or somebody else. |
| • School-based interventions have been implemented but have not resulted in adequate improvement in the problem symptoms. | • The student exhibits possible symptoms of psychotic behavior (such as auditory or visual hallucinations, abnormal or disconnected thought processes, or highly bizarre social–emotional behavior). |
| • The student of concern is willing, motivated, and has sufficient maturity and verbal skills to participate in direct intensive counseling. | • School-based interventions have been implemented but have not resulted in adequate improvement in the problem symptoms. |
| • The student's parents are willing to seek such additional help. | • There is a strong family history of mental health problems. |
| • It is not possible to implement the needed intervention services within the school setting. | • There are possible health or medical complications to the social–emotional problems. |
| | • The student's parents are willing to seek such additional help. |

chiatric medications, including excessive and unnecessary use, adverse reactions and effects, labeling and stigmatization, and parental opposition.

## Excessive and Unnecessary Use of Medication

One of the most common concerns in this area is that psychiatric medications are being used excessively and unnecessarily with children and adolescents. A drug given to a child for the purpose of keeping him or her calm and quiet, or otherwise reducing overtly disruptive or disturbing symptoms, is inappropriate when it is given to compensate for a lack of attention or interest from parents or teachers. Likewise, using medications to avoid inconveniencing parents or teachers whose attention and effort might otherwise help deal with the problems is a particularly poor use of psychopharmacology. Additionally, use of excessive dosages of specific medications, or combined use of several medications to remove symptoms, beyond what is in the best interests of the child, is a highly questionable strategy.

## Adverse Reactions and Effects

Another common concern is the negative physical effects that might result from psychiatric medications. Most of these medications provoke short-term side effects, some of which may be quite unpleasant. Although most psychiatric medications used with children and adolescents are not considered to be addicting, there are some exceptions (i.e., the benzodiazepines), and some medications may be difficult to reduce or eliminate after prolonged use. The long-term developmental effects of many psychiatric medications with children are simply unknown. For example, a medication that has been developed for the treatment of depression, field-tested, and approved for use with adults might also be frequently used with children on an experimental basis, particularly when other treatment choices have not worked or are otherwise not a valid option. Parents and mental health professionals need to understand that although such practices are common, they are indeed experimental, and one can only hope that there will be no untoward long-term effects on the development of the child.

## Labeling and Stigmatization

An additional, common concern related to using psychiatric medications for students' emotional and behavioral problems is that of being labeled or stigmatized. Students who take antidepressants, antianxiety agents, or other psychiatric medications may feel embarrassed or ashamed of using them. Parents may likewise feel that there is a negative stigma attached to their child's problems being "medicalized" or "pathologized," and may avoid disclosing the fact that their child is "on drugs" even to extended family members or close friends. Certainly, many of these concerns must relate to the history of misunderstanding, poor treatment, and social stigmatization regarding mental health problems in general as opposed to nonpsychological medical problems. However, such concerns must be recognized and respected, and it is simply foolish to dismiss them as unimportant.

## What If the Parents Are Opposed to Using Medications?

For a variety of reasons, many parents may be opposed in principle to the idea of having their child take psychiatric medications for treatment of behavioral and emotional problems. Some parents, because of their religious or philosophical convictions, may oppose medical treatment in general. Other parents may be concerned about possible adverse reactions or side effects, or unproven effectiveness of such medications. Because of the stigma that still seems to be attached to having psychological or mental health problems (as opposed to "physical" problems), some parents may disagree with the idea of treating emotional or behavioral problems with medicine, believing that it is a sign of "weakness," or may feel that if they just give the child more attention, change his or her diet, pray, or make some other changes in the child's life, then the problems can be resolved without medication. Although each practitioner who faces parental opposition to the suggestion that a student be considered for psychiatric medication treatment will have a unique reaction to the reasons for the opposition, it is important always to treat the parents' concerns seriously and respectfully. Dismissing their concerns as "superstitious," "ignorant," or "paranoid" will do nothing to help the student. The best course of action to take in such situations is to listen respectfully to the parents' concerns, try to address these concerns by educating parents regarding the process, and the potential benefits and risks of medication, encouraging them, and realizing that the final decision rests with the family. The only situations in which a school or mental health agency should consider actively challenging parents' decision not to allow their child to receive a medication is when there is reasonable evidence that failure to do so will likely put the child's life or health in serious jeopardy. Thankfully, such instances are rare; however, they do happen.

Each of the areas of concern addressed in this section may present very real barriers to the effective use psychiatric medications for depression, anxiety, or related internalizing problems with children and youth. Despite such inevitable challenges, in many situations, the use of such medications is truly the best alternative under the circumstances. Practitioners who are sensitive to these concerns and work respectfully and gently with students and their parents to address them will find that their efforts often result in the child obtaining the kind of help and support that is needed.

## MEDICATIONS FOR TREATMENT OF DEPRESSION

The most widespread use of medications to treat internalizing problems is for depression. This section includes brief descriptions of two classes of antidepressant medications, the tricyclic antidepressants (TCAs) and selective serotonin reuptake inhibitors (SSRIs). These two types of antidepressants are perhaps the best known and most widely used with children and youth. Additionally, included is a brief description of some other types of medications used to treat depression in young persons. As is true for this chapter in general, these descriptions are very brief and not technical or detailed. If you are interested in learning more about psychiatric medications, consult specific sources in this area. Before reading about specific medications in this section, please note that in cases where the brand name of a medication is noted, the first letter is capitalized, whereas when a medicine is referred to by its generic name, the first letter is lowercase. Some medications, such as imipramine, are more commonly referred to by their generic name. Other medications, such as Prozac or Xanax, are more commonly referred to by their brand name. In most instances in this chapter, both the brand and generic names of medications are used.

### Tricyclic Antidepressants

The first class of effective psychiatric medications developed for use in treating depression was the TCAs. These medications are no longer as popular as they were prior to the mid-

1980s because of the development of newer, safer drugs with fewer side effects that are equally or more effective. However, the TCAs have been used to treat depression in children and youth as well as adults for many years and continue to be used for this purpose in particular cases in which the child does not respond well to other treatments. In fact, many published studies in the child and adolescent psychiatry literature have documented the effectiveness of TCAs for treating internalizing disorders and related problems with children and youth. Some of the TCAs that are most commonly used with children include amitriptyline (Elavil), desipramine (Norpramine), imipramine (Tofranil), nortriptyline (Pamelor), and amoxapine (Doxepin).

Although the TCAs have been proven effective in reducing symptoms of depression and other related problems, their major drawback is the high incidence of adverse reactions and side effects they produce. The most common side effects of TCAs include dry mouth, drowsiness, blurred vision, constipation, decreased cognition, nightmares, and sleeping problems. In some cases, TCA use has been found to produce increased anxiety, seizures, and cardiac arrhythmia (irregular heartbeat). When used with individuals who have psychotic disorders (schizophrenia), TCAs may sometimes produce a worsening of conditions such as increased rate and intensity of delusions. Perhaps the most serious problem with TCAs is the very real threat of severe, even life-threatening reactions, from an overdose. Regarding overdoses and severe adverse reactions, it has been noted that children are more vulnerable to adverse and toxic reactions from TCAs than adults (Del Mundo, Pumariega, & Vance, 1999).

Even though TCAs are not as popular as they once were, because of the adverse reaction and side-effects problems, they are still used in certain cases and are a potentially useful intervention alternative when other treatments have not been effective, or when there is a complicated constellation of symptoms. For example, TCAs, especially imipramine, have been shown to exert broad therapeutic effects with children and adolescents and have been used successfully for treating bedwetting and other manifestations of enuresis, ADHD, sleep disorders, school phobia, and general anxiety disorders. Educators and mental health practitioners who work with children and youth who are taking a TCA under the care of a physician should be vigilant in observing and reporting any possible adverse reactions or side effects and also be aware that discontinuing use of TCAs must be done slowly, because of the possibility of negative reactions. Because TCAs are potentially lethal in an overdose, special care should be used in storing and dispensing these medications.

## Selective Serotonin Reuptake Inhibitors

The class of drugs that has become most notable and widely used in recent years for treating depression and related internalizing problems is the SSRIs. Prozac (fluoxetine), the first SSRI approved by the U.S. Food and Drug Administration (FDA), was introduced in the mid- to late 1980s, and very quickly became one of the most widely prescribed medications in the nation. The immediate widespread use of Prozac in the United States became evident in the intense media coverage it received, the use of the word Prozac in everyday language of typical Americans, and the success and impact of several popular books relating to the phenomenon, such as *Listening to Prozac* (Kramer, 1993) and *Talking Back to Prozac* (Breggin & Breggin, 1995). Following the launching of Prozac, other SSRIs were introduced in subsequent years, including Zoloft (sertraline), Paxil (paroxetine), Luvox (fluvoxamine), and Celexa (citalopram), and most of these medications have also become widely prescribed.

The widespread popularity of SSRIs is due in great measure to the fact that these medications are relatively effective in reducing the symptoms of depression and several related problems, without posing the same degree of risk from adverse reactions, side effects, and overdoses as the TCAs. Most comparative studies have indicated that SSRIs are equally as effective (or in some cases, more effective) as TCAs, but they seem to have less intense or obvious risks. For example, current evidence indicates that overdoses of SSRIs are very unlikely to be lethal or to produce severe permanent harm, whereas overdoses of TCAs are potentially life threatening. Also, the most common side effects of SSRIs, which include nausea, headache, diarrhea, insomnia, dry mouth, and sexual dysfunction (usually in males), tend to not be as severe or varied in most cases as the common adverse effects of TCAs. Another reason for the popularity of the SSRIs involves their ease of administration. Most persons who use SSRIs take a single dose daily, a much simpler endeavor than the twice- or three-times-daily schedule that is sometimes required with particular TCAs.

Although it is no overstatement to say that the SSRIs have had a major impact on the treatment of depression and other internalizing disorders, and that they might even be considered revolutionary medications, it is important to understand their limitations and to avoid the belief that these drugs are without problems. The percentage of depressed persons whose symptoms are noticeably improved by using SSRIs is probably about the same as that for TCAs—maybe 60–75% at best, a widely cited range. Therefore, understand that a significant percentage of persons, maybe one-third or more, will not be helped by these medications. Another potential problem is that although the side effects of SSRIs are fewer and less serious than those of TCAs, they are pronounced in some individuals, who simply cannot tolerate them. Finally, consider that with few exceptions, the SSRIs were initially developed and approved for use with adults rather than children and youth. Although there are some specific situations in which the FDA has approved some SSRIs for use with children and adolescents, most uses of these medications with young persons are based on the clinical experience of physicians rather than a long-term collection of studies. Given that SSRIs are a relatively new class of medications, it is unclear whether any long-term developmental problems will result from their continued use with children and youth. In Table 10.2, the five SSRIs presently available in the United States are listed, with additional information on their common uses and some potential problems.

## Other Medications for Treating Depression

In addition to the TCAs and SSRIs, other medications are sometimes used to treat depression and some closely related problems. Wellbutrin (bupropion), a relatively new

**TABLE 10.2. The SSRIs: Common Uses and Unique Characteristics**

| Medication | Most common uses | Some unique characteristics |
| --- | --- | --- |
| Prozac (fluoxetine) | Depression, eating disorders, obsessive–compulsive disorder | May produce agitation or irritability in some persons; remains in the body for at least 2 weeks. |
| Zoloft (sertraline) | Depression, obsessive–compulsive disorder, panic disorder | Remains in the body for at least 1 week. |
| Paxil (paroxetine) | Depression, obsessive–compulsive disorder, panic disorder, social phobia | Produces drowsiness or sedation in many persons. |
| Luvox (fluvoxamine) | Obsessive–compulsive disorder | Has been approved by the FDA for treating children with obsessive–compulsive disorder. |
| Celexa (citalopram) | Depression | Is thought to have fewer side effects and produce fewer adverse interactions with other drugs than other SSRIs. |

medication used to treat depression in particular circumstances, appears to have a more favorable side-effect profile than the TCAs. Wellbutrin, most commonly used with adults and adolescents, is increasingly being used to treat children who exhibit depression and, in some cases, children with ADHD characteristics. It is also used in cases where youngsters do not respond well to SSRIs. Other, newer medications that are sometimes used for treating depression in children and youth include Effexor (venlafaxine) and Remeron (mirtazapine). Both these medications are thought to have better side-effect profiles than TCAs and, like Wellbutrin, may be useful in particular cases of depression that do not respond well to other treatments, or when individuals cannot tolerate SSRIs. An older class of antidepressant is the monoamine oxidase inhibitors (MAOIs), such as Nardil, Parnate, and Marplan. Although these medications have been shown to be effective and are occasionally used with children and adolescents, such use is usually not recommended, and their adverse reactions and interactions with other drugs and certain foods are well known.

For depression that occurs in conjunction with intense mood swings, some rather specific types of medications are often used. The best known of these mood-stabilizing medications is lithium, which is often used to treat bipolar mood disorders. Although lithium is known for significant side effects and possible toxic reactions when its levels are too high in the bloodstream, it is clearly the best documented medication for treating bipolar mood disorders. More recently, Depakote (valproic acid or divalproex), originally developed to treat seizure disorders, has been used to treat severe mood swings and depression that is resistant to treatment or occurs in conjunction with other mood disorders. Like lithium, Depakote may produce numerous side effects and be toxic in an overdose. Therefore, its use is not nearly as widespread as that of the SSRIs, and it is more likely to be prescribed by psychiatrists than by primary care physicians.

# MEDICATIONS FOR ANXIETY-RELATED PROBLEMS

Like antidepressants, several classes of medication are commonly used for treating the symptoms of various anxiety-related problems. This section includes brief reviews of the benzodiazepines, antihistamines, SSRIs, TCAs, and Buspar, a newer drug that does not fit into any of the other specific classes. Again, in most cases, both the brand (first letter capitalized) and generic names for each medication are listed.

## Benzodiazepines

The benzodiazepines are a class of drugs that include such well-known medications as Valium (diazepam), Xanax (alprazolam), Ativan (lorazepam), Klonopin (clonazepam), and Tranxene (clorazepate), to name a few. This class of medications was first introduced into clinical practice in the United States in the 1960s and until about 1980 had the same rapid and widespread popular impact across the nation that the SSRIs would later have when Prozac was introduced.

Although each benzodiazepine has unique characteristics, they share several common properties: They tend to be relatively fast acting and are generally very effective in reducing muscle tension and spasms, nervousness, agitation, and insomnia. They are also effective in reducing various somatic symptoms, they usually produce drowsiness and an overall state of relaxation. The psychiatry literature contains convincing evidence regarding the effectiveness of benzodiazepines for short-term relief of anxiety-related symptoms. Some benzodiazepines are used primarily to treat and prevent panic disorder; others are primarily for treating general anxiety problems, and still others are used mainly for treating insomnia. The strength of the medicine prescribed (i.e., the number of milligrams of the medication in one tablet) is also a factor in determining which specific manifestations of anxiety are treated.

Although benzodiazepines are not as widely used as they were two decades ago, they are still popular because of their relatively favorable side-effect profile and their ability to relieve anxiety symptoms very quickly. These drugs are used mainly with adults, but children and adolescents seem to respond to them in a generally similar manner. Although they are usually very effective for short-term relief of anxiety symptoms, there are some very good reasons why they should not be considered the initial treatment of choice or even be used at all with most children and youth. When used with certain children, these drugs may produce the opposite reaction to what is desired or expected, an effect called *disinhibition*. When this reaction occurs, the child's agitation, anxiousness, sleeplessness, and so forth, tend to be aggravated rather than improved. Another concern in using benzodiazepines is that they can easily become habit-forming, and perhaps addicting. Once individuals have taken a benzodiazepine on a regular basis (say, daily) for a relatively long period of time (say, several months or a year), it is difficult to get them off the drug because anxiety symptoms may worsen and, in some cases, withdrawal-like symptoms may occur (such as sweating, diarrhea, pain, and even convulsions). Therefore, cessation of the drug is usually achieved by tapering the dosage very gradually and adding other nonaddicting drugs (such as antihistamines) during the tapering period to reduce the rebound of symptoms. Children and adolescents with a propensity for substance abuse problems are particularly poor candidates for treatment with benzodiazepines. As a practical matter, these medications can be a complicated treatment choice because of the drowsiness or sleepiness they often produce.

All things considered, benzodiazepines may provide a significant reduction in severe anxiety-related symptoms in children and youth when used properly. However, because of the problems that have been mentioned, these medications are usually not the first treatment of choice and their use should generally be for a short period of time to help with immediate relief of significant symptoms.

## Antihistamines

Although many people find this fact surprising, antihistamines, such as Benadryl (diphenhydramine) and hydroxyzine, were among the earliest medications used in treating emotionally troubled youngsters (Green, 1991). Although these medications are intended primarily to be used for treating seasonal allergies to molds, spores, pollens, and so forth, they are often used for treating anxiety-related problems. The main reason that some antihistamines arc used for this purpose is the well-know side effects that they produce. As virtually any allergy-sufferer will testify, most antihistamines are noted for causing drowsiness, sleepiness, and a general state of relaxation. Because of these properties, they are usually very effective for short-term treatment of agitation, insomnia, and the general state of nervousness or overarousal that often accompany anxiety. Antihistamines are also used to treat the sleeplessness or insomnia that may be a side effect of other medications, such as some of the SSRIs. Another benefit of many antihistamines is that they are quite safe and produce few interactions with other medications. However, some antihistamines can potentially produce negative interactions with other medicines. As a practical matter, antihistamines should generally be used for only short-term relief of symptoms because of the substantial drowsiness they usually produce (Wilens, 1999). Although parents can purchase several antihistamines (such as Benadryl) "over the counter," without a prescription, because of some of their potential negative effects, parents should not be encouraged to do so without first consulting their family physician.

## Selective Serotonin Reuptake Inhibitors

Although the SSRIs are usually thought of as antidepressants, some of these medications are known to be quite effective in treating anxiety-related symptoms, such as panic attacks, agitation, sleeplessness, general overarousal, obsessive–compulsive disorders, and even social phobia (see Table 10.2). Of the five SSRIs that were discussed in the section on medications for depressions, Zoloft and Paxil seem to be the most effective for treating anxiety symptoms, and Luvox seems to be a good treatment for obsessive–compulsive symptoms. Although they are usually not considered to be as effective as the benzodiazepines for treatment of general anxiety-related problems (Wilens, 1999), they are often the best choice, because they are not habit forming and may produce fewer adverse reactions or side effects. They are also an excellent treatment choice in cases where anxiety and depression symptoms co-occur, or when there are some very specific types of anxiety problems present, such as obsessive–compulsive behavior. Physicians who use SSRIs to treat anxiety symptoms usually start patients on lower doses of the medication and increase it gradually, because of the possibility that it may actually produce a worsening of anxiety symptoms in some instances.

## Tricyclic Antidepressants

Like the SSRIs, the TCAs are primarily thought of as medication for treating depression, but they are also known to have a broad therapeutic effect and can be quite effective in treating some types of anxiety problems. For example, imipramine has been used successfully for treating general anxiety symptoms and insomnia, and desipramine has been used successfully in treating panic disorders. Anafranil (clomipramine) is a TCA that has been shown to be especially useful for the treatment of obsessive–compulsive disorder. Although they may be quite effective for these purposes, the TCAs should be considered a second or third choice for treating anxiety-related problems, because of the potential for significant side effects and adverse reactions, as discussed in the section on using TCAs to treat depression. However, they may be an excellent choice in situations where anxiety symptoms co-occur with depression or ADHD, or when other treatments are not successful.

## Buspar

An additional medication that is used to treat anxiety-related problems in particular instances is Buspar (buspirone). This medication is a newer and somewhat novel drug that is quite different from the other drugs reviewed in this section. The advantages of Buspar include the fact that it tends to not produce extreme drowsiness and it has a very low potential for abuse or addiction, and a generally favorable side-effect profile. However, Buspar is not thought to be as effective as the benzodiazepines in treating serious symptoms (Wilens, 1999) and may have to be taken as many as three times a day. It is often used in conjunction with the SSRIs and is thought to enhance the properties of these medications in some instances for treating children with ADHD, aggressive behaviors, and serious developmental disorders.

## ALTERNATIVE INTERVENTIONS

It is important to recognize that mental health counseling services and psychiatric medications are not parents' only choices when it comes to seeking additional help for their children outside of the school setting. In fact, you might be surprised to know how many alternative treatments are actually purported to help alleviate symptoms of depression and anxiety. With a quick trip to your local supermarket or pharmacy and a little looking around, you will likely find a surprising array of products, ranging from herb-infused soft drinks and food supplements to homeopathic preparations touted as being helpful in promoting calmness, relaxation, and enhancing mood. Also, a number of possible intervention techniques outside of the mainstream mental health and medical fields are purported to help with these problems. It is impossible to evaluate fully all of these alternatives. Many of them, in my opinion, are little more than modern-day "snake oil" remedies that offer no more than a placebo effect at best, and some even cross the boundaries of rationality and move into the realm of the bizarre. There is also the possibility that some alternative treatments, such as various herbal preparations, may actually produce a treatment effect, as well as unwanted side effects and interactions. Parents of students with whom you work may feel the need to explore some or even many of these alternatives. It is important to be respectful to parents, but avoid recommending or encouraging alternative treatments for which there is no supporting evidence. However, within the general realm of alternative treatments are two that actually have received a surprising amount of support, and with which you may wish to become familiar. These two alternatives, St. John's wort for reducing depression and anxiety, and light therapy for treating seasonable depression, are discussed briefly in this final section of the chapter.

## St. John's Wort: Nature's Mood Enhancer?

St. John's wort (*Hypericum perforatum*) is an herbal preparation that has been used for at least 300 years in Europe as a treatment for mood problems (depression and anxiety), particularly in Germany, where it is very popular. During the past decade, St. John's wort has become increasingly popular in the United States and has been touted as a "natural antidepressant," or "nature's Prozac." A quick visit to most pharmacies, health food stores, and nutritional supplement centers in the United States will probably result in easily locating a display of St. John's wort.

Several well-controlled studies conducted in Germany over the past several years have concluded that St. John's wort is reasonably effective (i.e., more effective than a placebo) in treating mild to moderate symptoms of depression (Rosenthal, 1998a). The specific mechanisms of action are presently unknown. Currently, several studies are under way in the United States to replicate these findings and to identify optimum treatment doses. The most common recommended dosage for using St. John's wort to treat depression is to take a 300-milligram capsule of the preparation three times daily. However, it is unclear whether this dosage is optimum in various cases, or what factors should be taken into consideration in modifying the dosage. There seems to be a general consensus that St. John's wort produces fewer side effects than conventional antidepressants, and that individuals who take it should gradually build up to the full dosing schedule over a period of several weeks to avoid adverse reactions.

Despite the fairly impressive array of anecdotal evidence and some empirical evidence supporting the use of St. John's wort, there are also some lingering questions and concerns. Virtually all of the literature on St. John's wort has focused on its uses with adults rather than children or adolescents, and very little is known about both optimum dosing schedules for children and long-term effects or potential for adverse reactions. Because St. John's wort is considered to be a nutritional supplement rather than a drug, its manufacture and distribution are not monitored by any federal agencies, such as the FDA. Therefore, this preparation is produced and marketed by a startling large number of entrepreneurs, which raises questions regarding equivalency of potency or purity of the substance across different manufacturers. Because St. John's wort cannot be patented, pharmaceutical corporations have little financial incentive to research its effects and to seek FDA approval for its use as an antidepressant medication.

In summary, there seems to be a reasonable amount of evidence that St. John's wort may be effective in treating mild to moderate symptoms of depression in many individuals. Therefore, parents who choose to use this herbal preparation as a treatment option for a depressed child or adolescent may find that it will provide some symptomatic relief. However, it is important to realize that there are many questions that remain unanswered at the present time, and the same cautions should be used with St. John's wort as with conventional medications. Ideally, it should be administered under the direction of a health care provider who is knowledgeable about the preparation and its possible side effects. School-based practitioners should avoid specifically recommending or *prescribing* St. John's wort, but should become familiar with it, so they can work effectively with families who consider using it.

## Using Light Therapy to Treat Seasonal Depression

A relatively new treatment for mood disorders (particularly depression) that occur in a seasonal pattern is the use of light therapy. This treatment is becoming increasingly popular because of its documented effectiveness, ease of use, and lack of adverse reactions or side effects.

It is becoming increasingly understood that in some cases, there is a "seasonal" pattern to affective disorders, particularly depression; that is, symptoms may be more likely to emerge or worsen during particular seasons of the year. Norman Rosenthal, a research scientist at the National Institutes of Mental Health, is generally considered to be the preeminent authority on light therapy. He has compiled much of what is known on this topic in his excellent book, *Winter Blues: Seasonal Affective Disorder—What It Is and How to Overcome It* (Rosenthal, 1998b). He discusses the three primary causes for seasonal patterns of depression: *inherent vulnerability* (genetic and biological factors), *light deprivation* (lack of exposure to direct sunlight because of environmental or lifestyle constraints), and *stressful events*. For persons living in North America, the most common seasonal pattern of depression occurs in winter. Symptoms are worse during the winter months, and better during the summer months. In regions farther north of the equator (e.g., Minnesota as opposed to Texas), more people appear to experience adverse effects of seasonal patterns of depression, and those who are impacted may be impacted more severely. Rosenthal has estimated that in northern latitudes of the United States, and in Canada, as many as 20% to nearly 30% of the population may be adversely affected during the winter months, and between 5% and 10% of the population in these areas may actually suffer from a full-blown seasonal affective disorder (SAD).

Although the research in this area has focused mainly on adults, a few published studies have indicated that the same general risk factors and patterns appear to hold for children and adolescents (e.g., Giedd, Swedo, Lowe, & Rosenthal, 1998). However, *the incidence of seasonal patterns of depression and other affective problems appears to increase dramatically with the onset of adolescence*, and particularly during the high school years. The best evidence to date indicates that only about 1% of children in the early elementary grades suffer from SAD, but "by the senior year of high school, approximately 5 percent of schoolchildren report seasonal problems severe enough to qualify them as suffering from SAD" (Rosenthal, 1998b, p. 77). Thus, school practitioners should consider SAD or "winter worsening" a relatively small concern in the early elementary years that increases significantly by the high school years.

Treatment of SAD and winter worsening symptoms can include various types of interventions depending on the individual and the particular pattern of symptoms. Traditional interventions such as counseling or psychotherapy and antidepressant medications are often used, the same as for nonseasonal patterns of internalizing problems. However, during the past few years, an innovative and effective intervention has been developed and validated specifically for treatment of seasonal depression: light therapy. The basic principle behind light therapy is simple: Individuals with SAD, or "winter blues," benefit from exposure to more light. Although there are a number of ways that such treatment might occur, such as spending more time outside during the daylight hours or placing more lamps into one's living space or workplace, the best-studied method of providing a more therapeutic level of environmental light is through the daily use of a specially designed fixture or "light box." Such devices shine high-intensity light directly into the field of vision of the person being treated, from a relatively close distance (usually 1–2 feet). Research has indicated that the therapeutic range of light intensity is anywhere from 2,500 to 10,000 lux (a measurement of light intensity); most commercially available light boxes or fixtures used for this purpose are at the 10,000-lux level. The typical recommended range for exposure to the high intensity light is 20 to 90 minutes daily, with most persons benefiting from a 30- to 40-minute period of exposure. Most persons who use this form of treatment purchase specially designed light boxes for treatment of SAD. Such devices usually cost in the range of $200–500.

The research on using light therapy to treat seasonal depression, as cited by Rosenthal (1998b) is impressive. There should really be no question that for many afflicted persons, light therapy has proven to be a powerful and very effective treatment tool. The downside of using light therapy is minimal. It requires an initial expense, a daily time allocation for treatment during the darker months, and, in some very few cases, it might produce some mild side effects such as headache, eyestrain, overactivity, irritability, or insomnia. Almost all of the treatment research has been with adults, but there is no reason to think that adolescents and children who experience seasonal patterns of depression could not be helped by it as well, and there are certainly many case studies to back up this assertion. However, treatment should not be undertaken haphazardly, and should preferably be done under the initial guidance of a professional who is trained in using light therapy, and who understands the nuances involved. Because light therapy requires very close proximity to the treatment light source, it is probably not very realistic to use this intervention in school settings through adding light fixtures. More likely, effective use of light therapy for children and adolescents would need to be done in the home setting, under the supervision of parents.

## CONCLUDING COMMENTS

The current good news is that school-based practitioners now have many potentially effective tools that provide effective interventions for students who suffer from depression, anxiety, and related internalizing problems. The not-so-good news is that these school-based interventions are sometimes not sufficient to provide the help that is needed. Thus, school-based practitioners need to consider carefully their practices of making referrals for outside services, particularly mental health counseling services and psychiatric medications. The use of psychiatric medications and other biological interventions for treating internalizing problems of children and youth is becoming increasingly accepted. There have been some substantial advances in psychopharmacology during the past two decades. Perhaps the most significant recent advance has been the development of the SSRIs, such as Prozac, Zoloft, and Paxil, which are effective in treating various internalizing symptoms in many cases and are safer and less troublesome than older medications, such as the TCAs. Table 10.3 provides a summary overview of the psychiatric medications discussed in this chapter, and their most common uses. Although it is important to recognize that the use of psychiatric medications for treating internalizing disorders of children and youth is not necessarily a better or more effective intervention alternative than psychosocial or psychoeducational approaches, it is increasingly apparent that such medications may provide significant relief of symptoms in many cases, and, in some cases, may even be viewed as a "Godsend" because of the dramatic positive changes they produce. Despite the increased acceptance of psychiatric medications, there are still many problems to be considered. Many potential side effects or adverse reactions are possible, and many parents are outspoken in their opposition to this form of treatment for their children.

Clinicians should view psychiatric medications for children as one potentially useful treatment alternative and be open to their use when the circumstances warrant it. At the same time, mental health professionals and educators should be encouraged that the psychosocial and psychoeducational treatments advocated in this book are increasingly effective, and that, unlike psychiatric medications, these interventions may possibly produce long-term change through skills acquisition and changes in thinking and behavior patterns. At best, psychiatric medications and the effective alternative treatments provide the symptomatic relief that might create a climate in which psychosocial and psychoeducational interventions are optimized.

**TABLE 10.3. Classes of Medications Most Commonly Used for Treating Depression, Anxiety, and Related Internalizing Disorders**

| Class | Common preparations | Most common uses |
|---|---|---|
| Selective serotonin reuptake inhibitors (SSRIs) | Prozac (fluoxetine), Zoloft (sertraline), Paxil (paroxetine), Luvox (fluvoxamine), Celexa (citalopram) | Depression, anxiety, and panic disorder (Zoloft, Paxil); obsessive–compulsive disorder (Luvox); eating disorders (Prozac); social phobia (Paxil) |
| Tricyclic antidepressants (TCAs) | Norpramin or Pertofrane (desipramine), Tofranil (imipramine), Pamelor (nortriptyline), Elavil (amitriptyline), Vivactil (protriptyline), Ludiomil (maprotiline), Anafranil (clomipramine) | Depression, anxiety, and panic disorder (desipramine); obsessive–compulsive disorder (Anafranil); ADHD (Tofranil); enuresis |
| Benzodiazepines | Valium (diazepam), Xanax (alprazolam), Ativan (lorazepam), Serax (oxazepam), Tranxene (clorazepate), Librium (chlordiazepoxide), Klonopin (clonazepam), Halcion (triazolam) | Anxiety, panic disorder, and insomnia (Tranxene, Halcion); depression (Xanax) |
| Antihistamines | Benadryl (diphenhydramine), Vistaril or Atarax (hydroxyzine), Chlor-Trimeton (chlorpheniramine maleate) | Anxiety, panic disorder, insomnia, and weaning patients off of benzodiazepines |
| Monamine oxidase inhibitors (MAOIs) | Nardil (phenelzine), Parnate (tranylcypromine) | Depression |
| Mood stabilizers | Lithium salts (Lithobid, Lithonate, Lithotabs, Eskalith, or Cibalith), Tegretol (carbamezepine), valproic acid (Depakote, Valproate, or Depakene) | Severe emotional and behavioral swings or "lability" |
| Buspirone | Buspar | Anxiety, and to enhance effectiveness of SSRIs in particular cases |
| Bupropion | Wellbutrin | Depression and ADHD |
| Trazadone | Desyrel | Depression |
| Venlafaxine | Effexor | Depression |

# Appendix

# Reproducible Worksheets

# Social–Emotional Assessment Worksheet

*Page 1*

## 1. Student information

Name:                              School:

Grade:                              Age:

Major concerns regarding student; reasons for assessment:




## 2. Summary of Assessment Information

Most important test scores, observations, and information from interviews
or other assessment sources:




*(continued)*

---

## Social–Emotional Assessment Worksheet

*Page 2*

### 3. Problem Analysis

A. Major problems, concerns, diagnostic indicators, and so forth, that are indicated and supported by the assessment information.

B. Hypothesis regarding the possible origins and functions of any problems that are indicated. How might these hypotheses be tested?

### 4. Problem Solution and Evaluation

Potential interventions that appear to be appropriate for identified problems. Tools or methods that might be useful for monitoring intervention progress and evaluating the intervention outcome.

# Daily and Weekly Mood Log

For each day of the week, use the daily mood scale shown at the bottom of the page, and log your mood for that day in the space provided. This activity will help you to see how your mood changes from day to day and over time.

Log for week of (Monday through Sunday):

| Mon | Tues | Wed | Thurs | Fri | Sat | Sun |
|---|---|---|---|---|---|---|
|  |  |  |  |  |  |  |

Log for week of (Monday through Sunday):

| Mon | Tues | Wed | Thurs | Fri | Sat | Sun |
|---|---|---|---|---|---|---|
|  |  |  |  |  |  |  |

Log for week of (Monday through Sunday):

| Mon | Tues | Wed | Thurs | Fri | Sat | Sun |
|---|---|---|---|---|---|---|
|  |  |  |  |  |  |  |

Log for week of (Monday through Sunday):

| Mon | Tues | Wed | Thurs | Fri | Sat | Sun |
|---|---|---|---|---|---|---|
|  |  |  |  |  |  |  |

## Mood Scale

| 1 | 2 | 3 | 4 | 5 |
|---|---|---|---|---|
| very sad or depressed | somewhat sad or depressed | okay, about average normal mood | pretty good happy | great, terrific! very happy |

# Emotional Pie

Name _____ Time Period _____

This activity will help you describe how your feelings were divided up during a particular time, like a day or a week. Our feelings can be thought of kind of like a pie that is cut into slices of different sizes: Sometimes one feeling is bigger than another, in how much room it takes in our life. For the time period that you picked, divide the circle on this sheet into different sized "slices" to show how much room different feelings took in your life during that time. Pick at least two feelings, and label the slices of the pie using the first letter of that word. You might want to select the feelings from this list:

N = normal mood, okay     H = happy       S = sad
T = tense                 A = angry or mad    W = worried

Write down the names of the feelings, and the letters for them, that you are including in your chart:

# Thought Chart

**Directions:** This exercise will help you identify some of your "automatic thoughts"—those thoughts that seem to happen without warning, and without you realizing how they got there. When these thoughts are negative, they can lead to feeling depressed. Think of some situations from the past few days where you felt bad. Identify the situation and the specific feelings you had. Then, identify any "automatic thoughts" that seemed to go along with it.

| The situation | My feelings | My automatic thoughts |
|---|---|---|
|  |  |  |
|  |  |  |
|  |  |  |
|  |  |  |
|  |  |  |

# Identifying Thinking Errors

*Am I Making Any of These Thinking Errors?*

## 1. Binocular Vision
Do I look at negative things in a way that makes them seem bigger than they really are? Do I like at good things in a way that makes them seem smaller than they really are?

## 2. Black-and-White Thinking
Do I think about things only in extreme or opposite ways (e.g., good or bad, all or none, black or white)?

## 3. Dark Glasses
Do I think only about the bad side of things?

## 4. Fortune-Telling
Do I make predictions about what will happen in the future, without enough information?

## 5. Making It Personal
Do I make things my responsibility that I don't need to? Do I blame myself for things that I can't control?

## 6. Overgeneralizing
Do I make general conclusions based only on one event?

## 7. Labeling
Do I put simple, unfair, and negative labels on people or things that are really more complicated than the label?

## 8. Discounting the Positive
Do I ignore positive things or thoughts by telling myself they don't really matter? Can I accept a compliment from another person without thinking it isn't really so? Do I twist good situations into things that are bad?

## 9. Beating Up on Myself or Others
Do I insist or demand that things "should" or "must" be done a certain way?

---

# Are Things Really That Bad?: Three Questions

## 1. What's the evidence?
If something seems really bad, or if you are looking at something in a negative way, how much evidence is there that things are really as you think they are?

## 2. Is there any alternative evidence?
So, you are thinking that something bad is happening or might happen. Is there any evidence out there that indicates otherwise? Is there another explanation?

## 3. What if?
If the negative thing you are thinking of really does occur, what's the worse possible thing that realistically might happen to you? Have you been through worse things before and still survived? Have other people experienced this problem and still survived?

# Evaluating Positives and Negatives

| Situation | List the positive things ("pros") about this situation. | List the negative things ("cons") about this situation. |
|---|---|---|
| | | |
| | | |
| | | |

# My Daily Record to Spot Thinking Errors

**Directions:** Use this worksheet (a new worksheet for each day) to keep a record of some of the situations you experience where you might have made thinking errors. Use this worksheet to come up with some more realistic ways of thinking about the situation.

Name _____   Date _____

| What happened? | How did I feel? | My negative automatic thought | What thinking error did I make? | What is a more realistic way of thinking about It? | How do I feel after thinking about it in a more realistic way? |
|---|---|---|---|---|---|
| | | | | | |

# Changing Negative Automatic Thoughts

**Directions:** Use this worksheet to practice identifying your negative automatic thoughts and thinking errors. Identify some more realistic ways of thinking about these problems.

| What was my negative automatic thought? | What thinking error did I make? | What is a more realistic way of thinking about it? |
|---|---|---|
| | | |

# Increasing Positive Self-Statements

**Directions:** (a) First make a big list of possible positive self-statements to use in particular problem situations; (b) select from this larger list the positive self-statements that you think are the most realistic and will work the best for you; (c) write these statements on this worksheet and keep it in a place where you will be able to see it often.

| Problem situation | Possible positive self-statements |
|---|---|
| | |
| | |
| | |

## Changing Irrational and Negative Thinking the RET Way

- ## Identify your irrational and negative thoughts.

- ## Dispute these thoughts.

- ## Counter these thoughts with thoughts that are more realistic and positive.

### Changing the way you think
### can help you change the way you feel!

# Basic Steps to Self-Control and Self-Monitoring Interventions for Depression

1. Pay more attention to the way that you think about things, and to the number of positive activities that you get involved in.

2. Increase your involvement in positive activities, and increase your thoughts and statements that are associated with being in a good mood.

3. Pay attention to the later consequences of your behavior, not just the immediate consequences.

4. Pay attention to the positive things that happen after you do things that take a lot of work.

5. Set standards for yourself that are realistic and that you can reach with a little work.

6. Break down your personal goals into smaller steps.

7. Take credit for your successes, and don't always blame yourself for your failures.

8. Reward yourself more for thinking positively, for dealing with tough situations, and for getting involved in positive activities. Say to yourself: "Way to go!" or do something special.

9. Punish yourself less. Who needs it!

# The Learned Optimism Worksheet: Your A-B-C-D-E Record

Adversity (the problem):

Belief (my belief after the problem happened):

Consequence (how I felt):

Disputation (argue against the negative belief with a more realistic or helpful belief):

Energization (the new way that I felt after I disputed the old belief):

# Weekly Journal Entry Form

Your Name_____ Today's Date_____

Write about some of the *thoughts* you had during this past week, such as *what you were thinking* about yourself, your family, school, or things that you wanted to do.

Write about some of your *feelings* for the past week. For example, did you feel happy, sad, mad, bored, excited, or other ways at times this week?

Write about some of the *things you did* this past week, and tell about some of the thoughts and feelings you had during these activities.

Write down anything else that you think is important about this past week.

# Weekly Journal Entry Form with Mood Rating

Name_____ Entry Date_____ Week_____

Describe some of your *thoughts* about yourself, your world, and the future during this past week.

Describe how you often *felt* during this past week. For example, did you feel happy, upset, angry, bored, depressed, excited, or other ways at times this week?

Describe some of the activities that you did this past week. Also describe some of the thoughts and feelings you had during these activities.

Write down anything else that you think is important about this past week.

## Rate your *usual mood* for the past week (circle one):

| 1 | 2 | 3 | 4 | 5 |
|---|---|---|---|---|
| very sad or depressed | somewhat sad or depressed | okay, about average normal mood | pretty good happy | great, terrific! very happy |

## Weekly Planning Form for Scheduling Positive Activities

| | Monday | Tuesday | Wednesday | Thursday | Friday | Saturday | Sunday |
|---|---|---|---|---|---|---|---|
| Date | | | | | | | |
| Goals for positive activities | | | | | | | |
| Persons who will be involved | | | | | | | |
| Materials or resources needed | | | | | | | |

# Baseline Record for Positive Activities

| Activities | Days | | | | | | | | | | | | | | |
|---|---|---|---|---|---|---|---|---|---|---|---|---|---|---|---|
| | 1 | 2 | 3 | 4 | 5 | 6 | 7 | 8 | 9 | 10 | 11 | 12 | 13 | 14 | 15 |
| | | | | | | | | | | | | | | | |
| | | | | | | | | | | | | | | | |
| | | | | | | | | | | | | | | | |
| | | | | | | | | | | | | | | | |
| | | | | | | | | | | | | | | | |
| | | | | | | | | | | | | | | | |
| | | | | | | | | | | | | | | | |
| | | | | | | | | | | | | | | | |
| | | | | | | | | | | | | | | | |
| Total no. activities for each day | | | | | | | | | | | | | | | |

# Feelings Identification

**Directions:** This activity will help you learn to identify comfortable and uncomfortable feelings. *Comfortable feelings make people feel good. They can help you have fun and enjoy life. Uncomfortable feelings make people feel bad. They can also help people grow and change for the better. Uncomfortable feelings can help people notice and appreciate their comfortable feelings.* For one of the lists on this worksheet, put a + mark next to any words that you think describe comfortable feelings, and put a − mark next to any words that you think describe uncomfortable feelings.

## Feeling List 1

| | | | |
|---|---|---|---|
| happy | lonely | scared | bored |
| angry | sad | upset | surprised |
| strong | proud | lonely | glad |
| shy | worried | tired | love |

## Feeling List 2

| | | | |
|---|---|---|---|
| lonely | sorry | guilty | worried |
| happy | miserable | excited | proud |
| confused | strong | scared | loyal |
| crabby | surprised | upset | bored |
| serene | inspired | warm | angry |
| anxious | frustrated | thrilled | furious |
| compassionate | ignored | embarrassed | love |

# About My Feelings

**Directions:** Complete each of these sentences about feelings in your own words, using real examples about how you feel.

I felt afraid when _____

I am really good at _____

I get excited when _____

Most of the time I feel _____

I am happy when _____

I feel upset when _____

I am sad when _____

I am calm when _____

I was really mad when _____

I am thankful for _____

I am lonely when _____

# About My Feelings

**Directions:** Each of the sentences on this sheet include statements about feelings or emotions, but these sentences are not complete. Complete each sentence in your own words, using real examples from your own life.

I felt proud when _____

I am ashamed of _____

I get excited when _____

Most of the time I feel _____

I am happy when _____

I felt frustrated when _____

I am disappointed _____

I am calm when _____

I was really angry _____

I am thankful for _____

I hope that _____

# How Do You Feel?

**Directions:** From the list of feelings at the bottom of this sheet, choose words to write in after the "I feel" part of each sentence, and then use your own words to describe when you feel that way.

I feel _____ when _____

I feel _____ when _____

I feel _____ when _____

I feel _____ when _____

I feel _____ when _____

I feel _____ when _____

I feel _____ when _____

I feel _____ when _____

I feel _____ when _____

## List of Feelings

| | | | |
|---|---|---|---|
| happy | bored | joyful | thrilled |
| lonely | angry | thankful | safe |
| excited | proud | stupid | worried |
| scared | tense | hyper | upset |

# How Do You Feel?

**Directions:** From the list of feelings at the bottom of this sheet, choose words to write in after the "I feel" part of each sentence, and then use your own words to describe when you feel that way.

I feel _____ when _____

I feel _____ when _____

I feel _____ when _____

I feel _____ when _____

I feel _____ when _____

I feel _____ when _____

I feel _____ when _____

I feel _____ when _____

## List of Feelings

| | | | |
|---|---|---|---|
| happy | bored | joyful | thrilled |
| lonely | stimulated | inadequate | relieved |
| confused | accepted | contented | defeated |
| pressured | free | triumphant | enthusiastic |
| apathetic | angry | thankful | safe |
| excited | proud | stupid | worried |
| scared | tense | hyper | upset |

# Reacting to Emotional Situations

**Directions:** For each situation listed on this worksheet, describe the feeling you would probably have if it happened to you. Also, think about "why" you think you might feel that way.

| Situation | Feeling |
|---|---|
| You are invited by three different students to sit with them in the cafeteria. | |
| One of your friends doesn't want to spend time with you anymore. | |
| You can't think of anything to do. | |
| You get picked last to play on a team. | |
| You are home alone at night. | |
| You get picked first to play on a team. | |
| You don't want your mom or dad to see your report card, because of some poor grades you received. | |
| Your teacher says, "Great job. You got 100% right!" | |
| Your teacher says, "Your work is too sloppy. Do it over again." | |
| A student says, "I don't understand how to do this. Will you help me?" | |
| Your parents are having an argument. | |
| There isn't enough money to get something you want. | |
| Your mom or dad says, "You're too young. Wait until you're older." | |
| You are getting ready to go on a trip for which you have been waiting a long time. | |
| A family member is very ill. | |

# Expressing Feelings Inventory

**Directions:** For each of the feeling words listed on the rating form below, think about how easy or how hard it is for you to express those feelings to other people. Show whether it is *very easy*, *somewhat easy*, *somewhat hard*, or *very hard* for you to express those feelings, by putting an **X** in the appropriate box. This exercise can help you to see how much progress you have made, and can help you to set goals for changes you might want to make in the future.

| When I feel . . . | How easy is it for me to express this emotion to other people? | | | |
|---|---|---|---|---|
| | *very easy* | *somewhat easy* | *somewhat hard* | *very hard* |
| ANGRY | | | | |
| LOVE | | | | |
| SAD | | | | |
| WORRIED | | | | |
| JOYFUL | | | | |
| EXCITED | | | | |
| SURPRISED | | | | |
| FEARFUL | | | | |
| EMBARRASSED | | | | |
| JEALOUS | | | | |
| BORED | | | | |
| CONFIDENT | | | | |
| LONELY | | | | |

I think that I am a . . .

_____ very emotional person        _____ somewhat emotional person
_____ somewhat unemotional person  _____ very unemotional person

# Five Steps for Solving Conflicts

## 1. Define the Problem
- Begin with a positive statement.
- Be specific.
- Describe what the other person has done or said.
- No name-calling!
- Say how you feel.
- Admit your part and don't accuse.
- Keep it short and simple.

## 2. Generate Solutions
- Brainstorm as many solutions as possible.
- Be creative!
- No criticizing, judging, or evaluating yet.

## 3. Evaluate the Solutions
- How realistic is the solution?
- Why would this solution work or not work?
- Would this solution help all the persons involved in the conflict?
- Is this solution fair to all persons involved?

## 4. Choose a Solution
- Must be agreed on by both persons.
- Go back to item 3 if you can't agree.

## 5. Make and Seal an Agreement
- Each person states that he or she agrees and what he or she will do.
- Shake hands or write a contract with details.

# Listing and Rating Your Fears

**Directions:** You will be given 10 blank cards. On each of these cards, write down one of the 10 things or situations that you are most afraid of, or that causes you to feel the most fearful or uncomfortable. Describe the situation in a few words. After you have completed those 10 cards, you should assign each card a number that shows how afraid of that situation you are, or how uncomfortable you feel in that situation. The numbers you assign to each card could be anywhere from 10 to 100, in multiples of 10 (for example, 10, 20, 30, 40, and so on, up to 100). The higher the number, the more fear or discomfort that you would feel in that situation. Use the following guide to help you rate each situation:

**100**   The most fear of all; I would be extremely uncomfortable in this situation; I don't think I could stand it.

**90**

**80**

**70**   A lot of fear. I would be very uncomfortable in this situation, and would have a hard time dealing with it.

**60**

**50**

**40**   Some fear. I would be a little bit uncomfortable but would be okay, and I would be able to deal with it all right.

**30**

**20**

**10**   Very little fear or no fear. This situation would not bother me at all.

# References

Albano, A. M., & Barlow, D. H. (1996). Breaking the vicious cycle: Cognitive-behavioral group treatment for socially anxious youth. In E. D. Hibbs & P. S. Jensen (Eds.), *Psychosocial treatment of child and adolescent disorders* (pp. 43–62). Washington, DC: American Psychological Association.

Alberto, P. A., & Troutman, A. C. (1999). *Applied behavior analysis for teachers* (5th ed.) Upper Saddle River, NJ: Merrill/Prentice-Hall.

American Psychiatric Association. (1994). *Diagnostic and statistical manual of mental disorders* (4th ed.). Washington, DC: Author.

Bandura, A. (1969). *Principles of behavior modification*. New York: Holt, Rinehart & Winston.

Bandura, A. (1971). Psychotherapy based on modeling principles. In A. E. Bergin & S. L. Garfield (Eds.), *Handbook of psychotherapy and behavior change* (pp. 653–708). New York: Wiley.

Bandura, A. (1986). *Social foundations of thought and action*. Englewood Cliffs, NJ: Prentice-Hall.

Beck, A. T. (1967). *Depression: Clinical, experimental, and theoretical*. New York: Hoeber.

Beck, A. T., Rush, A. J., Shaw, B. F., & Emery, G. (1979). *Cognitive therapy of depression*. New York: Guilford Press.

Berry, J. (1987). *Every kid's guide to handling feelings*. Chicago: Children's Press.

Breggin, P. R., & Breggin, G. R. (1995). *Talking back to Prozac*. St. Martin's Press.

Brock, S. E., & Sandoval, J. (1997). Suicidal ideation and behaviors. In G. C. Bear, K. M. Minke, & A. Thomas (Eds.), *Children's Needs II: Development problems, alternatives* (pp. 361–374). Washington, DC: National Association of School Psychologists.

Burns, D. D. (1980). *Feeling good: The new mood therapy*. New York: Signet.

Cantwell, D. P. (1990). Depression across the early life span. In M. Lewis & S. M. Miller (Eds.), *Handbook of developmental psychopathology* (pp. 293–309). New York: Plenum Press.

Cicchetti, D., & Toth, S. L. (Eds.). (1991). *Internalizing and externalizing expressions of dysfunction*. Hillsdale, NJ: Erlbaum.

Clarke, G., Lewinsohn, P., & Hops, H. (1990). *Coping with adolescent depression course: Leader's manual for adolescent groups*. Eugene, OR: Castalia.

Del Mundo, A. S., Pumariega, A. J., & Vance, H. R. (1999). Psychopharmacology in school-based mental health services. *Psychology in the Schools, 36,* 437–450.

Eisenberg, N., Wentzel, N. M., & Harris, J. D. (1998). The role of emotionality and regulation in empathy-related responding. *School Psychology Review, 27,* 506–521.

Elias, M. J., Zins, J. E., Weissberg, R. P., Frey, K. S., Greenberg, M. T., Haynes, N. M., Kessler, R., Schwab-Stone, M. E., & Shriver, T. P. (1997). *Promoting social and emotional learning: Guidelines for educators.* Alexandria, VA: Association for Supervision and Curriculum Development.

Elksnin, L. K., & Elksnin, N. (1995). *Assessment and instruction of social skills.* San Diego: Singular.

Ellis, A. (1962). *Reason and emotion in psychotherapy.* New York: Lyle Stewart.

Flannery-Schroeder, E., & Kendall, P. C. (1996). *Cognitive-behavioral therapy for anxious children: Therapist manual for group treatment.* Ardmore, PA: Workbook Publishing.

Fuchs, L. S., & Fuchs, D. (1986). Effects of systematic formative evaluation: A meta-analysis. *Exceptional Children, 53,* 199–208.

Giedd, J. N., Swedo, S. E., Lowe, C. H., & Rosenthal, N. E. (1998). Case series: Pediatric seasonal affective disorders: A follow-up report. *Journal of the American Academy of Child and Adolescent Psychiatry, 37,* 218–220.

Green, W. H. (1991). *Child and adolescent psychopharmacology.* Baltimore: Williams & Wilkins.

Greenberg, M. T., Kusche, C. A., Cook, E. T., & Quamma, J. P. (1995). Promoting emotional competence in school-aged children: The effects of the PATHS curriculum. *Development and Psychopathology, 7,* 117–136.

Gresham, F. M., & Elliott, S. N. (1990). *Social Skills Rating System.* Circle Pines, MN: American Guidance Services.

Harrington, R. (1993). *Depressive disorder in childhood and adolescence.* New York: Wiley.

Hinshaw, S. P. (1994). *Attention deficits and hyperactivity in children.* Thousand Oaks, CA: Sage.

Hoier, T. S., & Cone, J. D. (1987). Target selection of social skills for children: The template-matching procedure. *Behavior Modification, 11,* 137–164.

Hoier, T. S., McConnell, S., & Pallay, A. G. (1987). Observational assessment for planning and evaluating educational transitions: An initial analysis of template matching. *Behavioral Assessment, 9,* 6–20.

Horner, R. H., & Carr, E. G. (1997) Behavioral support for students with severe disabilities: Functional assessment and comprehensive intervention. *Journal of Special Education, 31,* 84- 109.

Howard, B., & Kendall, P. C. (1996). *Cognitive-behavioral family therapy for anxious children: Therapist manual.* Ardmore, PA: Workbook Publishing.

Hughes, J. N., & Baker, D. B. (1990). *The clinical child interview.* New York: Guilford Press.

Jacobson, E. (1938). *Progressive relaxation.* Chicago: University of Chicago Press.

Kagan, J. K., Reznick, J. S., & Snidman, N. (1990). The temperamental qualities of inhibition and lack of inhibition. In M. Lewis & S. M. Miller (Eds.), *Handbook of developmental psychopathology* (pp. 219–226). New York: Plenum Press.

Kaslow, N. J., Morris, M. K., & Rehm, L. P. (1998). Childhood depression. In R. J. Morris & T. R. Kratochwill (Eds.), *The practice of child therapy* (3rd ed., pp. 48–90). Boston: Allyn & Bacon.

Kazdin, A. E. (1995). *Conduct disorders in childhood and adolescence* (2nd ed.). Thousand Oaks, CA: Sage.

Kazdin, A. E. (1998). Conduct disorder. In R. J. Morris & T. R. Kratochwill (Eds.), *The practice of child therapy* (2nd ed., pp. 199–230). Boston: Allyn & Bacon.

Kendall, P. C. (1992). *Coping Cat workbook.* Ardmore, PA: Workbook Publishing.

Kendall, P. C., Kane, M., Howard, B., & Siqueland, L. (1990). *Cognitive-behavioral therapy for anxious children: Therapist manual.* Ardmore, PA: Workbook Publishing.

Kendall, P. C., & Treadwell, K. R. H. (1996). Cognitive-behavioral treatment for childhood anxiety disorders. In E. D. Hibbs & P. S. Jensen (Eds.), *Psychosocial treatments for child and adolescent disorders* (pp. 23–41). Washington, DC: American Psychological Association.

Kramer, P. D. (1993). *Listening to Prozac*. New York: Viking.

Lewinsohn, P. M., Clarke, G. N., Hops, H., & Andrews, J. (1990). Cognitive-behavioral treatment for depressed adolescents. *Behavior Therapy, 21*, 385–401.

Lewinsohn, P. M., Clarke, G. N., Rohde, P., Hops, H., & Seeley, J. R. (1996). A course in coping: A cognitive-behavioral approach to the treatment of adolescent depression. In E. D. Hibbs & P. S. Jensen (Eds.), *Psychosocial treatments for child and adolescent disorders* (pp. 109–135). Washington, DC: American Psychological Association.

Lewinsohn, P. M., & Graf, M. (1973). Pleasant activities and depression. *Journal of Consulting and Clinical Psychology, 41*, 261–268.

Lewinsohn, P. M., Mischel, W., Chaplin, W., & Barton, R. (1980). Social competence and depression: The role of illusory self-perceptions. *Journal of Abnormal Psychology, 89*, 203–212.

Matson, J. L. (1989). *Treating depression in children and adolescents*. Elmsford, NY: Pergamon Press.

Meichenbaum, D. (1986). Cognitive behavior modification. In F. H. Kanfer & A. P. Goldstein (Eds.), *Helping people change* (3rd ed., pp. 390–422). Elmsford, NY: Pergamon Press.

Merrell, K. W. (1993). *School Social Behavior Scales*. Iowa City, IA: Assessment–Intervention Resources. (http://www.assessment-intervention.com)

Merrell, K. W. (1996). Social–emotional problems in early childhood: New directions in conceptualization, assessment, and treatment. *Education and Treatment of Children, 19*, 458–473.

Merrell, K. W. (1999). *Behavioral, social, and emotional assessment of children and adolescents*. Mahwah, NJ: Erlbaum.

Merrell, K. W., & Caldarella, P. (2001). *Home and Community Social Behavior Scales*. Iowa City, IA: Assessment–Intervention Resources. (http://www.assessment-intervention.com)

Merrell, K. W., & Gimpel, G. A. (1998). *Social skills of children and adolescents: Conceptualization, assessment, treatment*. Mahwah, NJ: Erlbaum.

Minuchin, S., Baker, L., Liebman, R., Milman, L., & Todd, T. C. (1975). A conceptual model of psychosomatic illness in children. *Archives of General Psychiatry, 32*, 1031–1038.

Minuchin, S., Rosman, B. L., & Baker, L. (1978). *Psychosomatic families: Anorexia nervosa in context*. Cambridge, MA: Harvard University Press.

Morris, R. J., & Kratochwill, T. R. (1983). *Treating children's fears and phobias: A behavioral approach*. Elmsford, NY: Pergamon Press.

Morris, R. J., & Kratochwill, T. R. (1998). Childhood fears and phobias. In R. J. Morris & T. R. Kratochwill (Eds.), *The practice of child therapy* (2nd ed., pp. 91–131). Boston: Allyn & Bacon.

Mufson, L., Moreau, D., & Weissman, M. M. (1996). Focus on relationships: Interpersonal psychotherapy for adolescent depression. In E. D. Hibbs & P. S. Jensen (Eds.), *Psychosocial treatment of child and adolescent disorders* (pp. 137–156). Washington, DC: American Psychological Association.

Mufson, L., Moreau, D., Weissman, M. M., & Klerman, G. L. (1993). *Interpersonal therapy for depressed adolescents*. New York: Guilford Press.

Nelson, R. O., & Hayes, S. C. (Eds.). (1986). *Conceptual foundations of behavioral assessment*. New York: Guilford Press.

Quay, H. R. (1986). Classification. In H. C. Quay & J. S. Werry (Eds.), *Psychopathological disorders of childhood* (3rd ed., pp. 1–34). New York: Wiley.

Rehm, L. P. (1977). A self-control model of depression. *Behavior Therapy, 8*, 787–804.

Rehm, L. P. (1990). Cognitive and behavioral theories. In B. B. Wolman & G. Stricker (Eds.), *Depressive disorders: Facts, theories, and treatment methods* (pp. 64–91). New York: Wiley.

Reynolds, W. M. (Ed.). (1992). *Internalizing disorders in children and adolescents*. New York: Wiley.

Reynolds, W. M., & Coates, K. I. (1986). A comparison of cognitive-behavioral therapy and relaxation training for the treatment of depression in adolescents. *Journal of Consulting and Clinical Psychology, 54,* 653–660.

Robbins, L. N. (1966). *Deviant children grow up.* Baltimore: Williams & Wilkins.

Rosenthal, N. E. (1998a). *St. John's wort: The herbal way to feeling good.* New York: HarperCollins.

Rosenthal, N. E. (1998b). *Winter blues: Seasonal depression—What it is and how to overcome it* (rev. ed.). New York: Guilford Press.

Sattler, J. M. (1998). *Clinical and forensic interviewing of children and families.* San Diego: Jerome M. Sattler.

Schwartz, J. A. J., Kaslow, N. J., Racusin, G. R., & Carton, E. R. (1998). Interpersonal family therapy for childhood depression. In V. B. Van Hasselt & M. Hersen (Eds.), *Handbook of psychological treatment protocols for children and adolescents* (pp. 109–151). Mahwah, NJ: Erlbaum.

Seligman, M. E. P. (1981). A learned helplessness point of view. In L. P. Rehm (Ed.), *Behavior therapy for depression* (pp. 123–141). New York: Academic Press.

Seligman, M. E. P. (1990). *Learned optimism.* New York: Knopf.

Seligman, M. E. P. (1998). *Learned optimism: How to change your mind and your life* (rev. ed.). New York: Pocket Books/Simon & Schuster.

Seligman, M. E. P., Reivich, K., Jaycox, L., & Gillham, J. (1995). *The optimistic child.* Boston: Houghton Mifflin.

Shapiro, E. S., & Kratochwill, T. R. (Eds.). (2000). *Conducting school-based assessments of child and adolescent behavior.* New York: Guilford Press.

Shinn, M. R. (Ed.). (1997). *Advanced applications of curriculum-based measurement.* New York: Guilford Press.

Shapiro, E. S. (1996). *Academic skills problems* (2nd ed.). New York: Guilford Press.

Sheridan, S. M. (1995). *The tough kid social skills book.* Longmont, CO: Sopris West.

Siegel, L. J. (1998). Somatic disorders. In R. J. Morris & T. R. Kratochwill (Eds.), *The practice of child therapy* (3rd ed., pp. 231–270). Boston: Allyn & Bacon.

Silverman, W. K., & Ginsburg, G. S. (1998). Anxiety disorders. In T. H. Ollendick & M. Hersen (Eds.), *Handbook of child psychopathology* (3rd ed., pp. 239–268). New York: Plenum Press.

Silverman, W. K., & Kurtines, W. M. (1996a). Transfer of control: A psychosocial intervention model internalizing disorders in youth. In E. D. Hibbs & P. S. Jensen (Eds.), *Psychosocial treatments for child and adolescent disorders* (pp. 63–81). Washington, DC: American Psychological Association.

Silverman, W. K., & Kurtines, W. M. (1996b). *Anxiety and phobic disorders: A pragmatic approach.* New York: Plenum Press.

Stark, K. D. (1990). *Childhood depression: School-based intervention.* New York: Guilford Press.

Stark, K. D., & Kendall, P. C. (1996). *Treating depressed children: Therapist manual for ACTION.* Ardmore, PA: Workbook Publishing.

Stark, K. D., Swearer, S., Kurowski, C., Sommer, D., & Bowen, B. (1996). Targeting the child and the family: A holistic approach to treating child and adolescent depressive disorders. In E. D. Hibbs & P. S. Jensen (Eds.), *Psychosocial treatments for child and adolescent disorders* (pp. 207–238). Washington, DC: American Psychological Association.

Sulzer-Azaroff, B., & Mayer, G. R. (1991). *Behavior analysis for lasting change* (2nd ed.). New York: Holt, Rinehart & Winston.

Wilens, T. E. (1999). *Straight talk about psychiatric medications for kids.* New York: Guilford Press.

Wilkes, T. C. R., Belsher, G., Rush, A. J., Frank, E., & Associates. (Eds.). (1994). *Cognitive therapy for depressed adolescents.* New York: Guilford Press.

# Author Index

# Subject Index